the Idler

ISSUE 32 | WINTER 2003

First published in Great Britain in 2003 by
Idle Limited
Studio 20, 24 - 28a Hatton Wall
London EC1N 8JH
Tel: 020 7691 0320
Fax: 020 7691 0321
e-mail: theidlers@idler.co.uk

ISBN 0-9536720-7-7

Editor: Tom Hodgkinson   Creative Director: Gavin Pretor-Pinney
Non-Executive Deputy Editor: Matthew De Abaitua
Deputy Editor: Dan Kieran
Designer: Sonia Ortiz Alcón
Assistant Editor: Sam Jordison
Managing Editor: Clare Pollard
Literary Editor: Tony White
Music Editor: Will Hodgkinson
Sports Editor: John Moore
Contributing Editors: Greg Rowland, Adam Higginbotham
Editorial Assistant: Christie Currie
Cover: Gavin Pretor-Pinney
Advertising: Jamie Dwelly at Cabbell 020 8971 8450

THE PERFECT CHRISTMAS GIFT

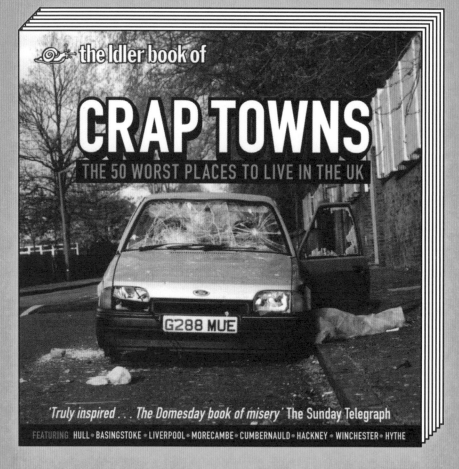

the Idler book of

CRAP TOWNS

THE 50 WORST PLACES TO LIVE IN THE UK

G288 MUE

'Truly inspired . . . The Domesday book of misery' The Sunday Telegraph

FEATURING HULL ∘ BASINGSTOKE ∘ LIVERPOOL ∘ MORECAMBE ∘ CUMBERNAULD ∘ HACKNEY ∘ WINCHESTER ∘ HYTHE

For Julia

Ged Wells

www.idler.co.uk

...

Where Idler readers write:

Crap Towns
The Sweet Smell Of Failure
The Rambler
Crap Jobs
Louis Theroux's Unfinished Jokes
Idle News
Felicitous Phrases
Record Of The Week

HANNAH DYSON

CHIN'S 33 HAPPY MOMENTS p100

Contents THE IDLER, ISSUE 32, WINTER 2003

SOPHIE LODGE

OVID: LATIN LOVER p142

More Contents THE IDLER, ISSUE 32, WINTER 2003

EDITOR'S LETTER

The tragedy of the world is that the good can't be bothered but the bad can. This is the aphorism I invented one winter night not so long ago. I was drowning in a sea of bureacracy and crap, mainly supplied by the crooks at BT. I was trying to be idle, I was doing my best, but everywhere there were people bothering me. It's such hard work, doing nothing. The struggle to be idle is a lifelong one.

And that is why it is and always has been the purpose of the *Idler* to give our readers comfort and inspiration in the fight against the Botherers. It is also the aim that Keats, surely our greatest sleep poet, gave poetry: "To soothe the cares and lift the thoughts of man" is how he put it.

Anyway, since this is our ten years anniversary issue – ten years! and how little has changed! – I thought I'd give a brief history of what has happened so far. Our other anniversary project has been to round up many of our previous interviewees and give them the Idler Questionnaire, which is designed to gain insight into the most important question of all, and that is, how to live. The questionnaires are dotted through the front section of the magazine. There are contributions from Damien Hirst, Charles Handy, Billy Childish, Will Self, Penny Rimbaud and many more.

I first had the idea for the *Idler* in 1991 or 1992. At the time, I was working in a lowly capacity on one of Fleet Street's worst Sunday paper supplements. I was toiling here in the mistaken belief that the experience would help my chosen career as a journalist. I then believed all that first-step-on-the-ladder nonsense. Lesson one: don't suffer in the present in the service of the future.

The name came from Dr Johnson's series of essays, published in 1758, which I had been reading in bed. It seemed to fit the time: all my friends were scrabbling around trying to get careers going and taking crap jobs. I personally was full of self-admonishment, and the *Idler*, as I conceived it, was a way of celebrating and embracing laziness rather than criticising oneself for it. As well as Dr Johnson and his 18th century literary loafing, I had been inspired by the San Francisco fanzine *Processed World*, which ran articles written by aggrieved temps and lowly office workers. I was also into UFOs and other Californian subjects, and I thought it would be fun to bring together an 18th century British sensibility with the emerging "slacker" trend. I also had loads of friends, such as James Parker, who were talented writers but were not getting published.

The first interview was with Terence McKenna, one of the many great thinkers we have met who have since died. I wrote a short essay on Dr Johnson and his concept of the *Idler* as a person who is not simply lazy, but who works to his own clock and cannot be tied down by standardised time.

I approached my old friend Gavin Pretor-Pinney who had recently art directed *The Modern Review* and asked whether he would help me. He liked the idea and so we spent a summer assembling issue one in his flat on his Apple Mac. Contributors included Gavin Hills, Zed Nelson, Greg Rowland and a little known journalist called Louis Theroux, whose older brother Marcel was also

an early contributor. Friends popped round to help sub-edit. I was on the dole at the time, and I went on a course for people who wanted to start their own business. It was largely a waste of time but I received one good piece of advice, which was to start small. We raised £800 from family and friends and were able to print 1000 copies. I found a distributor who agreed to take 300 copies. I went round to Rough Trade, where I had worked until in 1999, to borrow their franking machine for mailouts.

We held the first party at the Salon Des Arts, an elegant room in South Kensington whose founder, the late Danièle Dodd, was very generous to the magazine in the early days.

Right from the start it was clear that some would "get it" and some would not. A diary story in the *Daily Telegraph* reported on our launch, saying: "It's good, but editor young Tom Hodgkinson, 25, will need imagination to keep the joke going."

This scepticism was balanced by the reactions we were getting from readers. It was always the readers who encouraged us to keep going through the tough patches, and particularly the many letters we received which told us: "I thought I was alone in being an idler but reading your magazine has inspired me to do what I want."

We managed to sell a few copies and started to produce issue two, with further funding from friend and contributor James Parker, as well as a cheque from our friend Eraj Jayaratnam, who very sadly died a year or so later. Issue two featured Homer Simpson as cover star; this was pretty well ahead of the times as it was published in 1993 when most people had not even heard of *The Simpsons*. This issue also included an interview with Will Self, who went on to become a great contributor to and supporter of the magazine.

Later in 1993 the *Guardian* newspaper began to show interest in our magazine. They were, luckily for us, busy trying to create an empire of magazines. Issue five, which featured Kurt Cobain on the cover, was the last that we produced at home. In mid 1994, we moved into a corner office of Farringdon Road. The *Guardian* had agreed to help us with business advice, free phones and office space. I also contributed a few op-ed columns, the first was called "Why I Don't Want A Job". Over the next three years, the magazine expanded slightly and – paradoxically for a magazine that criticised the notion of jobs – Gav and I were given jobs by the *Guardian*, to run their their "new ideas" department. This was great fun for a year or so. *Private Eye* ran an item on myself and deputy editor Matthew De Abaitua, calling the *Idler* a "one-joke Will Self fanzine staffed by friends of the former junkie". This amused us and also encouraged us to think that in some way we had arrived.

In 1996 tragedy struck with the death of my great friend Gavin Hills. His departure led me to question what I was doing. The *Guardian* was generous enough to send me to a counsellor at the time, and she helped me to decide that I didn't want a job any more and so I suggested to Gav PP that we go freelance, giving us more time to work on the *Idler*.

We were also still partying hard at the time. The *Idler* had emerged from the ecstasy culture. There was a wave of creativity that emerged from the recession. No one could get a decent job and so therefore there was nothing to lose by starting your own enterprise. *Time Out* ran a feature on the new magazines of 1993: there was us, *Blow, Dazed and Confused, G-Spot*. Of these only *Dazed* had the commercial nouse to create a proper business, but there was a paplpable excitment in the air. And rave transmuted into Britpop. It was Gavin Hills who, before the coining of Britpop, first detected the emerging Sixties-style cultural self-confidence, most memorably expressed by Oasis, Blur and Damien Hirst. 1995 was a fun year. We interviewed Damien who gave us 25 signed cigarette butts to give to readers in a competition. Sarah Lucas created her image of the cigarette with unflicked ash first for the *Idler*. Alex James became a conributor and friend. We were also inspired by the Easy Listening revival, the semi-ironic fashion for cocktails and lounge music, which itself inspired the more mainstream cocktail bar culture of the mid to late nineties. Everyone was having fun.

The death of Gavin Hills was a massive blow to all his friends, and perhaps started us a more sober reflective course. We moved the magazine to Zone, which had made money out of selling Spice Girls stickers and *Manchester United* magazine and was looking for more creatively satisfying projects. We spent a year trying to commercialise the *Idler*. We changed our tagline to "Licence to Chill", put celebrities on the cover and the like, but failed to achieve a mass audience and were dumped by Zone in late 1998. This was a low point for the *Idler*, but we had a distraction in our absinthe-importing business. Conceived by the musician John Moore, it was one of those pub ideas that actually happened, and we found ourselves at the centre of a mass of publicity. Absinthe seemed to fit the nation's decadent mood at the end of the millennium, and for a while everyone seemed to be tottering around the bars of Soho with a green glass in their hand. We had a particularly memorable night out with Bez on the stuff.

After a year of dragging ourselves around various publishing companies, trying and failing to convince them to take on the Idler, we decided to relaunch the mag in book format and publish it independently. Winter 1999 saw the publication of the Man's Ruin issue,

300 pages of satire, interviews and stories. It didn't sell loads but gave us a creatively satisfying way of continuing the mag. I should say that the magazine was still a non-profit organisation but not deliberately so. By now our old ally from the *Guardian*, David Brook, was a director at Channel 4, and this led to us carrying out a lot of creative work for their marketing department, which paid the rent and allowed us the time to continue with the *Idler*.. Channel 4 also became one of our few advertisers, as did Sony Playstation, for whom we produce the *Pilchard Teeth* fanzine.

The *Idler* you now hold is the eighth to be published in book format. After ten years the *Idler* is still a tiny operation but we now believe that our Crap Towns project will help turn the spotlight on us. Certainly I believe that the issues we have always addressed – overwork, creativity, control over one's own time, quality of life – are more relevant to more people than ever, and that we are all beginning to see through the myths of money and work that have kept us toiling in the mills. As more and more people search out alternative ways of living, it's our hope that the *Idler* will connect with a wider audience. But if it doesn't, it doesn't really matter. We'll keep doing it just because we enjoy it so much. And we hope you do, too.

TOM HODGKINSON
tom@idler.co.uk

IDLER CONTRIBUTORS

Who are the idlers?

Matthew De Abaitua is always available

Marc Baines runs the Salty Cellar club in Glasgow

Scott Bradfield is author of *The History of Luminous Motion*, *Greetings From Earth: New and Collected Stories*, *What's Wrong with America*, and the forthcoming *Good Girl Wants It Bad*. He reviews for the *Times*.

Andrew Copeman is out on bail

Adolfo Crespo is the Gladiator

Christie Currie did work experience in the office and wrote about fans

Brian Dean runs the excellent www.anxietyculture.com

Bill Drummond is a serial father

Hannah Dyson draws anthropomorphic creatures and other beings

Jon Fortgang is a journalist and writer

Lucy Granville runs the Loose Review from her Clerkenwell HQ

Paul Hamilton has had an American battleship named after him

Jeff Harrison is a painter, illustrator and misanthropist from east London

Joe Harrison is a comical, talented all-round good guy, need we say more?

Damien Hirst lives in Devon

Will Hodgkinson is a journalist based in London

Sarah Janes (above) is a multi-tasking rock'n'rolling journalist, ex-shoplifter and writer who lives in Brighton

Fanny Johnstone (below) writes about sex and cars in the *Daily Telegraph*

Sam Jordison is a classics scholar from Minehead and now runs the *Idler*'s Crap Towns franchise with Dan Kieran

Dan Kieran is the *Idler*'s deputy editor and runs the Crap Towns franchise with Sam Jordison

Sophie Lodge is an animator who used to make dinosaurs walk, but now makes Famous Grouses famous and bulls behave like horses

Pete Loveday is a jobbing artist, self-buried in Devon. He created the legendary Russell comics. Find out more at www.ccnewz.com

Mark Manning is the author of *Collateral Damage* (Creation Books) and by night becomes Zodiac Mindwarp

Edwin Marney is an illustrator who generally works for dull business magazines. Visit his website at www.edwinmarney.co.uk

John Moore is a father, musician and philanthropist whose new solo LP will rock your world very soon

Zed Nelson is a photographer whose books include *Gun Nation*

Marcus Oakley has been baking flapjacks and learning to play hippie surf rock guitar

Sonia Ortiz Alcón helped lay out this mag and her work can be seen at www.foreignoffice.com

Mitch O'Connell is a comic artist whose work can be seen at www.mitchoconnell.com

and can only produce work when his mental state is a fine balance of energy and misery

Chris Watson invites you to sample some king-size art and design at www.chris-watson.co.uk

Tony White is the *Idler* Literary Editor. His novel, *Foxy-T*, was recently published to great acclaim

Chris Yates is a legendary fisherman, photographer, master of idleness and author of *The Secret Carp* (Merlin Unwin)

James Parker is a young Dad and writer living far, far away in Boston, Mass

Kevin Parr is a writer and angler. He can sometimes be found on the A33 near Winchester

Daniel Pemberton has finally left home

Nick Roberts is an illustrator. He lives in East London

Greg Rowland (above) is a legitimate businessman

Jock Scot (right) is a poet

Ivor Smullen is a freelance journalist whose books include *Taken For A Ride: A Distressing Account of the Misfortunes and Misbehaviour of the Early British Railway Traveller* (Herbert Jenkins, 1968)

Louis Theroux (above right) is a journalist and broadcaster

Gwyn Vaughn Roberts lives in Wales

NOTES FROM THE COUCH

THE IDLER'S DIARY

Crap Towns

AS YOU read this, the Idler's Crap Towns franchise should be in full swing. Crap Towns started life as a web project where we invited readers to nominate the worst places to live in Britian. The quality of the entries was so high that we decided to collect them in a book, complete with defences from local councillors, plus statistics and photos of rubbish heaps and concrete bunkers pretending to be libraries. *The Idler Book of Crap Towns: The 50 Worst Places to Live in the UK*, edited by Sam Jordison and Dan Kieran, is published by Boxtree and is priced £10. To attack or defend a town, or to browse the thousands of previous entries, go to our website at www.idler.co.uk

Delays, Apologies, Sabbaticals

WE APOLOGISE for the long gap between this issue and the previous one. This was caused by the fact that Tom and Gavin quit town for seven months to work on their book projects and lounge around. Gav moved his operation to the beautiful loafer's capital Rome, while Tom moved to a farmhouse in North Devon. We have often been criticised for working too hard on the Idler so our retreats were a chance to try to practise what we preach. You can read Tom's account of the country life – which is surprisingly strenuous – on the Idler's website at www.idler.co.uk.

Decline of the Club

GENTLEMAN'S clubs, established for well-heeled idlers to relax in congenial surroundings, seem to be on the decline, *writes Ivor Smullen*. In 1986 there were 70 London clubs and 96, including yacht clubs, outside the capital. Today both these figures are under 60. Still running but on its uppers is the Bishop Auckland Club in Co. Durham, founded in 1868, which has half as many members as nine years ago, is open only three nights a week, and has had to move premises in the fight against escalating costs. The club was notorious for its dress code and one member recalls being

JEFF HARRISON

reprimanded for wearing a V-neck sweater. "Only cardigans," he says ruefully, "were allowed." The secretary, Brian Shaw, remembers the general relief when the word went out, on a day of temperatures exceeding 80 degrees, that members could wrench off their ties without causing offence. Meanwhile, after a century and a half, the Leeds Club, believed by its members half way through the 19th century to be one of the finest in the land, was recently put up for sale. It has 200 members (now of both sexes) and boasts a huge ballroom; an ancient, high-backed porter's chair; and lockers for storing your own wine.

the Idler book of

CRAP TOWNS
THE 50 WORST PLACES TO LIVE IN THE UK

G288 MUE

'Truly inspired . . . The Domesday book of misery' The Sunday Telegraph

FEATURING HULL • BASINGSTOKE • LIVERPOOL • MORECAMBE • CUMBERNAULD • HACKNEY • WINCHESTER • HYTHE

OUR LONG-AWAITED COMPENDIUM OF BRITAIN'S MOST AWFUL SPOTS IS NOW OUT

Confessions of a Book Buyer

READERS searching for old out of print books at low prices should check out abebooks.co.uk. It's a fantastic website which searches the shelves of all the little antiquarian bookshops in the country and the world. For example, we recently purchased an 1893 cloth-bound copy of

Confessions Of An Opium Eater by Thomas De Quincey for just £3. So much more enjoyable and so much cheaper than the Penguin Classic.

The French Kill Fun

PROPOSALS by the right-wing French government to change the country's unemployment benefit scheme for artists, actors, dancers and technicians were greeted in the summer by a massive wave of strikes and cancellations. Most memorably, the Avignon Festival - France's equivalent to Edinburgh - was completely cancelled. The arts workers believe that the changes would lead to less choice in projects accepted, less autonomy, and greater reliance on private sponsorship. Pity the poor French: the work-obsessed Prime Minister recently announced his vision of a new moral order, saying: "Il faut reapprendere l'art de rêver tôt". The French must relearn the art of getting up early. From a nation of flâneurs to a nation of disciplined drudges: how the Republic has fallen!

Tony's Toil Laws

MEANWHILE, there is nothing to be smug about at home as far as the campaign for idleness goes. Tony Blair has recently got himself in trouble for refusing to accept a piece of Euro legislation which limits the working week to 48 hours. Blair believes that businesses would become less productive if staff did not toil for long 19th century-style working days. Under the cover of promoting freedom and choice - "everyone should be permitted to work as long as they like!" – Blair has come out as the consummate striver, sadly clinging to the religion of hard work. He has also made the age-old mistake of assuming that longer hours lead to greater productivity, and therefore believes that the 48 hour week would damage exports and everything. "Travailler moins, produire plus," is the truth, as the French, those lovers of paradox, are well aware.

Nation Of Time Servers

ACCORDING to recent government survey, retail staff work the longest hours. Anyone who has ever worked in a shop will also know that sitting behind a shop counter is possibly the most unbearably tedious way to spend an afternoon ever invented. And the same survey said that an increasing number of employees are working more than sixty hours a week: one in six surveyed said they were working more than 60 hours a week compared to one in eight two years ago. Idlers, where are you?

To Business

AFTER ten years of paying only the most fleeting attention to matters of commerce, we at the *Idler* have decided it is time to move our magazine closer to the centre of British culture. To help us to do this we are looking to appoint a Commercial Director, someone who knows the ways of the world, someone who can take this labour of love – and powerful brand – and turn it into a thriving enterprise. Idler fans with experience in magazine publishing should write to tom@idler.co.uk ☜

THE IDLER QUESTIONNAIRE:
JOHN MICHELL

JOHN MICHELL: MYSTIC, DAILY MIRROR COLUMNIST, THINKER

What time do you get up?
Midday.

Do you leap out of bed the moment you wake or lie slumbering?
Lie.

Do you smoke and drink, and if so, how much?
Much.

How many hours work do you put in on an average day?
All I can spare.

Do you take holidays?
No.

Where do you live?
At home in London.

Where do you work?
At home in London.

Where do you think?
All over.

What are your three greatest pleasures?
Resting, sleeping, staring about.

Do you like money?
When it comes.

Is the world a better or a worse place for idlers today than ten years ago?
Same.

Are you happy?
So far.

How many hours do you sleep at night/day?
Eight to ten.

What are you reading?
Mostly proofs.

If it came to the crunch, would you choose money or art?
Depends on the art.

What have you been thinking about?
Same as most men.

Who are your heroes?
Yehudi Menuhin.

Any advice for young people?
Don't worry, it's not your fault.

Do you like to go a-wandering?
Not too far.

What is paradise?
Other people.

READERS' LETTERS

Hello,

I very much enjoy dipping into the Idler website, especially at work. I have one question: Why are there no female idle idols or conversations/ interviews with women? I'm starting to think that maybe women, due to their cultural conditioning, are just not very good at being idle. What do you think?

Laura

Ed writes: This is a question that has foxed us for many years. Are women less lazy than men? And if so, why? Are they genetically programmed to toil or are they conditioned that way? Any readers with any suggestions for female idlers, celebrated or obscure, alive or dead, we'd love to hear from you. Write to me at tom@idler.co.uk

Hi there,

I absolutely love your website. I cried with laughter, then I came across the Chris Yates article and couldn't believe that – brilliant. One of my all time heroes.

Simon

Dear Idlers,

I'm just e-mailing to say thank you thank you thank you for writing such a brilliant magazine. Thank God for you guys, I was starting to feel I was the only Idler out there.

I'm a sixth form student, and, for some bizarre reason unknown to me, everyone around me suffers from this work ethic. Try as I might, people are determined to actually work, and try to force me to do the same. If it was up to me, I'd stay in bed 'til early afternoon, snoozing with my cat (who's also a great Idler, only ever going out for her "constitutional"), but I'm forced to get up at 7am. Its been proven that teenagers need to lie in 'til at least 10am to get their proper amount of sleep, so I don't know what the school system is on about.

However, I've managed to sneakily introduce the concept of idling to some friends, via your magazine, so hopefully I can set up a campaign to bring down this oppresive system...

Anyway, thanks guys, for letting me know there are other idlers out there.

Yours,
Laura Haslam

Dear Idlers,

I thought you might like to know about my book: "Healthy Man Does Not Need Work – Finnish Laziness."

In it, I define three types of Laziness, which have been specified in traditional Finnish proverbs. I would like to know from your readers: "are these types of people common in Britain?"

Type One: Depressed Lazy Bone. He attempts to work, but simply can't extend his efforts past waking up. He is negative, self-destructive and nobody likes him. Laziness will destroy him. Type Two: Idle Trickster. This man does what ever he wants, whenever he wants. He has a big mouth and irritates his company. When he feels like working, he is capable of working as hard as seven men, but he will make an arrogant show of his efforts. Once he has exerted himself, he will take pleasure in being (justifiably) idle for the next fortnight, avoiding work and talking his way out of things. Type Three: Buddha-like Lazy. Deeming "sitting around" an occupation in its own right, he will rise his hand for food and he will receive it.

He doesn't moan or complain, he is a professional lazy bones. He wants little and gets it for free.

Jyrki Piispa

Ed writes: Every country

has its own history of idleness to be written. We'd love to hear about others. Idlers of the world unite, you have nothing to lose but your chains. The global revolt starts here!

Send us your idle thoughts at: theidlers@idler.co.uk

THE IDLER QUESTIONNAIRE:
DAMIEN HIRST

What time do you get up?
No fixed time.

Do you leap out of bed the moment you wake or lie slumbering?
Leap out.

Do you smoke and drink, and if so, how much?
No.

How many hours work do you put in on an average day?
24.

Do you take holidays?
Yeah, but I always have ideas on holiday.

Where do you live?
Devon.

Where do you work?
Everywhere.

Where do you think?
Cabs.

What are your three greatest pleasures?
Wife and two kids.

Do you like money?
I like all the shit it gets you.

Is the world a better or a worse place for idlers today than ten years ago?
Slightly better.

Are you happy?
On and off.

How many hours do you sleep at night/day?
Eight.

What are you reading?
Al Quaeda and What It Means To Be Modern by John Gray.

If it came to the crunch, would you choose money or art?
Art.

What have you been thinking about?
Death.

HIRST: WORK IS PLAY

Who are your heroes?
Joe Strummer, Keith Allen, Gordon Matta Clark.

Any advice for young people?
Grow up.

Do you like to go a-wandering?
You have to step over the edge to find out where it is sometimes.

What is paradise?
Heaven on earth.

SKIVERS

HEROES AND VILLAINS...

The British Worker

CHEERING figures recently released by the Confederation of British Industry claim that bogus absences cost businesses £11billion a year.

Luxury Sheds Calender

A TRIUMPH of shed porn. Costing just £3.50, the 2003 Luxury Sheds calendar features twelve lovingly photographed sheds hand-picked from allotments round the country. Its manufacturers intend the calendar to celebrate what they call "allotment architecture" and we're pleased to see such winningly inelegant temples of indolence honoured in such style. www.the-sheds.com

---

Majestic Wine Warehouse

ALL SUMMER long we ordered case after case of Marston's Pedigree for just 83p a bottle - that's £9.96 per case, delivered free to your door. Now a press officer informs us this little holiday in the sun is over: the price is going up to £1.08 a bottle, she said, adding that Majestic do not, in fact, deliver beer, unless you order a case of wine at the same time. The fact that we were delivered to was the result of having a nice manager, she said. And no, she responded to my next enquiry, there is no chance of Majestic ever selling tobacco. Apparently, though, you can still get Youngs Special for 83p a bottle. But is Young's Special as good as Marston's Pedigree? Now we can't decide whether Majestic is a friend to idlers or not. What do you think? Real ale lovers please let us know at theidlers@idler.co.uk

---

The Internet

STILL A friend to the office-bound skiver, a recent survey claimed that "shopping online while at work is growing in popularity, with a whopping 31 per cent admitting to buying something online and on the sly while at the office." Consuming, though, is hardly an act of revolt, although it's perhaps preferable to working.

MAJESTIC MAY DLIVER FINE ALES AT LOW PRICES TO YOUR DOOR, IF YOU'RE LUCKY

STRIVERS
...OF THE IDLE UNIVERSE

The Grey Grafters

NEW socio-economic category to describe oldies who, bafflingly, continue to work after retirement. Example: Tony Shelley, 78, who toils as a butcher at Asda. In a recent piece of pro-work propaganda in the *Sun* newspaper, he describes his punishing schedule: "I am up at 3.30am and leave the house at 4.30am to get there by 5am. I then have a cup of tea and get ready to start work at 6am – then I'm on till 11.30am." In return for donating most of his life to Asda, Tony gets £6.14 an hour, or about £135 a week after tax. But, more baffling still, he will sometimes work for free. "I normally work 30 hours a week but if there's a job that needs doing I'll take the overtime – if not I'll finish the job anyway."

PRO-WORK PROPAGANDA
RECENTLY PUBLISHED IN THE SUN

Spam Email

THE IDLER replied to each and every email promising increased length, girth and satisfaction, and now our entire staff have 14-inch cocks.

Strimmers

THE STRIMMER is one of those so-called labour-saving inventions that doesn't actually save any labour. Rather, they make extra work. They break, they run out of petrol, they blind you with small pieces of grit, they are slow, tiring to use and expensive. And they shatter the peace of the countryside with their 2-stroke whine. You'd be better off with a pair of nail scissors. And anyway, what's wrong with long grass? Strimmers take Mother Nature's beautiful wilderness and turn it into flat bourgeois grass-scapes.

Cats

WE USED to think that these languid killers were friends to the Idler. No more. Having recently acquired two kittens in order to get rid of the mice, we found that the cats were a lot more trouble than the mice ever were. This is because of their turds. Everywhere. All over the house. Every morning. Stinking. Not to mention the entrails of poor little voles.

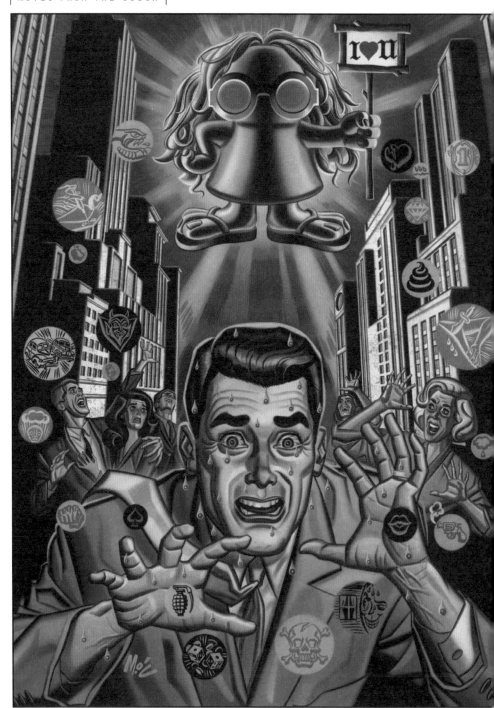

THE TRUTH

The world is nothing like as crime-infested, dangerous and damaging to your health as the *Daily Mail* would have you believe.
Here Brian Dean of *Anxiety Culture* presents some statistics to make you feel better.
Illustrations by Mitch O'Connell

THE ONE YOU LOVE (DETAIL) BY MITCH O'CONNELL · www.mitchoconnell.com

Deaths

Following figures are for England & Wales, 2002 – from the Office for National Statistics (they use the same categories/terms as the World Health Organisation, but these figures are more up to date than WHO's).

Total deaths (all causes)............535,356

HIV disease (AIDS*) 197
Diseases of circulatory system (eg heart diseases and strokes): 209,948
Neoplasms (cancer)................................140,453
Pneumonia................................32,769
Infectious and parasitic diseases 4,335
Asthma................................1,276

Total by accidents................................10,714
Transport related accident....................6,459
Accidental falls 2,511
Accidental Drowning/submersion................191
Exposure to fire/smoke................................352
Accidental poisoning................................1,648

Suicide/intentional self-harm.........3,319

Assault (total)................................385
Assault by "rifle, shotgun and larger firearm discharge" 7
(2001 figure; 2002 not available)
Assault by "other and unspecified firearm discharge" 24
(2001 figure)
Assault by "sharp object":................................118
(2001 figure)
Assault by "pushing from high place" 1
(2001 figure)
Assault by "hanging, strangulation and suffocation" 34
(2001 figure)

ONS/WHO categories for death by assault seem to differ from police definitions of homicide, so I'm not sure how the above figure of 385 deaths by assault fits with the recorded police homicide figure of 886. Possibly, if a heart attack occurs, that's categorised as such under ONS/WHO categories, but as homicide by police - but that's speculation on my part.

*"AIDS" isn't a category they use. They always say "HIV Disease". As far as I'm aware, everybody who has AIDS also has HIV Disease. But not everybody with HIV Disease is classified as having AIDS.

Miscellaneous death statistics (from 'Equinox', Channel 4 TV, 13/4/99):

• For every death from sexually transmitted diseases there were 20 a century ago.

• For every death from infectious diseases there were 130 in the middle ages.

• In Britain each year approximately 20 people are electrocuted by their alarm clock or bedside light.

• Another 20 are killed falling over as they get out of bed.

• 600 per year die from falling down the stairs.

Crime

Total recorded homicides 886
(England & Wales, for year 2001/2002)
(Source: British Crime Survey 2001/2002)

The homicide rate in Britain today is roughly the same as in the mid-19th century.
(The Independent, 25/9/1996)

For every one person murdered today, ten were murdered in the middle ages.
('Equinox', Channel 4 TV, 13/4/99)

One in three elderly women feels "very unsafe", but fewer than one in 4,000 will be assaulted.
(The Times, 11/9/96)

Total recorded child abductions 583
(England & Wales, for year 2001/2002):
(Source: British Crime Survey 2001/2002)

The number of children murdered by strangers (in Britain) averages below 10 a year. For example, Home Office figures show that the total in the decade from 1988-1997 was 57, an average of six a year.
(The Guardian, 2/8/99)

"The chances of a child aged one to four being killed by a stranger are less than one in a million, and have fallen by a third since 1988, while the risk to a child of five to 15 is even less."
(Quoted from a front-page Guardian story, 2/8/99, criticising scaremongering tactics of charities such as NSPCC)

According to the *Guardian*, 12/7/2002, the average person in Britain is burgled only once every 50 years. That seems unbelievable, but is confirmed by the recorded police figures (approx 200 domestic burglaries per 10,000 households per year):

Recorded domestic burglaries per 10,000 households 214
(England & Wales, 2001/2002)
Recorded domestic burglaries per 10,000 households..200
(England & Wales, 2000/2001)
Recorded domestic burglaries per 10,000 households..220
(England & Wales, 1999/2000)
(Source: British Crime Survey 2001/2002)

Half of all domestic burglaries have a value of property stolen less than £500.
(Source: British Crime Survey 2001/2002).

More from the British Crime Survey (generally accepted as the most authoritative source on British crime statistics) for 2001/2002:

"Between 1999 and 2001/02, crime fell by 14 per cent... This figure includes falls in domestic burglary (down 23%), vehicle thefts (down 14%) and common assaults (down 28%)."

"Almost one-third of respondents (30 per

cent) believed that crime had risen 'a lot', and a further third felt that crime had risen 'a little' over the previous two years. This is despite the total number of crimes reported to the BCS falling by 14 per cent between 1999 and 2001/02."

"There was a notable increase in the proportion believing that crime had risen 'a lot' in the first quarter of 2002, rising to 35% from 27% in the final three months of 2001. This period witnessed a heightened degree of press coverage on crime, which particularly focused on a claimed rise in crime... Readers of the national tabloid papers are much more likely to consider the national crime rate to have increased over this period, compared to broadsheet readers (42 per cent versus 26 per cent)."

"Since 1995, the BCS has reported a fall in crime at each survey. There was a 22 per cent fall in the crime measured by the BCS over the last five years from 1997 to 2001/02"

"The increase in violent crime recorded by the police, in contrast to the estimates from the BCS, appears to be largely due to increased recording by police forces.

Taking into account recording changes, the real trend in violence against the person in 2001/02 may have been a reduction of around five per cent"

Injuries

You are not very likely to be injured by a mad axeman. :

From the latest Statistical Abstract of the United States, (1999 figures):
Number of injuries involving
toilets.. 56,424
Number of injuries involving
lawn mowers 70,640
Number of injuries involving
ceilings and walls.....................................259,301
Number of injuries involving
beds..455,027

31,000 people per year in the US are injured by their "grooming devices", compared to 16,670 injured by hatchets and axes.
(The *Independent*, 4/10/99)

Meanwhile, in Britain, 60 people a year are seriously injured putting on their socks.
(*Equinox*, Channel 4 TV, 13/4/99) . ☯

NICK ROBERTS

KICK OUT THE JAMS

Why bother undressing for bed? Nadia Shireen celebrates the pleasures and practical benefits of sleeping in your clothes

The winter months leave us with a need to insulate and conserve heat. We struggle to remain cosy at any cost. The low temperatures and need to hibernate induce a habit I cling on to long after chills have left the air: sleeping in my clothes. It makes sense and feels great. Why expose flesh needlessly to the harsh atmosphere, why suffer the abrasions of removing trouser-wear, why allow for goose-pimples and undue physical strain? Make the journey from lucidity to slumber a short and easy one.

The feeling of waking up in your clothes is glorious. Like when you were a teenager and first woke on a stranger's floor after an enjoyable night out.

There's a sense of smug satisfaction, as if you've had a successful afternoon nap in the office stationery cupboard (if you have done this but do not work in an office, congratulations on your impressive narcoleptic terrorism).

It is the ideal way to ease into the day, and is also beneficial for people who tend to be late for things. The baying hygiene and fashion donkeys can be silenced by changing into fresh apparel in the afternoon, which is a much more pleasing time of day to stride around your home or place of work naked. If you absolutely must take off the clothes you are wearing, at least have the decency to do so in bed. Do not rush this process - take it in stages. You will probably find yourself exhausted, naked from the waist down apart from your socks. See? You were silly to even try. Now leave the rest of your clothes on, turn over and go to sleep.

Ladies may be wondering if sleeping in clothes will work for them too. Of course it will. Can you sleep in your bra? Yes. Will you wake up with misshapen breasts? Very possibly. But think of the time you've saved, and no-one selects underwear sensibly in the morning anyway.

There should be as few obstacles as possible between you and sleep. Contact lens wearers are always at an immediate disadvantage. They are cruelly interrupted from a blissful, hazy descent into oblivion before waking with a sudden jolt to remember that they still have to peel those plastic bits off their eyeballs. Which is why they above all should insist on sleeping in their clothes. It is their right, the poor bastards. In bed with someone else? Don't worry. If they have any carnal desires,

hang back and eventually the work of undressing will be done for you. If you are keen to look presentable in the morning, allow yourself five minutes of rolling, time so that you become, in effect, a human iron. It works quite well. Do not, however, get rid of your nightwear. Pyjamas are wonderful inventions, and do have their time and place. About mid-afternoon, on the sofa. ☻

THE IDLER QUESTIONNAIRE:
BILLY CHILDISH

CHILDISH: MUSICIAN, ARTIST, POET AND CHEERFUL CHAP

What time do you get up?
8.30/10.30.

Do you leap out of bed the moment you wake or lie slumbering?
I like to relax myself.

Do you smoke and drink, and if so, how much?
Eat chocolate.

How many hours work do you put in on an average day?
15, sometimes one.

Do you take holidays?
No.

Where do you live?
Chatham, Kent.

Where do you work?
At home, paint at my mother's and recording and playing music: out and about.

Where do you think?
In bed, toilet and kitchen.

What are your three greatest pleasures?
Eating, sex, laughing.

Do you like money?
Yes, and also dislike it a lot.

Is the world a better or a worse place for idlers today than ten years ago?
Worse.

Are you happy?
Yes.

How many hours do you sleep at night/day?
Eight.

What are you reading?
Don Quixote.

If it came to the crunch, would you choose money or art?
Art.

What have you been thinking about?
Re-modernism and a spiritual renaissance.

Who are your heroes?
Van Gogh, Dostoevsky, Christ and Buddha.

Any advice for young people?
Remember what you liked as a kid and do it: authenticity and not originality.

Do you like to go a-wandering?
Now and then I might have a quick wander.

What is paradise?
Contentment.

MR LAZY

Greg Rowland writes in praise of the great idler,
sleeper and revolutionary inactivist

t is long overdue, but let us now celebrate the
most famous narcoleptic in all of children's
literature — the astonishingly slack Mr Lazy.
  Mr Lazy is a Mr Man. The Mr Men are a group of
simply drawn entities, each of whom is dominated
by one overriding character trait. Thus Mr Strong
is strong, Mr Greedy is greedy and Mr Fussy is
fussy. Each character seeks to make his own
unique signifier palpable in actual experience (or
the "lifeworld" as Jorgen Habermas or some other
German refers to it, except he employs a long
German word to describe it. For further
information on the lifeworld and other long German
words please refer to the *Journal of Long
Pretentious Academic German Compound Nouns*.)
  Roger Hargreaves' Mr Men world (or
weltgeshunggshtickdreckherrzimmer) is often a
reactionary place. Those born with a
monomaniacal fixation on a single issue (like a
living embodiment of the Schopenhaurian "Will")
tend to be forced towards the bourgeois norm by
the close of the narrative. For example, the
powerfully-lunged Mr Noisy is studiously ignored
by local shopkeepers until he
modifies his decibilic register. Mr
Nosey, a subverter of bourgeois
notions of propriety and the
private Self, is similarly
ostracised for his own
transgressions until he learns to
modify his behaviour. Most
startlingly of all, in an
unpublished manuscript, Mr
Radical is subjected to torture
by means of electrodes inserted
into his oversized red brain, while
being anally raped by Mr
Conformity.
  However Mr Lazy is different.
Mr Lazy is unconscious for over
85% of the story. Hence,
because the narrative exists
outside of the restrictive
consciousness of the bourgeois
Self, even the conservative
Hargreaves seems unable to pull

the character back from his self-expression in the form of sleep.

Moreover, Mr Lazy lives in Sleepyland — a place which, like some post-revolutionary utopia, essentially denies the need not only for work, but for activity of almost any kind.

Hence in Sleepyland, the birds often fall from the sky because they don't flap their wings fast enough and everybody gets up in the afternoon. Modified by some quantum disturbance in the reactionary notion of linear time, even the conventional rules of physics do not apply to Sleepyland — a kettle takes four hours to boil. Sleepyland is a place ruled by the unconscious.

However, the forces of consciousness and the puritanical work ethic are strongly represented here too. The arrival of the besuited Mr Busy and Mr Bustle attempts to deform the idyllic somnambulance of Sleepyland and, more specifically, the indolent life of Mr Lazy.

They arrive with a set of instructions designed specifically to make Mr Lazy work really hard. Their inhumane demands on Mr Lazy — a list of energetic and practical tasks he must undertake — cause some form of synaptic rupture within Mr Lazy's neural pathways by way of response:

"Oh dear," groaned Mr Lazy in a daze. "The wood to clean and the beds to get and the floors to cut and the coal to cook and the windows to make and the plates to mend and the furniture to chop and the grass to wash and the hedges to dust and the clothes to clip?"

Nevertheless Mr Lazy is forced to undergo some kind of transformation into a patriarchal Charles Ingles figure as he, with increasing personal sorrow, sets about his allotted chores. Were that not enough, the tyrannical Mr Busy and Mr Bustle send Mr Lazy out on the longest walk he has ever been on:

"Now," they said when he'd finished, "it's time for a walk!"
And off they set on the longest walk Mr Lazy had ever been on.
Mr Lazy is one of those people who never walks when he has a chance of sitting down, and never sits down when he has a chance of lying down. But this day he had no choice. They made him walk for miles and miles, until he felt his legs must be worn right down to his body. Poor Mr Lazy!

Poor Mr Lazy indeed. The long walk is one of the most fiendish devices of torture ever created by the crapulent behemoths of late capitalism. And yet, Mr Busy and Bustle, on Mr Lazy's return to Yawn Cottage, seek to outdo themselves: "'Right. Now for a run!' said Mr Busy. 'Oh no,' groaned Mr Lazy.'"

Yet it is the very sound of the Mr Bustle's starting whistle that provides the means of liberation from Mr Lazy's activity-led bondage. It is the whistle that wakes Mr Lazy from this hideous dream of crypto-Protestant *ashlocharbeteinwelt*. It is not, as it turns out, Mr Bustle's whistle that stirs Mr Lazy, but rather it is the whistling of the kettle that he had put on the stove before falling asleep and being plagued by these demons of toil.

In an unexpected but joyously liberating plot-twist, the whole sad affair had been a dream — "Mr Lazy heaved a sigh of relief." Soon, while thinking about his dream, Mr Lazy falls asleep once again, at which point the text closes. The unconscious reigns supreme once more, and all activity is consigned to the dustbin of history. Mr Lazy remains undaunted by the forces of bourgeois industry and consciousness and finds elegant strategies for non-conformity by a consistent retreat into the world of the unconsciousness.

We can only hope that, as the forces of late capitalism crumble around our ears, that we heed Mr Lazy's vital revolutionary message — that the only genuinely subversive response to the horrors of the current social order is to go to sleep and forget about it all. ◉

THE FINE LINE BETWEEN

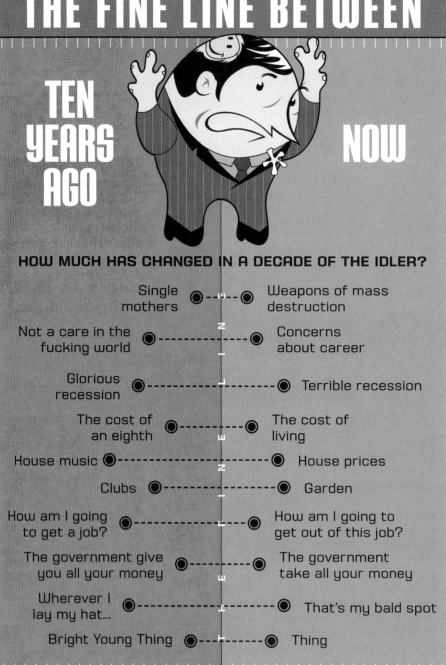

TEN
YEARS
AGO

NOW

NICK ROBERTS

HOW MUCH HAS CHANGED IN A DECADE OF THE IDLER?

Single mothers ●---F--● Weapons of mass destruction

Not a care in the fucking world ●------------● Concerns about career

Glorious recession ●------------● Terrible recession

The cost of an eighth ●------------● The cost of living

House music ●------------● House prices

Clubs ●------------● Garden

How am I going to get a job? ●------------● How am I going to get out of this job?

The government give you all your money ●------------● The government take all your money

Wherever I lay my hat... ●------------● That's my bald spot

Bright Young Thing ●------● Thing

THE WIT AND WISDOM OF

PETER COOK

Paul Hamilton presents choice cuts from the man who looked as if he was sitting on the funniest joke in the world, but couldn't be arsed to tell it

Perhaps the comedian Peter Cook didn't die. Maybe he discovered a method of being even more idle than he was prior to 1995. A loafer par excellence ("Indolent to the point of madness" was his self-description), the obituaries unanimously stated his was a talent wasted. Hmmm. Anybody who eared a cock to the gems he produced, be it the sixties revue *Beyond The Fringe* ("Now, we shall receive four minutes warning of any impending nuclear attack. Some people have said, 'Oh my goodness me – four minutes? That's not a very long time!' Well, I would remind those doubters that some people in this great country of ours can run a mile in four minutes."), the Derek and Clive LPs made with Dudley Moore, or the *Why Bother* radio series – now a CD – he made with Chris Morris might beg to differ... if they weren't otherwise preoccupied by laughing.

Rather than celebrate Cook's wayward, insouciant brilliance with an all-too-predictable cache of extracts of classic sketches from his supposed glory days of the sixties, we present a random selection of skewed views, comic riffs and contrarianism culled willy-nilly from eighties and nineties chat shows and press interviews. Peter Cook unfailingly detected the absurdity factor in

"I don't like working all that much. What's the point in working?"

everything, not least his own job at amusing people for profit. "My best performances are in private, in restaurants," he once reflected, "but I'd feel rather mean passing the hat round afterwards."

I set my other trousers on fire. I was in my garden with a friend the other night trying to light some candles. I said, "You've been to public school and been in the Boy Scouts, you light the fucking candles." Trouble is, if the candles aren't lit, you can't see them. So he lit several white flowers and I lit my own trousers. I had to jump into the pond I'd just built. I put my leg in it. Had I been really arseholed, I would have probably put the wrong leg in and wondered why I was still alight.

I've always slagged off Dudley and there is no reason for me to stop now that he's a Hollywood star. He complained to me that in Hollywood he's surrounded by fools and sycophants who laugh at everything he says. I reminded him that when he was living here he was surrounded by intelligent people who kept telling him what a toad he was

The ideal commercial I did was with Dudley and Ursula Andress, directed by Dick Lester, for a soft drink called Solo. I said, "For God's sake, Dudley, don't tell them what's wrong with this drink."

"What?" "The name for a start. It implies you drink it on your own, which is ridiculous. The second thing going against it is that it tastes absolutely disgusting!" The thing never got shown and we got a bundle of money. I am very much open to campaigns like that.

I don't think I could survive without television. I rely entirely on TV to breathe and live.

The biggest star in the world is Keith Richards. He defies death and has such wonderful make-up. I always like people who kick heroin and switch to Bourbon.

I saw Nirvana in Australia. I also like Guns 'N Roses. I've never met them but they behave like proper rock stars. I think they take their duties seriously. I don't like these fucking kids who don't smoke, don't drink and don't sleep around. I mean, what kind of rock star is that?

My beauty routine is a mixture of aerobics, isotonics, isometrics and a little bit of yoga. I basically follow a strict Buddhist drill every morning. To the uninitiated, though, it might look suspiciously like a fat middle-aged man lying in bed, drinking a cup of instant coffee and smoking a Silk Cut.

Q: You've got a reputation for being perverse, if I can put it that way. There's no other way of putting it, actually. You tend to like what other people don't like at the time.
PETER: Oh yes, it's pathetic. I mean, from the word go. If they prefer The Beatles, I'd say I preferred The Stones. I'd pick The Stones' least favourite number – the one they couldn't bear – and I'd say it's the best thing they ever did. When The Beach

Boys came along, I said Jan and Dean were much better. And I still am today. I mean, if pressed, I'd say that Donna Reed is a far better Miss Ellie [on Dallas] than Barbara Bel Geddes.

Q: Who's your favourite tennis player, now that Wimbledon's coming up?

PETER: Well, nobody likes him so I must say Lendl. It's very difficult being perverse. I mean, you glue yourself to Ivan Lendl and say "His charm doesn't come through on the court but it's all there in private." But Big Bill Tilden was my favourite. Big Bill Tilden was the only child molester to become champion at Wimbledon.

I just don't like working all that much. What's the point in working? It's good if it's funny and you enjoy the people you're with, but I'm really quite good at taking time off. It's a highly skilled thing. I do chat shows 'cos they're easy. I did one, *Whose Line Is It Anyway?*, then decided it was too far to go. If it's any good, people always say, "It's all worked out beforehand anyway", so what's the fucking point?

I'm not very busy. I'm very good at having holidays. I really am. A lot of people can't. I could have been born rich without having any of the horrible consequences. It wouldn't have bothered me. A lot of people have to go and work but I'm actually quite good at leisure. That's probably my major skill. And also I find – I don't remember jokes as such – but when funny things come out the first time they're immediately far better and once I try and repeat them it's really boring. I get most of that from conversations with people but there isn't a profession of just, you know, having conversations. I think I deserve a State Income just for being

alive, but I think you should retire at 20 and you get a huge pension until you're about 70 and then start a bit of work.

I have no ambitions but I am interested in being lazier than I already am. I like zoos and went to Melbourne Zoo where there are large amounts of space for the animals. I got lured into this great duckbilled platypus place. I'd seen them before but I thought I'd better go in again. We went in and there were these alarming signs on the wall saying "YOU ARE NOW ENTERING THE SILENT WORLD OF THE PLATYPUS – BE COMPLETELY QUIET!" and another sign saying "SHHH! ON NO ACCOUNT DISTURB THE PEACE OF THE PLATYPUS" on this huge tank of water. There were two old ladies peering at this tank, whispering very loudly to each other. One whispered, "Can you see it?" There was nothing in this tank at all. They were looking at water for about ten minutes – as indeed was I. I was with my girlfriend and about to come out with this bullshit – "They're masters of disguise..." Anyway, the old ladies cleared off and there was this shattering shout from the platypus attendant who barrelled in through the door shouting, "ALL OUT! ALL OUT! CLOSING DOWN!" I said, "What about the peace of the platypus?" He said, "They're not 'ere," and opened a trapdoor and pushed some through with a stick. They moved up and down twice and he said, "Right, that's enough. Out you go!" Now, his job is a bit too active for me but I wouldn't mind supervising him.

PETER: I feel a lot more upbeat.

Q: So you're going to go out there and grab life - ?

PETER: Grab life by the throat, wrestle it to the ground and kick it to death. 🔘

ROBERT
DEAN FRISBIE

In 1924, Robert Dean Frisbie, a disillusioned twentysomething, abandoned worldly duty and moved to a South Seas island, whose natives were a byword for indolence. By Dan Kieran

I was sitting in a pub a few months ago talking to an old friend I hadn't seen in years about the *Idler*. In the middle of the conversation he drew his head back as if something grand had suddenly entered his head. He smiled broadly and said, "Oh my God. You've got to read Frisbie."

I can't remember much of what he said about the man who I immediately assumed was the inventor of the flat, circular object you throw around in the park. And as always happens when you're in a pub and someone suggests an author you would like, I forgot about it as soon as I walked out the door and got on with my life.

A few weeks later the postman buzzed and handed me a box from Amazon. It was odd. I hadn't ordered anything, it wasn't my birthday, I racked my brain in case I'd got drunk and

bought a book that I'd forgotten about. Nope. It was a complete puzzler. So I tore open the box and out fell a green book with an American dollar price tag on the spine, "$5.95". I picked it up and read *The Book of Puka Puka - A Lone Trader On A South Sea Atoll*. Beneath the title there was a painting of a man walking with his arm around a beautiful island maiden in foaming white surf on a tropical beach. Under that it said simply, "Robert Dean Frisbie". I looked at the invoice in the box and read the short message, "I'm assuming you never got round to getting this - Love Brian."

It was an amazing feeling and a wonderful thing to do if you want to cheer someone up out of the blue. I felt slightly ashamed that I hadn't got round to getting it. God knows I'd remembered enough boring crap in the weeks that had followed, like changing my mobile phone tariff and paying my credit card bills, so I sat down and started reading it immediately. I read it cover to cover in one sitting. It was brilliant. So now I'm telling you, you've got to read Frisbie.

The following passage is from the opening chapter of *The Book of Puka Puka* - Frisbie's autobiographical account of his years on the island in the South Pacific. It's 1924, Frisbie is twenty-eight and, inspired by his hero Robert Louis

off the reef – eating, dancing, love-making on shore... You'll be very lonesome, and you know white men often go insane under such conditions as you find here. I'll leave you, if you're sure you want to stay; but if you've changed your mind, speak out now. I'll take you back with me and there'll be no harm done.

Frisbie mulls it over:

"...I thought of my long search in the Pacific for an island where I would be a law to myself and beyond the reach of even the faintest echo from the noisy clamour of the civilised world. I thought of my library of five or six hundred books boxed up in the hold, and of my half dozen kegs of fine old liquor smuggled from Tahiti. Then I visualised myself in a cool thatched hut, my brow fanned by the trade wind... Contentment's motherly hand already seemed to rest on me soothingly. Here no officious relatives or friends would cry: "Young man, you are wasting your life! Here you are, nearing thirty, with nothing accomplished, with no plans for the future, with no bank account! You must reform! It is your duty to keep the wheels of industry moving! Be efficient! Abstain from alcohol and tobacco! Join the church! Study Pelmanism!" I squeezed Viggo's arm. "No, I want to stay." I said. "Can I take my things ashore now?" 🌀

Stevenson, is on his way to open a copra trading station on the island of Puka Puka. There he hopes to live out the rest of his days and write his Moby Dick. He and the boat's captain, Viggo, have spent three months sailing across the Pacific Ocean to reach the island. As soon as they set eyes on Puka Puka, Viggo attempts, one final time, to persuade his companion not to leave the boat and go ashore:

Now there's Puka Puka for you," said Viggo, pointing towards the canoes. There was a slight note of resentment in his tone. "Everything is asleep here... The people see no reason at all for getting up in the morning, and most of 'em don't: they sleep all day, but at night they wake up, and you see them fishing by torchlight

Robert Dean Frisbie's *Book of Puka Puka* **is available from amazon.com for $5.95 or through abebooks.com. ISBN 0-935180-27-3 There are no UK editions of any of his books.**

THE IDLER QUESTIONNAIRE:
WILL SELF

SELF: DAYDREAM BELIEVER

What time do you get up?
7am.

Do you leap out of bed the moment you wake or lie slumbering?
I have a Professor-Brainstawm-style contraption which catapults me into my underwear and showers a bowl of Weetabix in my face. The customary nicotine and caffeine do the rest.

Do you smoke and drink, and if so, how much?
I smoke a pipe, a nice briar nowadays instead of the elegant glass ones I favoured in the past. As for the waters of Lethe, I have crossed over them and now sport in the meadows of sobriety.

How many hours work do you put in on an average day?
Seven or eight, difficult to say, given that as a Tantric consultant breathing is part of my work.

Do you take holidays?
Yes, I'm just off to the Door-dog-knee for a couple of weeks in a Villa with Condeleeza Rice. Lovely woman, very gentle.

Where do you live?
In a traditional Mongolian yurt next to the A303

Where do you work?
In London, and let me tell you the commute is hell.

Where do you think?
I think in the Chiltern Hills with Ian McEwan. You remember that advert for BBC4 which showed Ian wandering among some scrubby bushes on top of the Chilterns, flagged with the slogan: "Everybody needs a place to think"? Well, I'm hiding in the bushes.

What are your three greatest pleasures?
My family, my work and taking little trips (I prefer walking, but will daydream if pressed).

Do you like money?
Money - the anthropologist Mary Douglas sagely observed - is a supreme and specialised form of ritual. I prefer a black mass, but will take money if it's all that's on offer.

Is the world a better or a worse place for idlers today than ten years ago?
About the same, although the service centres on the M40 are a much needed innovation.

Are you happy?
I've never really thought about it, but I suppose I am.

How many hours do you sleep at night/day?
Between six and sixteen.

What are you reading?
The South Country by Edward Thomas, and a biography of CS Lewis by AN Wilson.

If it came to the crunch, would you choose money or art?
I'd choose Mart.

What have you been thinking about?
I haven't an idea in my sweet little head.

Who are your heroes?
My wife, Deborah Orr, and Hala Jaber, soigné Lebanese investigative reporter and pipe smoker.

Any advice for young people?
Throw yourself downstairs head first and arrest your growth.

Do you like to go a-wandering?
Yes, little trips (see above), I walked from my home in Stockwell, London to Harwich on the North Coast of Essex this summer. Four days, 110 miles, sheer bliss, saw no one, prelapsarian world of churches, fields and manor houses. Not an idea in my sweet little head.

What is paradise?
See above.

AN APOLOGY TO IDLERS

Our Sports Editor, the elegant musician and
wastrel John Moore, has a confession to make.
He's been working

y dear fellow Idlers. I have
let you down. I am a traitor. I
am unable to contribute to
this the tenth anniversary issue
of the *Idler* magazine because I
have become busy. It wasn't
deliberate. It goes against all my
principles and lifelong training,
but there you are, shit happens.
Perhaps even the laziest of us
have a few good weeks of work
in us every decade. I sincerely
hope that it is just a phase that
will soon pass, to be replaced
once again by sweet indolence,
intoxication and reverie. I'll tell
you what I am up to in a minute,
but first let me tell you how this
activity all came about.

I was recently entrusted with
the care of my young daughter,
and given the task of walking
her around the block to get her
off to sleep. An innocent and
inexpensive task you might
think. Usually so, but not always.
My favoured route for lulling the

tot into dreamland takes in a number of streets
with some rather good charity shops. Usually my
worst indulgence is a couple of quid for a set of
Russ Conway 45s or a Bernard Manning LP which
pleases me no end and gives the Missus an excuse
to call me an old git. On this occasion, however, I
returned home with one sleeping infant, two
exquisite Chinese silk dressing gowns – one a
beautiful half length smoking jacket of red and
gold, the other full length, of sea green silk with
embroidered dragons, and a rocking horse for the
child. Seventy pounds had been spent, which to my
mind was nothing – had these items been
purchased new on the open market, they would
have put a large dent in a thousand pounds. As is
so often the case, bargains turn up when you are
least able to afford them. However, experience has
taught me that whatever your financial situation, a
genuine bargain must never be ignored. I am not
digressing here, I am about to make a salient point.

The next afternoon, as I sat in the garden,
smoking roll ups and looking stylish, I was
telephoned by a journalist from the *Financial
Times*, who wanted to interview me as the leader
of a new economic sub-group to be featured in his
journal. Apparently my indolence is now a
recognised and respected economic category –

Later that day I learned that my current account balance was £248 – with no prospect of any more income ever

those who value time above money, and who so do the minimum work to enjoy the maximum leisure. Smugly, I waffled on for half an hour, giving soundbite after soundbite, all the time admiring the wonderful swirls and intricate patterns of my smoking jacket. Later that day, I learnt that my current account balance was £248 – with no prospect of more income ever. The royalties from Black Box Recorder's one little hit have dried up: it was good for a year, but now they're back down to one figure.

It was at this point that I realised drastic action was called for. I don't mean as drastic as looking for employment. Nobody could ever pay me what I'm worth. I decided to make another record all of my own... as a way of actually earning money.

I have been putting this off for years now, as much for the good of the public as myself – but I knew that I'd have to attempt it again one day. Black Box Recorder has been an easy ride – three people's effort lighten the workload considerably. Sadly, they also lighten the cash.

For these past two months, I have repaired to the countryside where I am endeavouring to make the next *Thriller*, in a boathouse on the river Loddon. I leave London on Monday morning and return on Friday evening. I wake at seven am, commence work at ten and knock off at midnight. The only contact I have with the outside world is a swan that nests beneath the boathouse and hisses at me until I feed her. At the weekend, I take control of my daughter – who wakes at six thirty and also knocks off at midnight.

This is the only serious work I've done in ten years so I can't complain too much. Also, I am thoroughly enjoying it. There is an end in sight, and if I get too worked up, I can go for a row. The power supply is a bit dangerous- when it rains, I get electric shocks from everything, but it gives the whole venture a sense of danger and nobility.

My intention is that with the success of this record, I'll make a fortune and retire again – until the next time. My family will lead lives of privilege and indulgence and thank their old man from time to time – even let him get drunk occasionally. I think there is some sort of lesson to be learnt here – not all work is bad, just most of it.

I've done the backing tracks and to my mind they sound excellent. I've been thinking about which finishing school to send my daughter to – I don't want her turning in to a snob – and which luxury car to purchase. It has to be fast, sporty and luxurious, yet big on safety features and refinements – I quite like the new Jags. Also, I'll require a country estate, London is just too poky nowadays. I'll need outbuildings, swimming pools, river frontage or beach and a secret garden for middle aged naturism and virgin sacrifices. I think I'll need five million minimum.

Next week I shall be adding my singing to the mix, so I may well have to settle for a hovel with an open cesspit, a rusty Ford Mondeo and custody visits. Still, at least I'll have a lot of spare time – and a smoking jacket. ☻

THE IDLER QUESTIONNAIRE:
ARTHUR SMITH

What time do you get up?
11am.

Do you leap out of bed the moment you wake or lie slumbering?
Leap up, but then leap back again.

Do you smoke and drink, and if so, how much?
Smoke - loads.
Drink - have been retired.

How many hours work do you put in on an average day?
Three.

Do you take holidays?
My life is a holiday.

Where do you live?
Can't remember. Oh! London (south).

Where do you work?
Three yards from my bed

Where do you think?
In the caff.

What are your three greatest pleasures?
Cigarette before, cigarette after.

Do you like money?
No.

Is the world a better or a worse place for idlers today than ten years ago?
Can't remember ten years ago.

Are you happy?
Yes.

How many hours do you sleep at night/day?
Eleven.

What are you reading?
Dante's *Inferno*, Richard & Judy's Autobiography.

If it came to the crunch, would you choose money or art?
I avoid the crunch.

What have you been thinking about?

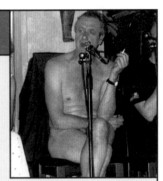

ARTHUR SMITH: BROADCASTER, PLAYWRIGHT AND NATURIST

Death.

Who are your heroes?
Alf Tupper, Joan of Arc, Lenord Cohen.

Any advice for young people?
Don't breed.

Do you like to go a-wandering?
Yes.

What is paradise?
The 3rd, most boring part, of Dante's trilogy. And my girlfriend's tits. (And her brain of course).

ENEMIES OF IDLENESS

THOMAS EDISON

Tom Hodgkinson claims that the great inventor
was merely a lackey of industrial capitalism

Like many enemies of idleness, the tragically dynamic inventor Thomas Edison is celebrated as a great man. It is our contention, however, that Edison actually did a lot of harm to idlers and and was instrumental in causing misery for millions. The world, we think, would have been better off without him and his infernal inventions.

Born in 1847 in Ohio, Edison was inducted into the work ethic a a young age and was already toiling at the age of 13. His job was to sell newspapers and sweets to train travellers passing through his town. When he wasn't hustling for cash in this way, he was improving his mind at home, reading technical books about the latest inventions such as the telegraph. It was this particularly American combination of commercialism and hard work that led to his enormous success.

By 16 he was a full time telegraph operator, and at 19 he was inventing things. His first invention, a machine for vote counting, failed, and after that Edison vowed only to make machines that would make him profit. He then invented a stock ticker device, and received the enormous sum of $40,000 for it and for some other capitalist toys.

Edison's diaries reveal a personality driven by the work ethic. He believed in hard graft (usually for others) and large profits (usually for himself). he was therefore on the side of the devil. Take the following shocking passage:

Most people overeat 100 per cent, and oversleep 100 per cent, because they like it. That extra 100 per cent makes them unhealthy and inefficient. The person who sleeps eight or ten hours a night is never fully asleep and never fully awake – they have only different degrees of doze during the 24 hours... anything which tends to slow work down is a waste. We are always hearing people talk about 'loss of sleep' as a calamity. They better call it loss of time vitality, and opportunity.

Edison claimed only to need four or five hours' sleep, which puts one in mind of Margaret Thatcher's self-advertising as a rejecter of long sleeping. Put together such a brutal personal philosophy with Edison's evident genius and you have a formidable enemy indeed.

How, Edison wondered, could we banish wasteful sleep? In the 1870s, he started work on a device that would rid us of that terrible inconvenience to capitalism, night. This would mean that the factories would be able to work non-stop, and one

excuse for sleep would be removed.

And in December 1879 – oh, dark day for the loafer! – Edison unveiled his greatest invention yet: the electric lightbulb. This cruel device opened the door for every mill-owner to press the workers into yet more misery than they were already used to. The early lightbulbs were rather dim; it was in 1913 that the tungsten filament lightbulb was invented and the light was lit. And it really did have a devastating effect on our sleep patterns. The academic Stanley Coren has shown that in 1910, people slept for an average of nine hours a night. Today, he says, that figure is just under 7 1/2 hours. "In other words," Coren concludes, "Edison can claim to have added more than 500 hours of waking time to every year we live."

Edison made vast fortunes from his dastardly invention, and became friends with that other great enemy of idleness, Henry Ford. It also became apparent that, like many moralists, he did not practise what he preached. One day, when Ford came to visit, he was surprised to find that the great enemy of sleep was asleep. The truth is that Edision was a great napper, and hypocrite.

During the first World War Edison worked for the military, inventing new ways to kill people. His final gift to humanity was the development of a cheap kind of rubber for car tires. He died in October 1931. Edison is taught today as a great hero in American schools; in other words, he is still doing a great deal of harm even after his death by promoting the slave's virtues of industry and work hours. I urge all readers to abandon him and instead to celebrate Edison's contemporary, that great American loafer, Mr Walt Whitman. ◉

BY PETE LOVEDAY

PAUL DAVIS

THIS LAZY RUBBING
OF A 50 PESOS PIECE
IS WORTH 25 QUID.

PAUL DAVIS

THIS EQUALLY LAZY
RUBBING OF A 2 EURO
COIN IS ALSO WORTH 25 QUID.

THANK YOU!

DAVIS

THE IDLER QUESTIONNAIRE:
DOUGLAS COUPLAND

COUPLAND: GENERATION X; HEY NOSTRADAMUS

What time do you get up?
11am. If I'm in New York, 2pm. My body has always wanted to wake up at 11am. It's why I went to art school, because I knew if I went there, I'd never be in a position to take a job requiring getting up at 10:59.

Do you leap out of bed the moment you wake or lie slumbering?
I dawdle until about 11:30.

Do you smoke and drink, and if so, how much?
I quit smoking on Halloween, 1988, but still consider myself a smoker. I have slip dreams all the time. I drink whenever. I can't drink red wine, though. Teenage trauma that remains unresolved. And gin reminds me of poison.

How many hours work do you put in on an average day?
Once I'm vertical, I don't stop.

Do you take holidays?
I don't believe in holidays for myself, as it implies that my life is the opposite of a holiday.

Where do you live?
Vancouver.

Where do you work?
Anywhere. My job is highly portable.

Where do you think?
Well, anywhere, obviously, but if I really need to figure out something, I get in the car and drive for four hours to Seattle or the BC interior with loud music blasting away. and then when I get there, it's magically figured out. I recommend it.

What are your three greatest pleasures?
Everything.

Do you like money?
I believe money is a crystallization of time and free will, the two characteristics that set us apart from everything else in the world. More money multiplies my ability to use time creatively, and to exercise my free will more forcefully. So for that reason, I like it. I get really disgusted when people collect money just to see how much they can collect.

Is the world a better or a worse place for idlers than ten years ago?
About the same. As a species we always seem to factor in enough wiggle room for idleness. And the internet has many many idling converts from the previously industrious.

Are you happy?
Only if I'm making things, or contemplating their making.

How many hours do you sleep at night?
Nine.

What are you reading?
At the moment nothing. I'm in the middle of a fruitful writing patch, and if I read anything but a newspaper, it throws me off.

If it came to the crunch, would you choose money or art?
Art.

What have you been thinking about?
Art.

Who are your heroes?
People who can wake up early and not feel like sludge for the rest of the day.

Any advice for young people?
Never do it for the money, because once you do, you can never go back to doing it just for the sake of doing it. And go to art school.

Do you like to go a-wandering?
I used to. Now the thought of airports makes me queasy. I've simply travelled too much since 1990. I can't look at magazine stands now because they remind me of airports. Or luggage. On the other hand, last month, for no reason other than curiousity, I flew to Newfoundland.

What is paradise?
Things as they stand.

IT'S A BANAL, BANAL, BANAL WORLD

The latest trend in employee training is a motivational system based on Malory's *Morte D'Arthur*, as a horrified Matthew De Abaitua discovers

The most over-trained and underemployed man is in town again, so we meet up for a drink. Since I have alienated most of my close friends and family by ripping off whole chunks of their private lives and turning it into fiction, let us give him a pseudonym, just this once: at random, we'll call him Sly Stone. Based in the personnel department of a major multi-national corporation, Sly Stone gets to go on all sorts of courses that necessitate him coming up to London. These training trips are so frequent that he has developed something of a routine. He dutifully attends the first day of the course, meets up with me afterwards, and then we drink manfully until it is time for me to hail a cab, and time for him to walk – Northern and frugal – through the metropolitan mayhem and back to his the Holiday Inn. During one of these sessions, Sly Stone tells me about a new consultancy who have been engaged to re-engineer his office culture. Their big idea is a motivational system based on Malory's *Morte D'Arthur*.

Essentially he and his colleagues have been taught to phrase their personal development in the terms of Glastonbury and Avalon. Glastonbury represents achievements others can see – that is, a convertible Golf Gti (or whatever those fuckers drive these days) or a new conservatory or a watch that has a dial which tells you how quickly you are drifting through the cold dead vacuum of outer space. Glastonbury is demonstrable material achievements: Avalon is your personal goal, unknown to others. Fulfilling Avalon is your secret destiny, the misty land that only you can see. Achieving one's Glastonbury goes some way to personal fulfilment, but it is only when you have reached your Avalon, the purpose of your soul, that you attain true inner peace.

"How does that work in the office then?" I ask, the ashes of a once-sane culture drifting about us. Sly Stone thinks about this. Then he says: "Well, if the manager dumps a

MIDDLE MANAGERS GET IN TOUCH WITH THEIR INNER AVALON

shitload of work on you in Friday afternoon and says, can you do this by Monday. And you say, well, I was hoping not to work this weekend, then they say, 'Sly Stone, I don't think you are really being true to your inner Avalon.'"

My indignation toward this abuse of the ancient legend of Arthur, a seam of Englishness that has long been a touchstone for the Idler, quickly gives way to the whoring money-grubber within me. I wonder: could I take a classic work of literature and transform it into an incredibly lucrative consultancy? A motivational seminar structured around Gulliver's Travels ("Problems are like Lilliputians, tying you down."). Or Chaucer ("Everyone in here today is a pilgrim, and you all have a tale to tell.") Are there any fruitful correspondences between Blake's mythic system as set out in epic poems of *Jerusalem* (I want the account team to play the role of the Four Zoas and I want the

"Why be heroes just for one day when you can be heroes five days a week?"

marketing executives to think of themselves as Los, and though your Spectre is divided it shouldn't be beyond your powers to build a new Jerusalem, here by – say - next Friday)? The problem with literature is this – it's just so élitist, so word-based, even dour. I need a more popular, entertaining mythic system for my corporate culture re-engineering seminars. Why not take "Yellow Submarine" as our model, ("And so, you can see that – in many ways – you don't just live in a Yellow Submarine. You work in one too.") or Bowie's "Heroes" ("But why be heroes for just one day when you could be heroes five days a week?")

Actually I've got a better idea. Why don't we take everything we have ever loved, all the art and culture that has ever moved us, gather up all the rare gold of our birthright as human beings, and turn it into a giant pair of 24-carat commemorative bollocks?

It's the Dark Ages out there. Our task is not to resist the tidal wave. It is to spirit away all that is precious, lock it up in a secret place, and guard it until the world is ready to behave itself again. ◑

THE IDLER QUESTIONNAIRE:
CHARLES HANDY

CHARLES HANDY: MANAGEMENT GURU TO THE IDLE

What time do you get up?
7am.

Do you leap out of bed the moment you wake or lie slumbering?
Slumbering for one hour.

Do you smoke and drink, and if so, how much?
3 glasses a day.

How many hours work do you put in on an average day?
Six.

Do you take holidays?
Sort of. Six weeks a year at our home in Italy.

Where do you live?
London.

Where do you work?
Norfolk.

Where do you think?
Norfolk.

What are your three greatest pleasures?
Eating & drinking with friends. Reading in the sun. Theatre.

Do you like money?
Enough is as good as a feast.

Is the world a better or a worse place for idlers today than ten years ago?
Worse.

Are you happy?
Extraordinarily so.

How many hours do you sleep at night/day?
Eight.

What are you reading?
Life of Pi and William Trevor's short stories.

If it came to the crunch, would you choose money or art?
Money. I guess. Art is all around for free.

What have you been thinking about?
My new book.

Who are your heroes?
Don't believe in heroes.

Any advice for young people?
Go with your heart.

Do you like to go a-wandering?
Not really.

What is paradise?
Lying in bed with my wife in the morning in Norfolk and not having to get up.

ELIZABETH HANDY

CRAP TOWNS

Grimy Cleator Moor, grim Grantham and snobby Thorpeness
come under fire. Go to www.idler.co.uk for the latest entries

CLEATOR MOOR
Population: 2,000

THIS wild west Cumbrian town is
a forgotten outcrop on a
forgotten part of England,
neglected since the Great
Depression destroyed it almost
100 years ago. It most closely
resembles the town in *Pale Rider*
– after Clint Eastwood's killed
nearly everyone, painted the
houses red and renamed it Hell.

There is one long, infinitely
desolate main street full of
dangerous pubs, smashed up
cars and heavily fortified shops.
The few bored inhabitants drift
around like tumbleweeds, looking
for someone like YOU to hit.
They're so hard that when they
die they use them to hold up
bridges. When they're alive
they're more dangerous than
sarin gas. And they have
generations of anger to expend,

HELL

rightfully pissed off at the way no one has ever
done anything to help them or their unhappy home.

The closest "outsiders" ever get to Cleator Moor
is when they tramp within a mile of its boundaries
on Wainwright's Coast To Coast walk. The
famously straight talking creator of the walk
advised anyone thinking of taking a diversion into
the town to "abandon hope". **"Billy Badmatches"**

GRANTHAM
Population: 33,000

GRANTHAM, Oh Dear God,
Grantham.

Truly there has never existed
before such a heady concoction
of boredom and inertia, such a
malevolent mix of dilapidation

and depravity. When Milton wrote about about the
crushing despair and misery of hell – it was clear
that the poor man had heard of Grantham. It's true
it has produced a clutch of famous characters;
Margaret Thatcher, Isaac Newton, the first female
police officer (already there is the distinctive
sound of a barrel being scraped) but in the main,
Grantham is fetid pile of dung.

The Earlsfield Estate has apparently got (or at
least had) the highest crime rate per capita of any

council estate in the country. Some accolade. This is because of Grantham's oppresive boredom; there is nothing to do but go drinking under-age and commit violent crime. On a Friday night, large herds of 14 and 15 year olds roam the streets, trying to get served in the towns' numerous pubs. When they don't achieve this exorbitant goal, they turn on each other, which usually results in either hospitalisation, or another teenage pregnancy.

It is a town somewhat devoid of morals, but what truly defines its sense of worthlessness is the eagerness with which its inhabitants continuously talk of leaving. It was voted the most boring town in Britain on a poll conducted by a national radio station, and, despite the afore-mentioned luminaries, the best thing to come out of Grantham (as revealed in another poll) is apparently the A1.

Save yourselves: Don't Go There.   **David Finch**

CRAP TOWN TRIVIA

Outside Grantham's Beehive pub, in Castlegate, is what's referred to by the tourist blurb as "The Living Sign". It's mentioned on a series of brown signposts dotted around the town. But it isn't a living sign. It's just a beehive stuck in tree. It's a real anti-climax when you find it.

IS THIS THE MOST BORING TOWN IN BRITAIN?

MOCK TUDOR CANNOT HIDE THE DARKNESS WITHIN

THORPENESS
Population: 1,000

MORE OF a golf club than a town, Thorpeness represents the apotheosis of middle England snobbery. Sure, the "floating house" and mock tudor thatched mansions are attractive, but no amount of twee flower arranging will hide the vile darkness of the inhabitants' souls.

"Don't even think of parking here," yell the signs. "Private. Members only". "Access for RESIDENTS ONLY". "Polite notice: if you can't afford to live here, fuck off".

IDLE PLEASURES: CLOUDGAZING

The Club 18-30 sun-fascists would have the clouds banished from our skies. But where would we be without them? The clouds are our friends. Aristophanes called them "the patron saints of idle fellows". To the Buddhists, they are the spiritual cousins of elephants. In Arabic, a lucky man is one whose "sky is always filled with clouds".

The beauty of a sunset is thanks to the clouds. They are

JOHN CONSTABLE, STUDY OF CLOUDS AT HAMPSTEAD, 1821

nature's countenance. To sit and watch its ever-changing expression is a pursuit worthy of any dreamer. So lie back and lose yourself in the poetry of the skies. Cirrus, stratus, altocumulus undulatus. Lenticular, mammatus, cumulonimbus pileus. Soon, you are a child again dreaming of their puffy white expanses. Take off your little shoes, tuck your tiny toes beneath you, and flop back into their cotton-wool curves.

How better to spend an afternoon than in the company of these old friends? How better than to lose oneself in the gentle drift of these sofas of the saints?

Gavin Pretor-Pinney

BILL & ZED'S

WE'VE FUCKED UP OUR LIVES ...

SIZE MATTERS

Dear Bill And Zed,
I receive over twelve emails a day concerning my penis. These unsolicited emails claim that - if I only invested in their scientifically-proven treatment - I could expand both the length and girth of my penis until I have a muscular monster cock, capable of "ripping her vagina apart". Each day, their promises become wilder and more obscure.

I shudder to think what my cock would become if I subjected it to each and every extension treatment and unguent they are touting. I would end up with a cock like a skinned cow.

Could you make them stop?
Average guy,
Kentish Town

ZED: My esteemed colleague and I have been ripping women's vaginas apart for many years, Mr Guy, and cannot impress on you forcefully enough the therapeutic benefits of having a massive fucking chopper. I am sending you a free sample of Bill and Zed's Miracle Bell End Magnification Cream. I can only urge you, young fellow, to stop being so negative and grow yourself the monstrous todger you know you and your underage girlfriend deserve.

BILL: Actually there is something I should add to the sound advice my fellow agony uncle has already imparted to you. We too had received similar unsolicited mail and as we obviously were not in the need of these treatments and unguents, but realised that others may, we decided to get into the market ouselves. Thus the Bill and Zed's Miracle Bell End Magnification Cream. It's been a winner. The market is big enough for many more go-getting guys like yourself to get into. What I

suggest is you collect up all the old bottles of pills that are knocking about your mum's bathroom cabinet, re-sticker the botltles with Average Guy No Longer labels. Email everyone in your address book with your scientifically proven average sized cock cure and watch the orders roll in.

LAND OF LAPS

Dear Bill And Zed,
While drunk, I allowed my friends to persuade me to visit a lap-dancing bar. By the end of the evening, they had to drag me away. I was convinced all the women wanted to fuck me. Is buying a lap dance ethically untenable? And how can I rid myself of this glee in paying women to strip for me?
Peter Pseudonymous,
Made Up Place,
Obviously

ZED: Why pay and why worry, you silly sausage? Find yourself a drunken whore, bugger her violently and then instead of paying good wanking money to the hideous disgrace in the

BAD ADVICE

... NOW IT'S YOUR TURN

face of Allah that she is, eviscerate the vile slattern with spectacular yet graceful elan and eat her liver. A cut throat straight razor manufactured at Salingen in Germany, I find, is quite excellent for this type of work, but at a pinch a traditional Stanley knife works equally well. Good luck and do send me a polaroid.

BILL: Lap-dancing? Ah yes, I remember fondly the time that my comrade and I made a sojourn to the North Pole via Lapland. While passing through these parts and marvelling at the magic of the aurora borealis we were welcomed by the indigenous people of Lapland. Any time I hear the word "lap-dancers" I think of the evening the pair of us were entertained (for free) by a bevvy of young Lapp females dressed in their traditional costumes. Why go through all the guilt stuff about supporting the sex industry when Easyjet are now offering very reasonable rates for flights to the heart of

Lapland where all young Lapp females enjoy indulging in their ancient tradtion of entertaining travellers from far lands.

GENTLEMAN'S RELISH

Dear Bill And Zed,
Tits or face?
Best,
Popbitch *reader*

ZED: I've always been a tradesman's entrance sort of non-procreative safe sex type fellow myself, Poppy darling. Kids, eh, who in their right fucking mind would want one of those hideous little cabbage rippers?
BILL: Popbitch? Isn't that some sort of website thing? Where they make up scurrillous rumours about those who have found fleeting fame in the world of pop? Face, tits, and even the trademan's entrance as my fellow Zen Master so crudely puts it, are all very well. But I always find it far more creatiive to use a handy Stanley knife to slice open a brand new orifice. That way you can always be

sure no one's been there before you.

MID LIFE MISERY

Dear Bill And Zed,
I hate my friends, I hate my friend's children, I hate my friend's lovers, I hate my job, I hate my work mates, I hate my employers and the trap they have sprung upon me, I hate this filthy city, I hate the homeless people and their whining, I hate the mewling of the middle classes and their gardens and their cancer-fears and their fucking elaborate cooking, I hate opinions, both my own and other people's, I hate my ideas, every word-spew I have dribbled out over the years, I hate America and each and every American (with the possible exception of Saul Bellow,

BAD ADVICE CONTINUED

although I doubt even he would be civil to me), I hate computers, magazines, adverts, cars and houses. You get the gist. What is my roadmap to peace? Hate etc
R.

ZED: Middle age, eh, dear Mr R. Well, with the right attitude it doesn't have to be completely shit. Pack your job in, tell that ungrateful nagging bitch of a wife that you don't love her and that her oral sex technique is and always has been appalling. Buy yourself the hugest most dangerous motorcycle you can find, fuck a couple of your daughters for good measure and then, noble silver-haired Saddhu, get

THE IDLER QUESTIONNAIRE:
DAVE STEWART

DAVE STEWART: SWEET DREAMS

What time do you get up?
8.30am.

Do you leap out of bed the moment you wake or lie slumbering?
Leap up.

Do you smoke and drink, and if so, how much?
Don't smoke. Drink three or four glasses of red wine, sometimes vodka martini or lemoncello.

How many hours work do you put in on an average day?
Twelve hours.

Do you take holidays?
Yes, usually to Jamaica.

Where do you live?
Covent Garden.

Where do you work?
Everywhere, on trains, buses, automobiles.

Where do you think?
From the heart (in the bath).

What are your three greatest pleasures?
Family, friends, music.

Do you like money?
I don't like or dislike it.

Is the world a better or a worse place for idlers today than ten years ago?
Worse.

Are you happy?
No.

How many hours do you sleep at night/day?
Seven.

What are you reading?
These questions.

If it came to the crunch, would you choose money or art?
Art.

What have you been thinking about?

Who are your heroes?
Nida Noodle, Morrissey, Mr. Macaroni.

Any advice for young people?
Don't take drugs in the dark.

Do you like to go a-wandering?
Yeah, always (let my mind off its lead).

What is paradise?
Lime Hall, St Ann, Jamaica; bunch of musician friends on the back porch, Lee Scratch Perry on the ghetto blaster, "Hal Cooking", Mrs Jacob's Rum Punch and her homemade trifle.

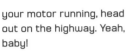

your motor running, head out on the highway. Yeah, baby!

BILL: All this hate, hate, hate is going to get you nowhere and as you aleready know it is a symptom of you being a failure in life. Start being a successs. Once you had dreams, it's now time to realise them. Once you do, all this hate stuff will just fade away and you might even stop hating yourself. Mind you, I might just take Zed's advice and see if that works better.

ONCE A TOSSER

Dear Bill and Zed,
Me and my friends have become tossers.
Any advice?
Klootie

ZED: Ever tried celebrity queerbashing, Klootie old pal? No? Well, don't worry, it's almost literally a piece of piss. Here's how: You and your tosser friends all go down a posh celebrity type nightclub like Sketch or something. You all go to the pissoir and start doing some pretend furtive tossing. Before you know it some nonceophile

celebrity mongoloid will be in there wanting to join in the fun and bingo! before you can say Karma Karma Karma George Michael Barrymore the fat fucking queer's out sparko on the floor wondering what the fuck hit him.

BILL: Now, I'm not too sure what is or is not correct behaviour in these post-politically correct days. It seems so Nineties to be un-PC but if retro is your thing, Zed's advice seems sound enough to me. Mind you, you probably were always a tosser, it's only now that you're getting to know yourself better.

NESTING INSTINCT

Dear Bill and Zed
I have recently bought a flat in South East London, and have been looking for a sofa for the front room. Unfortunately, none of the sofas in Habitat or IKEA will fit through my front

room. Any advice?
The Little Prince

ZED: Murder the wife and kids, burn down your house and then fuck your elderly dying mother up her crusty incontinent bottomhole. When you've done that go around to the nearest fun pub and run into the children's play area masturbating insanely with a huge gentleman's vibrator hanging out of your arse. Believe me, Johnny Sailorboy, after this artistic little performance your trivial domestic concerns will seem as nothing. A lovely cardboard sofa will be waiting for you in your own special room at Broadmoor.
Enjoy!

BILL: And if you don't want to do that, and you feel the need to make the world a better place, and you still enjoy starting fires, go burn down Habitat and

BAD ADVICE CONTINUED

IKEA, and make out you did it as a statement against globalisation. You will become an icon of our times. You will write your memoirs, call the book *Firestarter*. It will sell millions around the globe to all those people that bought *No Logo*. Hollywood will buy the film rights. And you will be able to buy yourself a flat big enough to accommodate the world's largest sofa.

DESIGNS FOR LIFE

Dear Bill and Zed
Even though I am 26 I am not a web designer nor have I had any ideas for websites. Is there something wrong with me?
Alan Beaslery

ZED: How's this for a beezer website idea? Take digital photos of your children and your friend's children having anal bukkake type sex with animals. Bill, who is a close friend of Gary Glitter, tells me that there is a huge Internet type market for this kind of thing. Glad to have been of assistance.
BILL: Yes, I am a good friend of Gary Glitter's. Only last week we were discussing who would be the greatest influence on the youth of tomorrow. Gary thought Mussolini, I thought it would be you, Alan Beasley. You would be the first person to recognise that the whole web designer thing is a bit 2003. In your bedroom, behind the chest of draws, you will find a plug. Pull that plug out. And the whole world wide web goes off. No more amazon.com, booking online, internet chat rooms, virtual this, that and the other, and all those website designers will have to go back to being juniors in regional graphic design companies. Of course, Gary didn't believe me. But you will.

WORLD OF PAIN

Dear Bill and Zed
I have just returned to working life in London after seven months' blissful loafing in Rome. I have developed a pain in my lower back which I attribute to the stress of readjustment. I would love to hear your thoughts on how to destress myself.
Ky Ro
Cheam

ZED: Rape and murder, dear boy, an excellent tonic for all ailments.
BILL:You need more stress and not less. I've had pain in my lower back for decades and I've learned to love it. You can too. Get yourself on the next low-cost flight back to Rome. Buy a violin, a big box of matches, and a can of kerosene. Then get to work. While Rome burns all around you, start fiddling. The lower back pain willsubside and your stress levels will... well, who the fuck cares about that now.

THE IDLER QUESTIONNAIRE:
PENNY RIMBAUD

RIMBAUD: ARCHITECT OF CRASS, QUALITY THINKER

What time do you get up?
I never get up before I need to (need being an indulgence rather than an imperative). What determines the need varies – a sunny morning, a bad headache, a thirst for coffee, inspiration to write a poem – it could be any time, it could be no time at all.

Do you leap out of bed the moment you wake or lie slumbering?
It all depends on the needs explained above – whereas I'll leap up for a sunny morning, I'll take it easy if I've got a headache, either way, I'm glad the floor's still there.

Do you smoke and drink, and if so, how much?
I smoke a lot and a drink a little, but I usually get horribly pissed after performances (poetry readings), it's a way of blotting out.

How many hours work do you put in on an average day?
I don't recognise a difference between work and whatever work isn't – play perhaps? It's all one of the same thing – being and keeping alive.

Do you take holidays?
I sometimes go to different places, but I'm not sure that I understand the concept of holidays. I'm myself wherever I am and I don't need to get away from anything, so I guess I'm not holiday material.

Where do you live?
Like most people, I live at home, but, more important to me, I live mostly in my own head.

Where do you work?
In my own head.

Where do you think?
In my own head.

What are your three greatest pleasures?
What are (Western) pleasures but self-indulgences reflecting personal prejudice? Everything is a pleasure or nothing is.

Do you like money?
Money is the meanest form of energy. Much like modern Western man, money has no meaning but tokenism, no value but itself and what's more it is owned by the bank.

Is the world a better or a worse place for idlers today than ten years ago?
Better than what? Seasons might change, but the world doesn't. Dinosaurs come and go, empires rise and fall. Our egocentricity is ill-equipped to cope with the dynamics of inevitability.

Are you happy?
I don't accept (or like) the implication of this question. Why should it be a consideration? What is happiness but the mirror deluding itself?

How many hours do you sleep at night/day?
As many as it takes.

What are you reading?
My word processor.

If it came to the crunch, would you choose money or art?
The crunch came a very long time ago – art.

What have you been thinking about?
The nature of these questions.

Who are your heroes?
Heroes are psychic paper tigers – the matches are in the kitchen.

Any advice for young people?
Don't forget the matches.

Do you like to go a-wandering?
A-walking.

What is paradise?
A stupid bourgeois contrivance.

CONVERSATIONS

EASY WRITER

Paul Hamilton **meets film director** Joe McGrath **for a leisurely chat about** Terry Southern (right), **genius screenwriter and friend to the stars**

T his does not sound too promising.
I am on the tellingbone to Joe McGrath, asking whether he's up for a bit of a chat about Terry Southern. Joe (if that really is his name) directed the film of Terry's book *The Magic Christian* way back in 1969 when some of you were as old as I am now.

"All I seem to do these days is talk about dead people," he sighs. "It's the price one must pay for outliving your friends. I've just been interviewed for a Peter Sellers documentary – this must be the third or fourth one I've done; there've been two Peter Cook TV things in the

WILLIAM CLAXTON

Terry Southern
as an in-demand
writer came to
a full-stop in 1970
and the quarter
century until his
death was
a wasteland

last month; and I had only just been a talking head for a Spike Milligan Heroes of Comedy when he dies and then I've got these talk radio people calling up asking the usual idiotic questions – 'Was Spike as funny offscreen?' I mean, give me a break, you know? Can I have a minute to grieve for my friend?"

Well, it's been seven years since Terry Southern went tits up for the last time, a respectable enough distance between initiation and reflection. It's a good time for confabulation.

"OK. Why not? How about next Tuesday, the 28th, about 2 o'clock?"

Fine. I'll bring a bottle of wine, or two.

"Great. But, er, will any of your readers have even heard of Terry Southern?"

A good question. Time for a mental filling. Be patient and open wide.

I n his heyday, the late fifties through to 1970, Terry Southern was the Wonder Boy, American literature's very own Lenny Bruce, opening fire on the smugness, complacency and hypocrisy of an uptight buttondown world with a sawn-off typewriter. On the strength of his novel *The Magic Christian*, he was summoned by Stanley Kubrick to England in 1962 to transform his Cold War nuclear fear filmscript from a well-meaning but dull grey slab of grimmo frowny seriousness into the brilliant black comedy *Dr Strangelove*. All those scatological or sexually rampant names – Merkin Muffley, Buck Turgidson, Mandrake, Premier Kissoff, Bat Guano – are Southern inventions. After Strangelove, Southern forsook the Quality Lit Game (i.e. novels) for film and *Easy Rider*, *Barbarella*, *The Loved One* and *The Cincinnati Kid* all in their diverse ways display the hallmarks of prime Southern – the American Way of Death seen through his absurdist telescope.

But Southern-as-successful-writer came to a full stop in 1970 and the twenty-five years up till his death in 1995 was a wasteland barren but for jettisoned projects, collapsed deals,

JUNKIE AND CLUNKIE:
WILLIAM BURROUGHS AND TERRY SOUTHERN, LATE SEVENTIES

disappointments. What happened? Had his brand of salacious satire fallen out of favour? Was he a victim of a Hollywood blacklist (most of his screen work was for European or US indie productions)? Had druggen drinkiness taken its toll on his creativity? Maybe IRS harassment robbed him of his concentration to write. Whatever it was that bedevilled him, Southern rarely lost sight of his principles. When Victor Bockris interviewed him in 1989 and tried to analyse Terry's career from a financial perspective he earned this rebuke:

"You're thinking of it as though my view is that of some professional, career-minded writer. I don't think writing is calculated. [...] You're assuming that I was [writing] for some kind of monetary response. It was all much less conscious and calculated. Are you saying that you can't comprehend creative work that isn't done to try to please somebody outside yourself? You seem to be, correct me if I am wrong, ruling out any comprehensive stimuli other than psychological peer-group approval power, or just straightforward money. You don't think that some of these things just happen almost on the level of, say, doodling when you're on the phone? Kafka's best writing is in his Diaries, I think, and he didn't want them to be seen by anyone."

Joe McGrath went to film after a few fantastic years of directing BBC TV comedy, most famously Peter Cook and Dudley Moore's first *Not Only... But Also* series. His movie-directing debut was the calamitous *Casino Royale*. It could only get better and productions like *The Great McGonagall, The Strange Case of*

TERRY SOUTHERN WITH A LOAD OF LONGHAIRS

The End of Civilisation As We Know It and *Thirty Is A Dangerous Age, Cynthia* are testaments to his freeform, loopy, just-for-the-hell-of-it vision. This conversation happened on a warm March afternoon in Joe McGrath's jazzy top floor flat in a Castle Draculaesque house in Swiss Cottage. Steadily filling our heads with Chilean red we talked of cabbages and kings and Terry Southerny things...

PAUL HAMILTON: Did you know of Terry Southern before Peter Sellers asked you to work on a *Magic Christian* film script?

JOE McGRATH: I had read the book, yeah, and Peter, Spike and me were chatting one evening and Peter was saying how difficult it all was to find a film that he really wanted to do. And *The Magic Christian* was mentioned and he was, "Oh, yeah, yeah! Why don't we get Terry in and try and get it off the ground?" We were beginning to work on *Magic Christian* in late '65 when we got the call

from Sellers saying he's got the offer to do *Casino Royale* – "Stop everything! You've got to save this script."

PAUL: *Casino Royale* doesn't make a word of sense. What was the plot supposed to be?

JOE: Don't ask me! The producer, Charlie Feldman, already had the script passed through lots of writers and I was finally handed this huge weight. Wolf Mankowitz had written a 230-page script. That's a three-hour movie we're talking about. And that was a jumble as well.

Terry didn't want to work on *Casino Royale* but when Charlie Feldman flashed the money – two grand a week, a hell of a lot of money for 1966 –

PAUL: Quite a pretty penny now, actually.

JOE: - well, Terry said, "Yes, of course I'll do it."

PAUL: What was Terry like as a person? One reads accounts where's he's a shy, bookish Texan and others where he's the gregarious life-and-soul-of-the-party type.

JOE: Well, he'd lost a lot of his Texan accent. He worked at losing it. Didn't want to be known as a Texan redneck. I mean, in New York he hung around jazz clubs with Miles Davis and the art scene with Larry Rivers so he was consciously cultivating a new identity. So his accent, that "downhome thang", he definitely strove to lose. But he could do it when the occasion arose. In *Dr Strangelove* when he's writing the Slim Pickens role [Major "King" Kong, the bomber pilot] – 'Sheeyitt'. Yeah. And all that bullish redneck stuff George C Scott spouts in *Strangelove* is pure Terry.

PAUL: In the early sixties, his book *Candy* was a literary sensation, wasn't it? It sold millions of copies and Terry should have been a millionaire from the sales but due to contractual and copyright fuck-ups he didn't earn a red cent. Did he ever strike you as bitter and twisted about his misfortune?

JOE: He never was bitter and twisted about it. Not to me, anyway. But Terry – well, Terry was out of his head on drugs a lot of the time.

PAUL: What sort of drugs were these?

JOE: Benzedrine and coke. He never was on heroin, never. But he was on stuff to keep him awake. He would say, "I'm on the sleeper leapers." You know, you take one to go to sleep, another to wake up and stay up. It's the Judy Garland syndrome. And he was drinking a lot. And Peter Sellers was drinking a lot – and on Valium. So it was a pretty interesting time, making *Casino Royale* with those two. Oh dear. I ended up quitting the movie, got paid off and pissed off. Meanwhile Wolf Mankowitz was going mad and screaming, "Let's go back to my screenplay!" What – the 230-page script that doesn't make any sense? Wolf is on record saying McGrath, Southern and Sellers fucked it up... He's probably

> "Wolf Mankowitz is on record saying 'McGrath, Southern and Sellers fucked up Casino Royale'"

right. [Laughter]

PAUL: Did Terry merely do a polish job on the dialogue for *Casino Royale* or did he create new scenes?

JOE: He wrote some good stuff. The lovely Woody Allen bit where he's being taken out to be shot by firing squad and he escapes by jumping over the

'Terry Southern is the most profoundly witty writer of our generation' Gore Vidal

The overall obsessions with Terry were sex, death, money and some more sex

wall, only to be shot at by another firing squad on the other side of the wall – that was one of our ideas, concocted with Woody. They got on well, Terry and Woody.

PAUL: It doesn't surprise me because the overall obsessions with Terry were sex, death, money and some more sex, and

in *Sleeper* Diane Keaton asks Woody, "You don't believe in God – so what do you believe in?" Woody says, "Sex and death. They both happen once in a lifetime but only one of them makes you wake up at two in the morning feeling nauseous."

JOE: Yeah, they definitely shared that New York sensibility, yeah. He was great on character writing, Terry. You know immediately when, like on *Strangelove*, these guys start talking who and what they are. Like Terry said, "You gotta know where they're coming from. We don't want to talk plot. We don't want to say, 'And which university did you go to?' and have someone talking about their background for the next five minutes." That's the great secret of screenwriting. He said there were two ways of writing screenplays – there's draw poker or it's the other sort of poker. He said, "You show your hand and the audience know what you're doing or, the better way, is you turn one card up at a time so you don't know what's coming next." He said, "A terrible screenplay is when you get a couple of guys in a car, they've known each other twenty years, yet they're talking about their backgrounds. They wouldn't do that!" Producers would say, "But the audience have to know." But Terry swore that was something he would never do – and he never did.

PAUL: There's no expositional dialogue in *The Magic Christian* film.

JOE: No, none at all.

PAUL: Like, when at the beginning Peter Sellers as Sir Guy Grand meets Ringo Starr in the park – they're meeting for the first time – you don't hear a word that is said; the dialogue is smothered by a Badfinger song.

JOE: Right. You don't need to hear it. What's he going to say? "Hello, I'm the richest man in the world and I want to adopt you." – "Fuck off, cunt. Explain yourself." – "Well, I have this idea of making jokes of humanity." – "Oh, that interests me. Yeah, I'll do it." That's what they would say but you don't want to hear that. You want the audience to think, "What is this guy up to? Is he trying

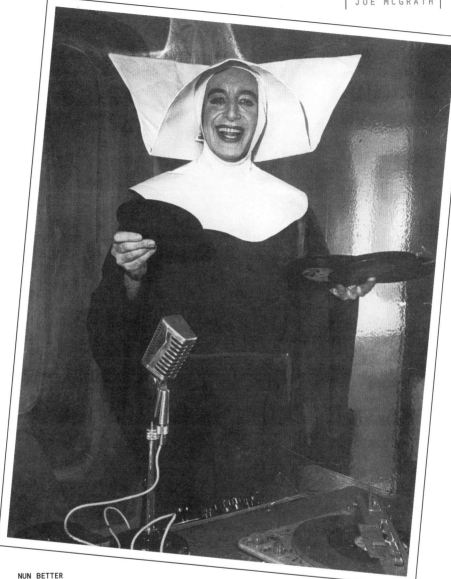

NUN BETTER

to pull this kid?"

PAUL: When you see photos of Terry from the sixties and his dark, brooding features, you'd think this was some vicious, acid-tongued chappie all-too-ready to lacerate and berate anyone foolish enough to stand in his way. Was that the case – or are appearances deceptive?

JOE: No, he wasn't like that. Terry and I got on very well right from the beginning because we had the same terms of reference. We liked the same type of music. Sidney Bechet and up to 1950s be-bop. Jazz.

RINGO: TERRY FAN

The Rolling Stones. The Beatles liked him.

PAUL: Yes, he's on *Sergeant Pepper.*

JOE: Yeah, Ringo loved him, just thought he was the most marvellous thing in the world. And quite rightly. He was a great writer but he just had this obsession with celebrity.

PAUL: Do you think his form of groupiedom blunted his edge as a satirist?

JOE: No. What blunted his edge was the excess of drugs and drink. Definitely. He couldn't get up in the morning. When I was shooting *Magic Christian* he wanted to be on the set working as he did on *Strangelove.*

PAUL: Yeah, with *Strangelove,* he would set off to the studio at four in the morning with new pages of script and watch the filming, making suggestions, a really active, integral part of the process.

He just loved that whole Miles stuff and Chet Baker and the West Coast relaxed bop. And we dug the same movies. He loved Ealing films. That was his trip. And Terry was the ultimate groupie of all time. He loved meeting and hanging out with famous people. If there was somebody famous in a room or a bar he would hand you a camera and say, "Quick, take a snap of me with -" whoever. I mean, it was embarrassing. But these people knew and liked his work too – it was probably a two-way thing – so no one really minded. He went on tour with

JOE: Yeah, but by 1969, you know, we'd send a car to pick him up and he wouldn't arrive until two in the afternoon. Because he'd been partying all night. He'd appear: "OK, what have you shot?" He'd see rushes and say, "Oh, you should do that again, I've got this idea," and I'd go, "No we can't. You should be here." So he'd promise to be in the next day. Send a car and once again he'd be late. I think he only managed to turn up at the set on time for thirty per cent of the shoot.

PAUL: Tell me about the writing of the screenplay. The credit is Terry, you and Sellers.

JOE: Well, it should be "Terry Southern and Joe McGrath, with additional material by Peter

Sellers, John Cleese and Graham Chapman."

PAUL: How did you and Terry work? Did you write scenes independently of each other and then collate them or – ?

JOE: No, no. Together. And Terry's agent, a real heavyweight agent called Cindy Deginer, was amazed when I went to the States to write with him. She said, "In all the years I've known Terry I've never known him to sit down and write for eight hours a day. Usually he would makes notes and get his collaborator, if he's working on a film, to go off, write it all up. The next day Terry would make adjustments and cuts, and then do a little more." We did it all in his flat on East 33rd Street in New York. Very enjoyable. But Terry's workroom – how could you describe it? It was a mess. Posters, records, books, scripts all lying on the floor, nothing tidied up. And – first time I had ever seen such a thing – there was what Terry called "a monstro TV screen". It was like four foot by three foot and he said, "We're gonna watch TV as we write." He would turn the telly on but leave the sound off: "This is valuable stimulus!" And he was right because you're staring at sheathes of paper and you look up and there's something happening on the screen and Terry'd be, "Gad! Look! What!??! Make a note of that!" He would scream and shout and laugh at the television. What's interesting is Peter Blake, the English Pop painter, tells me that when he paints he has a big TV screen on as well, with the sound down. He says that when he takes a break he'll have a cup of tea and look at the screen. It stops him developing tunnel vision about the work, all that "My God, what am I doing?"

But Terry – he was untidy. His flat was untidy, and he'd be drinking wine all day, but the desk we wrote at was like a surgeon's operating table. Immaculate, in order. The typewriter there; the pages pristine; pencils sharpened; fountain pens ready to use.

PAUL: Why was *The Magic Christian* translocated from America, where the book was set, to England?

JOE: It was always going to be set and shot in

The shit vat scene is the climax of the film, when a huge tank is filled with urine and excrement

England. But the shit vat scene was originally to be filmed beneath the Statue of Liberty. This was agreed by the film's backers, Commonwealth United, but at the last moment they backed down: "The legal department won't give us clearance and also it's showing America up in a bad way." Terry said, "That's the whole fucking idea! Why did you ever get involved in this movie?"

PAUL: We should explain that the shit vat scene is the climax of the film, when a huge tank is filled with urine, excrement and blood and then sprinkled with paper money.

JOE: Yes, and the generals and Wall Street moneymen were to wade into it, picking out hundred dollar bills.

PAUL: Sledgehammer subtlety.

JOE: Oh yes. Commonwealth went behind our backs to the authorities so we couldn't even sneak on and get some shots of Liberty to use as plates so we could put the scene together back in England during post-production.

Sellers suggested we film it on

"I don't believe in censorship. If Pasolini filmed someone fucking a goat, they should allow it"

the South Bank in London, where the National Film Theatre is, so there's St. Paul's in the background, and the City, so we're still making a statement about money and power and corruption. The film company refused to pay for this scene so Sellers paid for it out of his own pocket.

PAUL: How did Peter Sellers get a writing credit?

JOE: Oh, we showed him pages, scenes, and he might suggest lines or business and we would incorporate any good bits in to the script.

PAUL: Would he suggest something that was so profane or oddball that you and Terry just had to reject it?

JOE: Oh, no, no. Terry and I felt the same – "You can't go too far." I don't believe in censorship at all. If Pasolini filmed someone fucking a goat, I think they should be allowed to show that. You don't have to see the movie and if it's on the telly you can turn it off. Terry said, "They won't allow us to see fucking but they'll show

someone being shot in the eyes. A head being blown off in slow motion – that's pornographic."

PAUL: And making distinctions between erotica and pornography was the theme of his *Blue Movie* novel.

JOE: These judges, tastemakers, laying down the rules of what should and shouldn't be seen, but they own Picassos, Bonnards, Matisses and they were interested in erotica. I mean, if we were to live by these stern rulings, you know, we wouldn't be operated on in hospitals. Stubbs with his horse paintings, Rembrandt, Leonardo, people who knew about anatomy, they flayed bodies and opened them up to find out what was happening inside and that's how people are living till they're 90 today. That area was banned for years – "You can't cut up bodies, you can't even see them."

PAUL: Who brought in Graham Chapman and John Cleese to write for *The Magic Christian*?

JOE: That was Peter Sellers.

PAUL: Why? Didn't he have any faith in you and Terry?

JOE: Well, Peter was funny in those days – 'cos he was alive! But he was funny because of his total insecurity. He was aware of Cleese and Chapman.

PAUL: This was pre-Monty Python –

JOE: - right, and he thought, "Let's get these wonderful, up-to-date young guys in to help with this stuff." And he did that, Sellers, with any screenplay. He tried to bring people in because he thought "We might just get one funny idea." I mean, that whole nuclear bomb sequence at the end of Strangelove with Vera Lynn singing "We'll Meet Again" over it – that was Peter bringing Spike Milligan in. Spike wrote that.

PAUL: No he didn't.

JOE: Yes he did.

PAUL: No.

JOE: Yes he did. Because Kubrick filmed a custard pie fight which didn't work and Kubrick didn't know how to finish the film so Peter went to Spike and said, "We got this thing with the bomb, how the fuck do we finish it?" and Spike said "Get Vera Lynn with the BAOR and 'We'll Meet

Again'." Peter told Kubrick and he agreed. That's how that is in the film.

PAUL: Hmmm... No, surely –

JOE: Kubrick never knew anything about the BAOR and "We'll Meet Again".

PAUL: Perhaps, but Southern would have. He was ...

JOE: No he didn't, no he didn't.

PAUL: He served during the War, he was an Anglophile –

JOE: No. Terry told me he was annoyed. Because Peter said 'This is it' and it went in. There was no controlling Peter. Terry was annoyed about Cleese and Chapman being brought in by Peter but what can you do?

Cleese is on record as saying Southern just didn't know what the fuck he was doing. Now for somebody like John Cleese to say that about a writer like Terry Southern is totally out of order and wrong. Terry was a much better screenwriter. He could wipe the floor with somebody like Cleese.

PAUL: Yes, *Fierce Creatures*.

JOE: Yeah, God almighty. Then look at Terry – *Strangelove, Cincinnati Kid* –

PAUL: *The Loved One, Barbarella* –

JOE: - you name them. *End Of The Road*, that's a great one. But Cleese was in some magazine saying, "Peter handed us the script and the opening scene which describes Sir Guy Grand's bedroom and it mentions an ormolu clock on the mantelshelf. And we knew then that this script was rubbish. Why mention an ormolu clock?" Now the reason for the mention of the clock was a) it shows Guy Grand's elegance, and b) it's an ormolu digital clock, which shows the eccentricity of Guy Grand. And then you pan off it to Big Ben visible outside the window – dong, dong, dong. So the point being made is he's living in London, he's rich, he's eccentric and he's next to Big Ben. Where the hell does this guy live? And then you suddenly see he's living in Westminster School Yard.

PAUL: So you've set up the character in a couple of lines of stage directions, without recourse to reams of dialogue.

JOE: And Cleese misses that whole thing.

[Joe notices a book amongst the interviewer's clutter]

JOE: What's that book there?

PAUL: Ah, this is Lee Hill's biog of Terry: *A Grand Guy*.

JOE: Any good, is it? Let me have a look.

PAUL: It's a frustrating read. Hill lists the stories

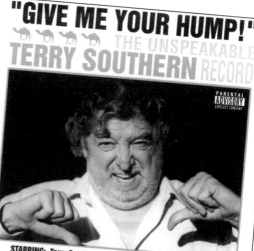

"GIVE ME YOUR HUMP!"
THE UNSPEAKABLE
TERRY SOUTHERN RECORD

PARENTAL
ADVISORY
EXPLICIT CONTENT

STARRING: Terry Southern, Marianne Faithfull, Allen Ginsberg, Martin Mull, Michael J. Pollard, Jonathan Winters, Sandra Bernhardt, Michael O'Donoghue, and Mary Jenifer Mitchell as "Candy" written, the scripts and novels, all that area, but you don't grasp any sense of Southern the man. He's noted when things were written but not the how and the why. He doesn't delve into why Terry scripted a porno movie and how he felt about it.

JOE: When did Terry script a skinflick?

PAUL: About 1980, I think. He was skint and that was the only offer on the table.

JOE: Yeah? I don't think there's anything wrong in that. Terry would have written skinflicks from 1960 if he could.

PAUL: Why would he do that?

JOE: That was just his attitude. Think of his favourite authors – Verlaine, Rimbaud. Anything is fair game for humanity. Like we mentioned Woody Allen earlier – his sex film with Gene Wilder in love with a sheep. But there's nothing wrong with porn films. Terry would have wanted to have made a great porno film, and he'd've been right to want to. Because they are just not good. And there must be a way to make a really great erotic film.

PAUL: Did you stay in touch with Terry after *The Magic Christian* in 1970?

JOE: Phone calls occasionally, and he nearly always used someone else's phone, but the last words he said to me on the telephone were, "I'll be in touch, Joe, but meanwhile be on the lookout for absurdity at all levels." I told his son this and he went, "That's so Dad."

PAUL: In 1990 you were working on a film with Terry that never got made.

JOE: *Festival.*

PAUL: How did this project kick off?

JOE: A guy called Walter Robin told me, "*Magic Christian* is my favourite movie of all time" and wanted to produce a film directed by me. Walt had an idea for a naughty, satirical film, *Starlets* he called it originally, about the Cannes film festival about how young girls go there and wander around and will do anything, you know.

The synopsis Walt had very mild and didn't really go as far as it could in terms of what the Cannes film festival is about. We worked on it but it wasn't really going anywhere so I suggested we get Terry Southern in. So we went to see Terry in his big old house in East Canaan and he liked the idea very much. He said, "Yes, it's a cattle market, these girls are being bought and sold!" and gets into this whole thing. Walt starts worrying – "What? Wait a minute, we're treating these women like meat." And I said, "Yes, but that's what you like about *Magic Christian* – the idea that humans can be bought. It's just the same thing; these girls are being bought. They'll do anything to get on." We quietened him down and he paid Terry some money to work on the script. Walt was a hustler, you know. He went and raised money for the project at Cannes, including some from women. That blew Terry's mind: "Women are paying for this film?"

We wanted George Segal to play the lead, this monstro film producer, a kind of Michael Douglas /Gordon Gekko character, the bastard who will sell his children, his wife, he'll take a fucking, anything to get a deal to make his film. He's surrounded by these girls who come once a year to Cannes who are just the same as him. They'd do anything to get into movies. And we brought in people from the newly-liberated USSR because suddenly the whole idea of Russia had changed and Cannes, the year we went there, was full of Russian prostitutes who came in from the Black Sea and up the Mediterranean. Terry saw this and said, "This is incredible! There's a whole new

element here. Communism meets Capitalism."
And all his books attack Capitalism.

Other than the meat-market theme, what was
great – from a film-maker's point of view – is that
at Cannes everybody is being filmed. You can't
walk three yards without a microphone being
shoved in your face and "Who are you? Are you
anybody? What do you think?" I had a flash of
inspiration and said to Terry, "How about the
paparazzi played by the Keystone Kops?" and
have thirty people dripping in cameras zipping en
masse like a swarm of bees over here, there and
everywhere: "Where's the story? Is it here? No, it's
over there! ZZZIPPP!! Arghh! Flash, flash, flash!"

It would have been great had it been made but
Walt ran out of money, Terry died; you know, it's
a shame. Because the film ends in terrorists
blowing up the festival and the girls are held
hostage and no one'll pay the ransom because
"the girls aren't important". If they took the
producers or the stars hostage it'd be a different
matter. It mixes sexual politics, religious politics;
it's a strong, strong idea. And it's mixing up reality
and film. Terry had a script about the assassination
of the pope and couldn't get backing for it - "It's
too dangerous and it's not real" – and then an
assassination attempt was made on the pope. That
September 11/Twin Towers episode: I'm sure
extremists must have seen those Bruce Willis and
Arnold Schwarzenegger films and said, "Look, this
is a fucking piece of cake. Let's do it!" And Terry
always saw possibilities: "Anything can happen!"
Nile's trying to get *Festival* made as a film. Three
quarters of the script is there, done, and we know
what the ending is, so good luck. It'd be a great
entertainment – men and women fucking each
other and fat slob film producers wading in the
sea, doing offshore deals. Twenty yards offshore!

Oh, Walter Robin – Terry called him "Big Walt"
and he was a big Walt. The size of Orson Welles.
Terry always familiarised names. His sort of slang –
cool, groovy, hip – is all 1940s, 1950s jazz jive.
There's a song called "I'm Hip" that Blossom Dearie
recorded that's so like Terry. Do you know it?

PAUL: No. How does it go?

JOE: "I'm hip, I'm no square,
I'm alert, I'm awake, I'm aware.
I'm always on the scene, doing
the rounds, digging the sounds. I
read *Playboy* magazine because
I'm hip. I dig, I'm in step, when
it was hip to be hep I was hep. I
don't blow but I'm a fan, look at
me swing, ring-a-ding-ding. I
even call my girlfriend 'man' cos
I'm hip. With my suit buttoned
tight and my suedes on, I'm
getting my kicks, watching arty
French flicks with my shades on.
I'm too much, I'm a gas, I'm
anything but middle-class…"

PAUL: Is there any more?

JOE: Yes, it goes on with, "I'm
deep into Zen, meditation,
macrobiotics, and as soon as I
can I intend to start getting into
narcotics. 'Cos I'm cool as a
kuke – "

PAUL: What?

JOE: K-u-k-e.

PAUL: Shouldn't that be k-o-o-
k, kook?

JOE: Hang on. "'Cos I'm cool
as a kuke, I'm a cat, I'm a card,
I'm a kook."

BOTH: ("Kuke" penny drops):
CUCUMBER!

JOE: You've had too much to
drink.

PAUL: Nonshensh.

JOE: "I get so much out of life,
really I do, Scooby-de-doo! One
more time play 'Mack The
Knife', let her rip, I may flip
but… I'm hip!"

PAUL: That's fantastic!

JOE: Fred Ebb wrote those
words. And it is absolutely Terry
Southern. ◉

FEATURES

WHY CUNTS SELL SHIT TO FOOLS

ATTN DESIGN DEPT.

Dear Sir/Madam

Your slippers are all very comfortable and all that - but my feet are shaped like this [TOES]

& your slippers are shaped like this ⌒

Its as if you were making hats for people whose heads were shaped like this ⌂

Has no-one else complained? Surely this is the female line. Any chance of BROAD TOED STYLE. ITS SO crushed up + sweaty.

yours in hope E. Mellor.

Damien Hirst says don't buy it.
Photograph by Mandy Lee Jandrell

The above letter, written by the late Joe Strummer, is a wonderful example of a successful communication between customer and manufacturer, so why am I left with a feeling that the letter actually went in the bin?

It's not just because I'm a cynical @!%&>^!, it's also because the world's !£@$@$<!

Why are exchanges of letters like these so rare in this day and age? Why do the cunts (powers wot be) sell shit (crap) to fools (you and me)?

I'm assuming rightly that the people who are running the world won't be reading this rant; they'll be far too busy running – or ruining – this beautiful world of ours.

A-ha: first point. I just detected something in what I was saying. TRUST – yeah. I assumed that they (the cunts) were actually running the world and not just lying in bed doing £@$! ALL! And we all know what assumptions make and furthermore that assumption was based on trust. When someone says, "trust me" I just know that they're gonna truss me up like a chicken! "Yeah I'll truss ya, truss ya up like a @£!$%^! chicken."

Buy one get one free! What the £@$! is that all about? I don't need two!

Forgive me if I wander from the subject and rant. It's all part of the piece and it's by its nature a wandering piece. Oh, and if you could hang on in there and read beyond the swearing and bad grammer and punctuation...

OK. All set.

So: money is a tool. It works like a key. The problems start when the tool is over-worshipped. It's easy to forget its lower function, which is to open the !@$£%&*! door. I mean, you wouldn't keep a screwdriver in your pocket for so long that you forgot what it was supposed to do.

Don't talk to me about discounts, *I'm just NOT !£@$%^&! BUYING IT AND THAT'S THAT!*

Money's the key and we understand absolutely that without money, the cunts wouldn't be able to sell shit to us fools. But do you know what? They fucking would. They are such cunts that they would find a way. They'd sell us ideas.

've always said that art is about life and the art world is about money.

However, the buyers and sellers, the movers and shakers, the money men, will tell you anything to hide the fact that their real motivation is profit. This is because if you realised that they would sell your Granny to Nigerian sex slave traders for fifty pence (ten bob) an' a packet a Woodbines, then you're unlikely to believe the other shit coming outta their mouths, the stuff they say to make you buy the garish shit hanging on the wall in their posh shops.

And if that's true then it's true in all businesses. It's true for art dealers and art; for car dealers and cars; for drug dealers and drugs, and even for politicians and politics. The four are the same !@£@$%! thing. They are all – most of the time – selling shit to fools, and it's getting worse. They may tell us that what we are buying into is not "transport but transportation" but we're beginning to realise that it just ain't getting us from A to B any more. And as usual we're doing nothing except £@$!%$! moaning.

If we accept that the cunts rule the world, then the collapse of quality in the time of the cunts is a given, and also we need to discover the reasons for the rise of the cunt. Could it be because someone took their eye off the ball? I'm not mentioning any names, but have a look in the mirror.

This collapse in quality is particularly noticeable in the music industry. The main reason for this is that the people who have the most control are the furthest away from the creativity. A friend of mine in a well known band was asked to sign a contract saying he wasn't allowed to change his look! Can you imagine the Beatles signing a contract like that in 1961?

Special offer! I'll give you a special offer – suck my cock, yeah, yeah, yeah, special offer. Everything must go! Closing down sale now on, $£@! off now! And you won't get punched – yeah there's a special offer in my underpants – all you can eat for £2.99.

I remember a joke when I was at school. Two kids are playing at shops and using leaves as money and one kid says to the other: "how much for that flower?" And the other kid says: "fifty leaves" and the first kid says: "do you think money grows on trees?" It's a bit like the one about the two Jewish guys in bed gently touching each other and gazing longingly into each other's eyes, and one says to the other urgently: "Turn over," and the other says, "about 12.8 million last year, how about yourself?"

The origins of money: exchange and swapping. (I need to speak to someone about this bit, a philosopher or historian to know what the $£@! I'm on about... or not bother.) Take two farmers, one with a field of wheat and the other with a field of sheep: they will always find a way to end up taking cold lamb sandwiches to work on a Monday morning, it's the way the universe works. Bartering came before money, then it was only a matter of time before some cunt introduces the idea of *money*, which will fill that gap between the lambs being slaughtered and the wheat being ground into flour. I think you get the drift. Yeah, that's right: now you can buy things out of season, something with value that you can save, no more scraping pounds of rotting lamb out of your pockets on a Friday, something small and convenient that won't perish and – bosh! – we've got a banker and then a bank and then several banks, and then insurance and loans.

It seemed like a good idea at first.

Now the value of our goods has been handed over to a third party. Of course they claim to have

Money's the key and we understand absolutely that without money, the cunts wouldn't be able to sell shit to us fools

And cars, what a tragic, sad, fucking horrific, wasteful, money-grabbing, planet-destroying piece of corporate shit we've bought into there

our best interests at heart, but as always happens with money, greed sets in. They (the cunts) tell us that possesion is nine tenths of the law. And guess wot? They've got our money! Worse still, we gave them our money!

It's your own fault, so don't be a fool and stop buying shit from these cunts! OK! OK! I hear ya babe. The Holy Trinity, The Three Stooges, yeah, you got it, come on down! Let's hear it for the Father, the Son and the Holy Ghost, the magnificent capitalist pub chat subjects, the big lies, the big three: cars, batteries and light bulbs. Yeah, hip hip, hooray! Designed to fuck up with in-built obsolescence. Oh, and you can add CDs to the list. Do I remember being sold the idea of CDs being indestructible? Yes, I think I do. I remember seeing a guy on TV telling me that you could drill a 5mm hole through a CD and it would still work! What cunts! They fed us such bullshit, but we ate it, and we deserve the blame. ("Don't ask what you can do for your country but what some cunt can do for you", A. Falliss 2002.) We didn't have to eat it! We swallowed it. And we knew it tasted bad. Or as Dino Felluga says:

> According to Karl Marx, the entrance into capitalist culture meant that we ceased to think of purchased goods in terms of use-value, in terms of the real uses to which an item will be put. Instead, everything began to be translated into how much it is worth, into what it can be exchanged for [its exchange value]. Once money became a "universal equivalent", against which everything in our lives is measured, things lost their material reality (real-world uses, the sweat and tears of the labourer). We began even to think of our own lives in terms of money rather than in terms of the real things we hold in our hands: how much is my time worth? How does my conspicuous consumption define me as a person? As the things we use are increasingly the product of complex industrial processes, we lose touch with the underlying reality of the goods we consume. A common example of this is the fact that

most consumers do not know how the products they consume are related to real life things. How many people could identify the actual plant from which is derived the coffee bean? Starbucks, by contrast, increasingly defines our urban realities.

And cars, what a tragic, sad, fucking horrific, wasteful, money-grabbing, planet-destroying piece of corporate shit we've bought into there.

Do you remember the TV repair man? Try and get something repaired these days, it's nigh on impossible. I've got two DVD players at the Sony Centre, which have been there for three months. They cost about three pence less to repair than buying a new one and the people who work there try everything in their power to get you not to mend it but to buy a new one instead.

Now I'm going to give you a quote. It relates to the subject and I could wait all day for a nice place to put it in, but I'm gonna use it now, to relieve the monotony of my search for truth. You can work out exactly how to relate it to the subject, it's about time you did something anyway, and got off your arse! It's sitting on your arse that got us in this situation in the first place.

"The easiest way to attract a crowd," Houdini wrote, "is to let it be known that at a given time and a given place someone is going to attempt something that in the event of failure will mean sudden death."

And here is Houdini's biographer:

Myths are often about the inescapable, about the painful discovery of powerful constraints, they don't tend to be stories about people who get away with things, but rather stories about people who try to; people whose transgressions turn out to be a lesson for us all. Oedipus, Prometheus, Narcissus and Antigone all, in their different ways, suffer the most violent of all sentimental educations. That there must be some things that no creature can elude – whether they be laws (natural or moral), desires (variously deemed moral or

immoral), or biological limits (the need to breathe, eat and die) – and that they must be discovered, recognised and observed are integral to our sense of ourselves, and the ways in which we question who we are. When a constraint can be described as something else – when the earth becomes round so we can't fall off it, when the notion of sin is seen as seen as a devious form of social control, and so on – we change our place in the world. When a constraint can be re-described, it can make the world – the way things are - despite our intentions seem more robust, more solid.

Take the rise of Ginsters and other purveyors of shit food – how did that happen? How did we let it happen? (their new ads in service stations feature the bare-faced lie "Real Honest Food").

You're wedged up and looking good and looking for a good buy? Get down the nearest art school and buy with your eyes, not your ears. Use yer noggin'. If it looks good, it is good. It's the same thing with music. If it sounds good, it is good. What's there to not be sure about, you cunts! Why should you care what other people think? So if your room feels a bit bare and lonely then get down to your nearest art school, just walk in and if you see something nice make an offer and buy somat to

brighten the room up. It'll be cheap and at the same time you get the added bonus of cutting out the middle men.

A word of advice for those considering "buying for investment" – don't bother! Money under the bed's no good any more, it's not safe and they keep re-designing it. I can hardly keep up. Is it getting smaller or is it me getting bigger? Buying something because you like it is the best investment anyone can make.

So where the %$@! are we now? I'll explain the story so far for the slow to catch on:

The reason why cunts sell shit to fools is two-fold, with a third point. Three elements – cunts, shit and fools.

(1) The fools behave as they're supposed to – as fools!

(2) because of (1), the cunts come out of the woodwork and make a killing!

But that's not the whole story. Points (1) and (2) work together as a force which in turn creates a decline in quality, and produces (3): this is the "shit" in "why cunts sell shit to fools".

I hope that will wrap the whole thing up even for the hard of hearing and the infirm among you. It's your own fault you're buying it; if you stop buying it then they'll stop selling it.

And if this rant feels too true, too close for comfort, and you're the kind of person that needs hope, all I know is this:

"There are no pockets in a shroud!"

That's me story an' I'm stickin' to it – so gerrit thru yer thick 'ed an' lerrit stop thee're lad. DON'T BUY IT!!!!!!!

"The tragedy of the world is that the good can't be bothered and the bad can." (T. Hodgkinson, 2003). ⊚

SON OF ALBION

New dad James Parker, living in
America, argues that Marc Bolan was
a master of English nonsense

ILLUSTRATION BY GEORGE UNDERWOOD
FROM 'ELECTRIC WARRIOR' BY T REX, FLY RECORDS, 1971

Milligan was good. Oh, Milligan knew what he was doing. "On the Nong Ning Nang all the mice go CLANG!" - that's hard to beat, that image of hollow metal mice in pitiless collision. That's nonsense, dude. Then again, if you ever heard him read it aloud you'll have picked up the harsh Goon note in his recital, the stridently silly voice, the (forgive me) spike-iness, as if he's making fun of foreigners somewhere. Too cruel. No, for melodiousness, absurdity and general charity to the fallen soul of man, I am naming MARC BOLAN as the Last Great English Nonsense Poet Of The Twentieth Century.

To give this assertion some context: I am 35 years old, an Englishman living in America, I've been writing for the *Idler* for

PHOTOGRAPH BY SPUD MURPHY.
FROM 'ELECTRIC WARRIOR' BY T REX, FLY RECORDS, 1971

ten years, and I have a one year-old son. If you're a dad you know what this means. You've met the other dads on the street, pushchair to pushchair, had the brief low-voiced dad-chats or maybe just given the dad-nod, stoic but searching, in which immense volumes of male sympathy are communicated: "I know you, brother, drab husband, ex-man, petitioning your wife for the weekly shag, your once-buoyant balls grown heavy and autumnal - I know you. And yes, I know also that you cry hot invisible tears of pride for your offspring, your child, your CHILD, this baby, this fragrant drop of fat, this precious little gentleperson, this soft-fingered surface-explorer, professor of corners and undersides, of joints, hinges and buttons, a diligent appreciator of LIFE in all its angles! This too I know!" Perhaps you've had this moment, or one similar. And perhaps, like me, you find yourself watching a lot of Teletubbies.

Teletubbies, as I'm well aware, is old news: the cultural property of mid-morning spliff-artists from the late Nineties. Nonetheless for me this time, in the company of my son, was the first time. And homesick as I am, as I watched Dipsy and the rest of them bounce and jiggle in Blakeian glee across that strange pruned landscape I got authentic pangs and visions of Albion. Those smooth, even tumuli, the sealed or blazing skies, the dozy rabbits lummoxing by... mangled England on a summer afternoon! Half-fairyland, half-traffic island! This is part of the expat condition: all phenomena relating to your mother-country are suffused with ancestral glory. I see an image of cheap-lit Heathrow Airport on ABC news and feel, like a flutter in my gut, that particular English sense of scale, that lovely English crappiness. I eat an overpriced import Curly Wurly and taste my childhood. And music! Music, first among the arousers... I listen to the dollop-drumming of early Killing Joke and seem to hear the ancient, savage pulse of England, woad-covered men beating their cauldron-bottoms in a trance... Hawkwind, and Arthurian spectres arise from their psychedelic barrows (like the one the Teletubbies live in)... hippy-era T Rex, and two men squat in a druidic bush on a railway cutting in Hackney Downs, half-arsedly tapping a bongo and murmuring the poetry of the ages... This kind of thing. And all of this, somehow, these expatriate longings, the hardcore infantilism of the Teletubbies, multiple readings-aloud of "The Owl and The Pussycat" and so on, combined in me to produce this conviction of Bolan's nonsense-majesty.

His song-lyrics from this era are redeemed by his potty locution - the vowels curlicued, the consonants dizzily relished

Strictly speaking of course he didn't write poems at all. Although unfortunately he did. In 1969 he published your archetypal slim volume, *Warlock of Love*, and wow it's bad: Dylan Thomas if he'd been sitting unguarded in London Fields for three days without a drink, eating clods of earth and chewing his tambourine. "Yon ravelling Mage/Crisp sunseanian sage... Tarragon seed whim/is a coin in the swim of your skin." It's all in that vein. Naturally we must acknowledge the possibility that he was, quite simply, taking the piss. I mean, come on - "Grand, grand, grand O prawn of time"? His song-lyrics from this era are a similar kind of waffle, although redeemed by the bright necessity of RHYME and also Bolan's extraordinary, potty locution – the vowels curlicued, the consonants dizzily relished, every word humming with imaginative overload, like a lavish beast-headed doodle in the margins of an illuminated manuscript. His reaubes of chintz were melting in the sneaus... My friend and colleague Josh Glenn, on hearing "Hot Rod

Mama", remarked that Bolan's pronunciation of the word "motorcycle" was "completely aestheticized" which I think brings the matter to the mark. There is some great nonsense on *Unicorn* and *Beard of Stars* - "He stalks in style like a royal crocodile" - although really only the occasional line bobs up intact from the general Tolkien-soup, the hippy gumbo. If you read the Bolan-related interviews in Jonathon Green's Sixties history *Days In The Life* (wonderful book) you'll find a concensus among the fractious old groovers that he was "a little shit", an untrue hippy, a careerist, a chancer, a dirty dancer, a red-legged prancer – all standard attributes of the trickster-role it was his destiny to fulfil. In this sense his early nonsense is impure; it is politic nonsense, cunning medievalist flim-flam to keep the flower children happy. As long as they sat cross-legged and big-eyed at his feet he would sing, in the accent of an upper-caste elf, of Dworns and mages and the sweet harmless Children of Rarn. Only when he made the electrified mutant leap into GLAM – the shamelessness, the absurd, teetering phallic presence – did he begin to write pure lambent rock'n'roll nonsense. Look at the cover of *Electric Warrior*, look at that phantom embodied out of blackness, as in some psychic experiment, by gold dust and the blast of a

BEAUTIFUL BOLAN

O Girl
Electric witch you are
Limp in society's ditch you are
(Girl)

Lightning
All the heavy world is frightening
I'm a child in the sand
On the beach of the land of you
(Lean Woman Blues)

Metal guru is it true
Metal guru is it true
All alone without a telephone
(Metal Guru)

I bought a car
it was old but kind
I gave it my mind
And it disappeared
(Spaceball Ricochet)

I have never never kissed a car before
It's like a door
(The Slider)

PHOTOGRAPH BY PETE SANDERS. FROM COVER OF 'UNICORN' BY T REX, CUBE RECORDS, 1969

monster amp, and fall down before the new god, the new voice: Beneath the bebop moon, I wanna croon... Praise him!

A word on nonsense: Teletubbies is not nonsense. Teletubbies, virtuous and child-centred production that it is, hails the dawning of sense, of things adding up and finding their places. The baby sun-god rises over Teletubbyland, quizzical at first but then laughing, golden-eyed, in a Biblical manner pleased. He knows this place, these creatures. My son always greets this image with a shout – it touches his sense of divinity, I think – except for one day, when our TV reception was poor and the wonky TV-waves granted him the profane and terrible sight of a RED baby sun-god. Teletubbyland must be familiar – everything there performs its function, from the nozzle-nosed vacuum-mother Noo Noo to the tiny trapped voices of the flowers ("Water! Lovely water!" they squeak when rain falls.) No, nonsense is stranger and more eruptive than that. Nonsense goes more like: "Far and few, far and few, are the lands where the Jumblies live..." Or "'Twas brillig..." or "Dancin' in the nude, feelin' such a dude – it's a rip-off!" This was the greatness of Glam T Rex. "I drive a Rolls Royce 'cos its good for my voice" – it's worthy of Mr Lear.

So clearly I've made a discovery here, I'm sitting on a literary-historical goldmine. This will give birth to university courses – the prawn of Time shall know my name. Should I write a book about it? I don't know. As an essayist-reviewer I've made money but never felt quite comfortable or authentic, not being one of those powerful, spiteful minds that can float Mekon-like on their little saucers of critical authority.... Anyway, at the moment nobody's paying me for my *bon mots* and what with one thing and another I might even be feeling a little discouraged, professionally speaking, were it not for the fact that last night I slept with the bitch Inspiration, the yellow horns of her toenails dragging on my legs (ecstasy!), and the child of our union is a poem that begins: "This is the story of Sid the snail, who went round the world on the back of a whale..." ☙

He would sing, in the accent of a half-caste elf, of Dworns and mages and the sweet harmless Children of Rarn

CHIN'S 33 HAPPY MOMENTS

We reprint a classic of Oriental philosophy and invite you to submit your own thoughts.
Illustrations by Hannah Dyson

Chin Shengt'an was a 17th century Chinese playwright who once found himself stranded with a friend in a temple for ten days because of a rainstorm. While thus secluded, the pair compiled a list of the truly happy moments in life.

The wonderful thing about Chin's Happy Moments is their lack of piety. Material pleasures are not rejected in favour of loftier ones, and some moments involve the misfortunes of others.

We reproduce them here and invite *Idler* readers to submit their own. The form is simple: describe your happy moment, and then add: "Ah, is this not happiness?" See idler.co.uk for more details.

1 It is a hot day in June when the sun hangs still in the sky and there is not a whiff of wind in the air, nor a trace of clouds; the front and back yards are hot like an oven and not a single bird dares to fly about. Perspiration flows down my whole body in little rivulets. There is the noonday meal before me, but I cannot take it for the sheer heat. I ask for a mat to spread on the ground and lie down, but the mat is wet with moisture and flies swarm about to rest on my nose and refuse to be driven away. Just at this moment when I am completely helpless, suddenly there is a rumbling of thunder and big sheets of black clouds overcast the sky and come majestically on like a great army advancing to battle. Rain-water begins to pour down from the eaves like a cataract. The perspiration stops. The clamminess of the ground is gone. All flies disappear to hide themselves and I can eat my rice. Ah, is this not happiness?

2 A friend, one I have not seen for ten years, suddenly arrives at sunset. I open the door to receive him, and without asking whether he came by boat or by land, and without bidding him to sit on the bed or the couch, I go to the inner chamber and ask my wife: "Have you got a gallon of wine like Su Tungp'o's wife?" My wife gladly takes out her gold hairpin to sell it. I calculate it will last us three days. Ah, is this not happiness? (*Note from ed: that's nearly two bottles of wine each per day.*)

3 I am sitting alone in an empty room and I am just getting annoyed at a little mouse at the head of my bed, and wondering what that little rustling sound signifies – what article of mine he is biting or what volume of my books he is eating up. While I am in this state of mind and don't know what to do, I suddenly see a ferocious-looking cat, wagging its tail and staring with its wide-open eyes, as if it were looking at something. I hold my breath and wait a moment, keeping perfectly still, and suddenly with a little sound the mouse disappears like a whiff of wind. Ah, is this not happiness?

4 I have pulled out the *hait'ang* and *chiching* [flowery trees] in front of my studio, and have just planted ten or twenty green banana trees there. Ah, is this not happiness?

5 I am drinking with some romantic friends on a spring night and am just half intoxicated, finding it difficult to stop drinking and equally difficult to go on. An understanding boy servant at the side suddenly brings in a package of big fire-crackers, about a dozen in number, and I rise from the table and go and fire them off. The smell of sulphur assails my nostrils and enters my brain and I feel comfortable all over my body. Ah, is this not happiness?

6 I am walking in the street and see two poor rascals engaged in a hot argument of words with their faces flushed and their eyes staring with anger as if they were mortal enemies, and yet they still pretend to be ceremonious to each other, raising their arms and bending their waists in salute, and still using the most polished language of *thou* and *thee* and *wherefore* and *is it not so?* The flow of words is interminable. Suddenly there appears a big husky fellow swinging his arms and coming up to them, and with a shout tells them to disperse. Ah, is this not happiness?

7 To hear our children recite the classics so fluently, like the sound of water pouring from a vase. Ah, is this not happiness?

....

8 Having nothing to do after a meal I go to the shops and take a fancy to a little thing. After bargaining for some time, we still haggle about a small difference, but the shop-boy still refuses to sell it. Then I take out a little thing from my sleeve, which is worth about the same thing as the difference and throw it at the boy. The boy suddenly smiles and bows courteously saying, "Oh, you are too generous!" Ah, is this not happiness?

....

9 I have nothing to do after a meal and try to go through the things in some old trunks. I see there are dozens of IOUs from people who owe my family money. Some of them are dead and some still living, but in any case there is no hope of their returning the money. Behind people's backs I put them together in a pile and make a bonfire of them, and I look up to the sky and see the last trace of smoke disappear. Ah, is this not happiness?

....

10 It is a summer day. I go bareheaded and barefooted, holding a parasol, to watch young people singing Soochow folk-songs while treading the water-wheel. The water comes up over the wheel in a gushing torrent like molten silver or melting snow. Ah, is this not happiness?

....

11 I wake up in the morning and seem to hear someone in the house sighing and saying that last night someone died. I immediately ask to

find out who it is, and learn that it is the sharpest, most calculating fellow in town. Ah, is this not happiness?

12 I get up early on a summer morning and see people sawing a large bamboo pole under a mat-shed, to be used as a water-pipe. Ah, is this not happiness?

13 It has been raining for a whole month and I lie in bed in the morning like one drunk or ill, refusing to get up. Suddenly I hear a chorus of birds announcing a clear day. Quickly I pull aside the curtain, push open a window and see the beautiful sun shining and glistening and the forest looks like having a bath. Ah, is this not happiness?

14 At night I seem to hear someone thinking of me in the distance. The next day I go to call on him. I enter his door and look about his room and see that this person is sitting at his desk, facing south, reading a document. He sees me, nods quietly and pulls me by the sleeve to make me sit down, saying, "Since you are here, come and look at this." And we laugh and enjoy ourselves until the shadows on the walls have disappeared. He is feeling hungry himself and slowly asks me, "Are you hungry, too?" Ah, is this not happiness?

15 Without any serious intention to build a house of my own, I happened, nevertheless, to start building one because a little sum had unexpectedly

come my way. From that day on, every morning and every night I was told that I needed to buy timber and stone and tiles and bricks and mortar and nails. And I explored and exhausted every avenue of getting some money, all on account of this house, until I got sort of resigned to this state of things. One day, finally, the house is completed, the walls have been whitewashed and the floors swept clean; the paper windows have been pasted and scrolls and paintings are hung up on the walls. All the workmen have left, and my friends have arrived, sitting on different couches in order. Ah, is this not happiness?

16 I am drinking on a winter's night, and suddenly note that the night has turned extremely cold. I push open the window and see that snowflakes come down the size of a palm and there are already three or four inches of snow on the ground. Ah, is this not happiness?

17 To cut with a sharp knife a bright green water-melon on a big scarlet plate on a summer afternoon. Ah, is this not happiness?

18 I have long wanted to become a monk, but was worried because I would not be permitted to eat meat. If I could be permitted to eat meat publicly, why, then I would heat a basin of hot water, and with the help of a sharp razor, shave my head clean in a summer month! Ah, is this not happiness?

19 To keep three or four spots of eczema in a private part of my body and now and then to scald or bathe it with hot water behind closed doors. Ah, is this not happiness?

20 To find accidentally a handwritten letter of some old friend in a trunk. Ah, is this not happiness?

21 A poor scholar comes to borrow money from me, but is shy about mentioning the topic, and so he allows the conversation to drift along on other topics. I see his uncomfortable situation, pull him aside to a place where we are alone and ask him how much he needs. Then I go inside and give him the sum and after having done this, I ask him: "Must you go immediately to settle this matter or can you stay awhile and have a drink with me?" Ah, is this not happiness?

22 I am sitting in a small boat. There is a beautiful wind in our favour, but our boat has no sails. Suddenly there appears a big lorcha, coming along as fast as the wind. I try to hook on to the lorchas in the hope of catching on to it, and unexpectedly the hook does catch. Then I throw over a rope and we are towed along and I begin to sing the lines of Tu Fu: "the green makes me feel tender towards the peaks, and the red tells me there are oranges." And we break out in joyous laughter. Ah, is this not happiness?

23 I have been long looking for a house to share with a friend but have not been able to find a suitable one. Suddenly someone brings news that there is a house somewhere, not too big, but with only about a dozen rooms, and that it faces a big river with beautiful green trees around. I ask this man to stay for supper, and after the supper we go over together to have a look, having no idea what the house is like. Entering the gate, I see that there is a large vacant lot about six or seven mow, and I say to myself, "I shall not have to worry about the supply of vegetables and melons henceforth." Ah, is this not happiness?

24 A traveller returns home after a long journey, and he sees the old city gate and hears the women and children on both banks of the river talking his own dialect. Ah, is this not happiness?

25 When a good piece of old porcelain is broken, you know there is no hope of repairing it. The more you turn it about and look at it, the more you are exasperated. I then hand it to the cook, and give orders that he shall never let that broken porcelain bowl come within my sight again. Ah, is this not happiness?

....

26 I am not a saint, and am therefore not without sin. In the night I did something wrong and I get up in the morning and feel extremely ill at ease about it. Suddenly I remember what is taught by Buddhism, that not to cover one's sins is the same as repentance. So then I begin to tell my sin to the entire company around, whether they are strangers or my old friends. Ah, is this not happiness?

....

27 To watch someone writing big characters a foot high. Ah, is this not happiness?

....

28 To open the window and let a wasp out from the room. Ah, is this not happiness?

....

29 A magistrate orders the beating of the drum and calls it a day. Ah, is this not happiness?

....

30 To see someone's kite-line broken. Ah, is this not happiness?

....

31 To see a wild prairie fire. Ah, is this not happiness?

....

32 To have just finished repaying all one's debts. Ah, is this not happiness?

....

33 To read the Story of Curly-Beard [who gave up his house to a pair of eloping lovers then disappeared]. Ah, is this not happiness?

....

KING OF THE LOAFERS

The great American poet Walt Whitman lived like a king and loafed like a god. Here's an extract from a 1926 biography, *The Magnificent Idler*

The sub-editor of the *Daily Aurora* arose from his desk at a half after ten one morning and with an air of expansive luxury lit a cigar. It was his last cigar after lunch, for the editor, Mr Walter Whitman, disapproved of tobacco. In perusing a file copy of the *Long Island Democrat*, a journal with which Mr Whitman had lately been connected, the sub-editor had noted with pleasure that Mr. Whitman had written to the effect that "a segar generally has a smoky fire at one end, and a conceited spark at the other." The sub-editor now found his cigars, not noticeably choice ones, infinitely more to his taste. He always smoked one at a half ten and strutted between the window and desk as he did so. At eleven he threw the stub away, opened the window and awaited the editor.

The editor of the *Daily Aurora* arrived at his office in the morning between eleven and half past. Sometimes he came later. The sub-editor, having thoroughly aired the room, reflected on the easy routine of those in authority, and arranged the daily and exchange papers in the executive's den, returned to his desk as Mr Whitman, his top hat at an amiably rakish angle, his light whangee [bamboo cane] slapping against a modishly trousered leg and the blue boutonnière in his well-cut coat still dewy fresh, bade the staff of the *Daily Aurora* an affable good-morning.

The staff greeted him in unison like the chorus of the antique play. They looked upon him with admiration and affection and some envy. They envied him his youth, his health, his pleasing and impressive eye, and the way, and the way his coat fitted upon his magnificent shoulders. They liked him for his inexhaustible and bland good-nature and his entire lack of autocratic assertiveness, and they admired him for his obvious creative abilities of which he gave proof in nearly every other journal in New York but their own.

In the meantime, Mr Whitman, the editor, had reverted to Walt the magnificent Idler. He was wonderfully content

In the meantime, Mr Whitman, the editor, strolling down Broadway to the Battery, had reverted to Walt the magnificent Idler. He was wonderfully content. The tenebrous moods of Jamaica and the Brenton household had not returned to oppress him, and he was beginning to find life an uninterrupted pathway of pleasant experience. He was becoming known in the city as a young author of strength and imagination and he was appearing with a gratifying regularity in the pages of the *Democratic Review* with such contributors as Hawthorne, Bryant, Longfellow, Lowell, Thoreau, Whittier, and the tragic Mr Poe. Walt twirled his whangee. Good company to move in. It was true that his position upon the *Daily Aurora* did not interest him overmuch, but it carried with it a certain distinction and an undoubted regularity of wage and he had so arranged the hours of his attendance at his office that the best part of his day was spent upon the streets, his mind like blotting paper absorbing faces and voices, and sights and sounds. He drank huge draughts of beer with shaggy labourers come so recently from the rainy west of Ireland that their speech resembled soggy vowels and consonants. With the same transparent interest and confidence that as a child had characterised his conversations with the dockhands of the Fulton Ferry, he questioned men whose faces interested him and drew from them opinions and sometimes confidences whose intimacy, when he had strolled on, astonished them. They looked at this broad departing back with stupefaction and cursed themselves for loose-tongued fools, imparting their private hopes and worries to a perfect stranger simply because there was something in his eye that impelled their trust and loosed their tongues ere they could say what now.

They had, such of them that did so, no cause to worry. Walt's unconscious integrity never unlocked a confidence thus made to him, and as time went on his street acquaintances turned to him as to a bank to deposit all manner of personal problems. There was about his presence a solidarity that radiated dependability. They sought

With a debonair flourish of the whangee Mr Whitman entered his den and commenced the work of the day, looking over the newspapers there laid out for him by the sub-editor. This duty occupied him for an hour, after which he sauntered out again. The sub-editor called himself to his attention and asked if there were any orders to be executed. Mr. Whitman thought not but observed that he would return at two or three o'clock and at that time he would attend to whatever affairs had arisen during his absence. Once again he flourished the whangee in a comprehensive gesture of farewell and vanished through the door.

The staff of the *Daily Aurora* resumed its duties with renewed zest. The genial atmosphere that its editor carried with him lingered in his wake and made the office more habitable and the air less heavy with strain of labour. Labour found no place in Mr. Whitman's atmosphere.

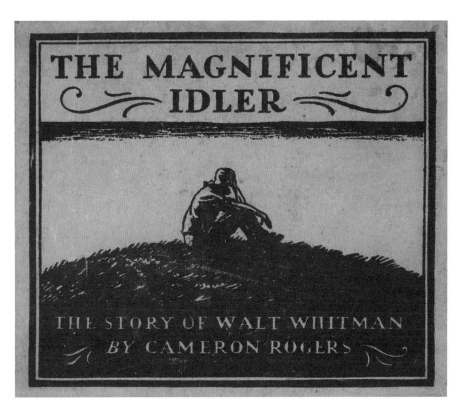

THE MAGNIFICENT IDLER

THE STORY OF WALT WHITMAN
BY CAMERON ROGERS

to know nothing of his antecedents, his occupation, or his means, but they paid him the rare compliment of believing that whatever his livelihood it was gained honestly and with distinction.

Upon Broadway he spoke to or was bespoken by a ship-builder, a carter, a butcher, and a fireman in swift succession. Clothed like one of the young bucks of the town, his top hat and light stick and fashionably tailored coat failed nevertheless to bully his personality into subservience. The latter swallowed the somewhat foppish former completely and easily and his acquaintances, roughly dressed themselves, felt no embarrassment before his splendour.

At the Battery Walt conversed for an hour with the mate of a new clipper-ship bound on the morrow around the Horn for the coast of California. It was after two when he returned to his office and shortly after five he left the Daily Aurora. The sub-editor had during that time sub-edited with passionate energy so that Walt's absence had in reality affected but little the progress of the journal. The sub-editor did not wish Mr Whitman considered incompetent. He himself considered him remarkably lazy but his laziness was a thing of gorgeous thoroughness and his charm was inexhaustible. Mr Whitman wished everyone a very good night, smiled delightfully, allowing his fine grey eyes to rest for a moment on those of each member of the staff, and took his way back to the parliament of the pavements.

He dined with a friend, the pilot of one of the Long Island Sound steamboats, Johnny Cole, a bronzed cylinder of a man whose conversation was a perfectly mixed amalgam of stout oaths, shrewd observations, hearty if coarse comment on the buxom Dutch girl who served them, and curiously tender reminiscence of a comrade recently drowned, and who ate enormously through it all, his bright little eyes observing Walt with affectionate curiosity and satisfaction.

Walt filled his spacious being with bread and meat, washing it well down with beer, and listened with attention. When they arose together and walked up two low steps and out on to Broadway, the appetising odour of the German kitchen still clamouring in their nostrils, they presented an impressive picture of well-fed and contented strength. Twilight was already aboard and the city gentry with it in well-brushed beavers and elegantly arranged cravats, little boots gleaming and side-locks and whiskers admirably curled and arranged. Walt and Johnny Cole moved through the crowd like sloops of war through a fleet of bouncing fishing smacks. They were going to the old Park

Theatre where years before Walt had first fallen beneath the spell of the drama and had revelled in the glittering declamations of Henry Placide. Junius Brutus Booth the elder was there playing his classic Richard the Third, for almost two decades the unrivalled Shakespearean performance in England or America.

Walt attended its performance at every opportunity, and Johnny Cole never visited New York without going to some play and applauding or denouncing with vigour the delivery and deportment of the actors. He had a voice of the same hoarse resonance as a foghorn but it possessed a far wider range. He also possessed the talent of being able to crack his fingers with such explosive sharpness that actors who had seemed to him inadequate entertainers often fled into the wings on hearing reports which seemed to be caused by a number of pistols in the possession of a great red choleric tun of a man who bellowed threats at them as he shot.

Walt deprecated his digital activity and Cole promised to abstain from it, but at those lines delivered by the first murderer to stab the unfortunate Clarence, "take that, and that; if all this will not do, I'll drown you in the malmsey-butt within," a series of terrific reports shattered the awed silence that filled the auditorium.

The first murderer, in the midst of his bloody villainy, was seen to shake visibly. Consummating his crime he made his exit without loss of time. Walt frowned at his companion but the harm was done. The second murderer quavered his despairing wish, like Pilate, he could wash his hands of that most grievous murder, expecting that the next volley would not fail to send him after the late duke.

With terror in his eyes the first murderer reappeared. He engaged with trepidation to censure his failing colleague and then concluded the act with his five lines of callous planning, ending:

For this will out, and then I must not stay

True to his threat he stayed not an instant. Though he could perceive no puff of smoke in the body of the house, the ominous crack of the vividly imagined pistol clove his eardrums like the thunder of doom. He was gone before his words had even reached the expectant audience. The curtain hid the stage while the spectators speculated loudly and with discontent upon the cause of his panic. Johnny Cole, his great hands hidden, vented sheepish excuses.

"Why, blast me, Walt, that boy's a terrible play actor. He's got no guts. Why, he never took his knife to the dook at all. The dook was dead as mutton before he was ever properly stuck. And look at the way he skipped about, like a dancing master he was, and him supposed to be a killer."

But Walt was adamant.

"Snap those crazy fingers again, Johnny, and home I go as sure as shooting." But even Johnny Cole sat transfixed as Booth filled the great lines with a brave roaring wind and blew them out to pit and stalls like a fleet of golden galleons. Walt's spine seemed to ripple in chilly, prickling waves.

Have mercy, Jesu! – soft! I did but dream – O coward conscience, how dost thou afflict me!

The house held its breath. Later Walt and his friend walked the streets in a ruminative silence that had followed hard upon a period of profound emotion. The expressive digits of Johnny Cole snapped faintly now and then, but in a spirit now of awed appreciation. Booth, he considered, possessed a quarter-deck delivery second to no actor upon the boards or bluewater bucko master afloat. On the Battery, the two men shook hands, Cole taking the South Ferry to Brooklyn and Walt directing his steps once more up Broadway.

"Walt, he's a jim-dandy, ain't he?"

This was admitted.

"Well, so long, Walt. Yes, sir, a jim-dandy! Well, so long."

He smote Walt on the back, peering at him tenderly. Walt smote him on the back. "Take care of yourself, Johnny, old soldier."

Walt, sauntering into his office at his usual near noon-hour, was aware of a certain ominous atmosphere

On Broadway Walt walked with the added dignity of an assimilated presence. Booth's royal habit of port became him extremely. With a noble flourish of the whangee he intoned valiantly:

Fight, gentlemen of England, fight, bold yeomen!
Draw, archers, draw your arrows to the head!
Spur your proud horses hard, and ride in blood!
Amaze the welkin with your broken staves!

A few days later Walt, sauntering into his office at his usual near-noon hour, was aware of a certain ominous atmosphere, anxious unrest about the desks of the staff of the *Daily Aurora.*

The sub-editor seemed distraught with nervousness. At Walt's entrance he made gestures of warning with his right hand and jerked his left thumb over his shoulder in what struck Walt as being admirable

FOXY-T

TONY WHITE

ff

comic pantomime. He laughed amiably and asked for a clue to all this. The sub-editor, his efforts at a mysterious silence thus rendered abortive, collapsed.

"Mr Whitman, the senior prop's in your den, sir. He's been there since half-past nine, steaming like a kettle." Walt, to his agonized astonishment, beamed.

"Well, well, I must go right in and see him."

Straightening his cravat, he ambled through the doorway while the sub-editor mopped his brow. "What a man," he said, "what a man."

His smile touching the condition of the senior proprietor was apt. He was indeed steaming like a kettle.

"Mr.Whitman, may I make so bold as to ask you if this is your regular hour of attendance at this office, sir?"

"Why, yes, sir, though sometimes I get in a little earlier or a little later."

"But, good sir, do you expect to edit a city paper by showing up at your office at lunch time? Are you occupied with other concerns that claim your attention during the remaining hours of the morning?".

Walt smiled with perfect good nature.

"Why, no! I have a very able assistant and he attends to much of the work as well as I could. Better, perhaps. I come every day, but I find my work pretty regularly cleaned up for me."

The senior proprietor in the face of this bland and infrangible benignity felt not unlike a kettle no longer steaming but filled with water warm which was growing rapidly cooler. He waggled his hands.

"Mr.Whitman, I regret very much to say that the interest of the *Daily Aurora* demand a man who will work for them early and late. I shall be, we all shall be, exceedingly sorry to lose your services but there you are. If I may say so, Mr.Whitman, if a man old enough to be your father may say so, you are a very remarkable young man but you are to my mind without any doubt the laziest fellow who ever undertook to edit a city paper. But mark me here, Mr Whitman, it is not that which brings us to the parting of ways. Not that at all. It is, shall we say, a point of editorial policy upon which we differ. Let us have no hard feeling. You are, Mr Whitman, a young man who will go very far. Very far, I am sure of it, but the *Daily Aurora* –"

He was out of breath. Startlingly red and panting, he gazed at Mr.Whitman in pathetic inarticulateness. His eyes held a frantic pleading. Walt smiled his charming smile.

"My dear sir, say no more about it. It has been a pleasant connection for me, very. I trust for both of us. I shall miss the *Daily Aurora* but doubtless it will thrive without me. Good-morning, sir."

He emerged from his den, now his no longer, into the arms of the bereaved sub-editor.

"Mr.Whitman, it has been an honour to know you, sir, and a pleasure to work for you."

The sub-editor had heard the tidings for himself. The staff echoed his words. Walt shook hands with them all, and tipping his top hat just a shade to the right, sought Broadway, again and as usual; very cheerfully, a free man. ☙

Search for The Magnificent Idler *by Cameron Rogers (Heinemann, 1926) in second-hand bookshops or websites such as www.abebooks.co.uk*

INSTITVTVM PATAPHYSICVM LONDINIENSE

Palotin 130 EP   *April 2003 (vulg.)*

The Office of Patentry
a Department of

THE LONDON INSTITUTE OF 'PATAPHYSICS
issues this General

CALL

for applications for OffPat Patents

𝕻𝖗𝖔𝖑𝖊𝖌𝖔𝖒𝖊𝖓𝖔𝖓. Humanity is in thrall to the functional, and the useful has inflicted its dreary utilitarianism upon the whole world. OffPat resists this unquestioning servitude by issuing legally worthless patents to the creators of inutilious inventions and innocent machines.

𝕳𝖔𝖜 𝖙𝖔 𝕬𝖕𝖕𝖑𝖞. Send a specification or description, as technical as necessary, and a visual rendering (drawing or photograph) of your invention to the LIP (c/o Bookart-bookshop, 17 Pitfield st., London N1 6HB). An anonymous committee will consider your application. If the invention is deemed to be useful, it will be rejected (and this is the *only* ground for rejection). Judgement will be subjective, and final. Applicants will be notified of the committee's verdict. Successful applicants may then purchase a sumptuous Off-Pat patent certificate for the sum of £11 plus £2 p&p.

𝕮𝖔𝖓𝖉𝖎𝖙𝖎𝖔𝖓𝖘. Applicants agree to the publication and/or exhibition of their applications whether they be successful or not. Rejected applications will be returned only if accompanied by an s.a.e., although the LIP will retain a copy. Applicants will, naturally, be informed of any exhibition or publication containing their work.

JULIA HEMBER

Julia, who's been our most regular and loyal photographer for nine years, lost her battle against leukemia in June. We decided to reprint some of the photographs she's taken for us over the years.

JULIA HEMBER (1970-2003)

We first met Julia at Joshua Compston's art fête in Hoxton in 1994. She came up to our table, bought a T-shirt, and declared that she wanted to take pictures for us. I told her we paid close to nothing. She said she wasn't planning on retiring on the fees and wanted to do something she believed in.

We ran her first image in Issue six, Cocktail Nation. From then on, not an *Idler* went by without Julia's photography in it. Six of our covers were her images. We made her a contributing editor.

She did the portraits for so many of our interviews, including Jeffrey Bernard, Bruce Robinson, John Cooper Clarke, Bill Oddie and Patrick Moore. She was instrumental in our eccentric forays into fashion, notably photographing Inaction Man in Issue 21, A Day Out in Hastings in Issue 23 and Jo Guest And The Holy Grail in Issue 24. She also documented the *Idler* retreats in France and in Devon.

We miss her enormous contribution to the magazine and to our lives. **Gavin Pretor-Pinney**

JEFFREY BERNARD,
ISSUE 8, FEBRUARY 1995

ABOVE: FROM "FASTER PUSSYCAT" FASHION STORY, ISSUE 22, APRIL 1998
OPPOSITE: JOHN COOPER CLARKE, ISSUE 17, NOVEMBER 1996

LEFT: FROM THE "INACTION MAN" FASHION STORY,
ISSUE 21, FEBRUARY 1998
ABOVE: BRUCE ROBINSON, ISSUE 12, DECEMBER 1995

POSITE: BEZ, ISSUE 21, FEBRUARY 1998
OVE: FROM "SHUT UP AND ENJOY YOURSELF!" FASHION STORY, ISSUE 23, JUNE 1998

BELOW: JOHN MICHELL, ISSUE 16, AUGUST 1996
OPPOSITE: ALEX JAMES AND PATRICK MOORE, ISSUE 28, SUMMER 2001

ON THE BUSES

The top deck is the VIP room
for the common man, says
Fanny Johnstone. Louis
Theroux and Bill Drummond
add their thoughts.
Photography by Adolfo Crespo

T he next time you're depressed about having
to take a bus because you can't afford or find
a cab, take comfort in the fact that fat-cats in
taxis and celebrities in limousines miss out on
one of life's most spectacular perspectives – the
views from the top deck. Despite all their VIP
advantages they don't know, or perhaps have
forgotten, that being on the top deck is a window
onto other lives, other angles. Up there you're with
the pigeons, the architecture, the tree tops and the
views.

The lower deck is the haven for the obese, the pregnant, the old, the laden, the injured, the lonely

As biographer Edouard Drumont said of Victor Hugo:

The morning, for him, was consecrated to sedentary labours, the afternoon to labours of wandering. He adored the upper levels of omnibuses – those "travelling balconies" as he called them – from which he could study at his leisure the various aspects of the gigantic city. He claimed that the deafening brouhaha of Paris produced in him the same effect as the sea.

Life on the lower deck feels more tense, vulnerable and claustrophobic because, as a Brit, there's always that slight fear that someone's going to speak to you. The lower deck is the haven for the obese, the pregnant, the old, the laden, the injured, the lonely. So there's a sort of unwritten rule that if you're fit enough to climb the stairs then you climb them. And when you get there, a slightly adolescent feeling embraces you that you're with the cool kids now. Inevitably, you adopt a certain detachment, equal to walking down dangerous city streets on which you're compelled to employ a confident gait. One that marries persuasive authority with a carefree attitude.

Life on the top deck with its 360° surround ventilation and visibility, has got its own liberated feel. It's where the young, the funky, the single, the newly loved and the sexy sit. In a recent survey 28% of the people questioned had enjoyed sexual encounters on the top deck with their partners. The favoured seat was at the back, next to the staircase, a long way from the driver's periscopic vision through the mirror. But with the arrival of CCTV those days are over now, unless you want to be recorded providing some en route entertainment. And you can't have a post-coital cigarette either since London Regional Transport banned smoking on buses in February 1991. It's all bad news for frisky lovers.

But if you've taken a route often enough it becomes engrained in your heart like a well-thumbed love (or hate) letter. Some bus routes can read like a potted history of a particular era in your life. In later years, when you've moved on to postcodes new, but find yourself having to take that old bus route again, there's that quiet internal hub-bub of revisiting one's past. Looking down to the streets below you can see yourself as a naïve teenager, getting off at a familiar bus-stop on your way to a club with friends; or as a hungover twenty-something making your way to work each morning, grateful that the bus knew the route so that you didn't have to think until it gently deposited you at your destination.

Whatever your stage in life the familiar rhythms of the top deck generally molly-coddle its passengers with soothing sounds. The ding-ding of the bell, the rumble of the engine, the chattering of the bus-conductor's ticket dispenser. But at each bus stop there are also those moments of quiet anticipation of who's climbing up the stairs and

TOP DECK LOLLING: VICTOR HUGO CALLED BUSES "TRAVELLING BALCONIES"

what they'll contribute to this vehicular eyrie… A newspaper to read over their shoulder? Aggravating habits? Armed robbery (as on the 253 recently)? Unexpected flirtation? Love-potential? Or unwittingly hilarious conversations… such as one naïve and embittered male student saying huffily to another "My flatmate's got delusions of grandeur. He shops at Marks & Sparks and all that crap."

Having delusions of grandeur is not something the Routemaster can be accused of. It's been afforded iconic status all of its own in film over the years. Even James Bond drove a bus. In *Live And Let Die*, Bond steals Solitaire and manages to escape from Mr Big's henchmen on a London Transport AEC Regent III, which he decapitates while driving through a tunnel. The Spice Girls each had a personalised area on the top deck of their Union Jack-decorated bus in their excitingly titled film *Spice Girls: The Movie*, jumping on the double-decker bandwagon of Cliff Richard &

Co in *Summer Holiday* over 30 years before. Peter Sellers spent a lot of time getting on and off and riding buses in *Only Two Can Play* and Albert Finney in *A Man of No Importance* plays Alfie Byrne, a 1960s poetic bus conductor in Dublin who, partly because of his closeted homosexual empathy with Oscar Wilde, rules his bus as a fey king would a country by charming his passengers with Wildean quotations. A passage from the film goes:

Robbie Fay: Don't you be dirtying that nice clean bus, now.

Alfie Byrne: You have it lovely, Bosie. I can see myself in it, like Narcissus.

Although there are all sorts of livery colour co-ordinations and Routemaster vanities, according to London Transport Museum there's no documented reason for why London buses were painted red. But the accepted answer is that when various bus companies merged to form the London General Omnibus Company in 1907 the predominant company was Vanguard, whose livery was the vibrant scarlet we know and love

BILL DRUMMOND **ON THE MAGIC BUS**

When suicide creeps up and dark thoughts abound, like "what's the fucking point of it all? And who gives a shit anyway?" When your girlfriend has dumped you and she's told you what you already suspected: "It wsn't just because you smelt, weren't funny, had bad dress sense, no, I could have coped with all of that. What really did it in the end was that you were a crap shag." Yeah, when it gets that bad, there is only one thing to do – no, not go and get pissed, that only makes matters worse, and will probably only lead you to making late night calls – no, the thing to do is take a bus ride. It can be a bus ride to anywhere, or from anywhere and just a couple of stops can do the trick, as long as it is a double decker and there's room up top, preferably the front seat. From up there, you get get a better view of things, get everything in proportion. You can look down on the other people's little lives as they pass by and, to use that overused phrase of the counselling profession, "move on", literally and maybe even emotionally. You can even check out the talent, consider your options, and there are always more than you thought before the bus ride began. And when you get off, you can still phone her up, and say al those things that you know you will regret, but needed to be said anyway. Ooh, aah, the Magic Bus!

"Red is a very powerful colour, associated with a high level of energy and stimulation"

today. For obvious reasons such as distance visibility in London's perennially grey weather, red was retained as the livery company colour. How apt then, that as the life force of the city red double-decker buses carry its workers about like red cells distributing oxygen. But according to Suzie Chiazzari, a

colour psychologist, "Red is a very powerful colour, associated with a high level of energy and stimulation. It goes hand in hand with adjectives such as courageous, anti-depressant, assertive, determined, friendly, warm, and sensual."

The first prototype wasn't exhibited until the 1954 Commercial Motor Show, with the first release entering service on route 2 (Golders Green to Crystal Palace) on 8th February 1956. The first production Routemasters entered central London routes during the summer of 1959.

Nearly sixty years after their first appearance just under 1,000 still exist in the British Isles out of the 2,876 built in total. 600 of these are still used everyday in London, and the Golden Jubilee prompted some of them to be painted gold. Many of the others are international ambassadors. London's red double-deckers transport wedding parties in Brussels, tourists in Manhattan, peace-activists in Baghdad, Jade Market trippers in Hong Kong and Bollywood wannabees in Bombay. And in 1956 the British Tourist Authority scored a triple whammy using a London bus to host Bing Crosby, Bob Hope and Dorothy Lamour as they toured

LOUIS THEROUX ON THE PLEASURES OF THE TOP DECK

One side benefit of buying a scooter eight months ago is that I now catch buses rarely enough that I actually enjoy riding them. Not Hoppers, those shoeboxes on wheels which are forever getting stuck in stand-offs in too-narrow streets. But double deckers. Is there anything more reliably reassuring than the sight of *your bus* appearing in the distance like a friendly monster? You pay your seventy pence, maybe stopping to think of the money you are saving by

not taking the tube or a taxi (and pretty good for the ozone layer, too!).

Then up the narrow stairs you bound, feeling a little like a cabin boy climbing into the crow's nest of a sailing ship. You trim against the motion of the vehicle as it moves off and make your way forward to one of the front two seats to take in the view, and there you reside, on your travelling observation deck. London passes by in a slow cavalcade. You sit and watch, willing the

America to promote Britain. Less glamorously, in Pakistan, their boarding steps have been so laden with people over the years that they've buckled, so that they grind along the road, sparks flying up, while the roofs remain dented after giant hailstones have battered them during the monsoons.

But for Londoners they remain one of the few stable, traditional elements of English life. A Londoner in question might be the ubiquitous "Man on the Clapham Omnibus". This fictional man is used in legal parlance to indicate a reasonable person. This man "is an abstraction and could be described by his lack of particular qualities rather than a list of qualities owned, because he is 'the man on the Clapham omnibus' who is not as courageous as Achilles, has not the wisdom of Ulysses or the strength of Hercules, nor the vision of a clairvoyant. He will take precautions where experience has shown this to be necessary. He is not a perfect citizen nor a paragon of circumspection."

But it is stunt legend Evel Knievel with whom double-decker bus trivia is normally associated. It was on 31 May 1975 at Wembley Stadium that Knievel crashed his motorbike after clearing thirteen double deckers. Knievel's sexual analogies, like many playboys, also revolved around buses. "Women are like buses. Good to ride on for fifteen minutes. But they forget that if you get off, there'll be another one along in fifteen minutes. And another one, and another one." A comforting notion for both men and passengers. Ding-ding. ◉

bus onward through the amber lights, past the request stops, listening to the passengers around you, happy to be on your way. Living in London as another Winter approaches, facing the daily purgatory of long dreary streets and dark evenings, we must take our consolations where we can. Let us hope there will be buses aplenty, and on time, if possible, too. ◉

BUS BY XTINA LAMB

DOLE DIARIES

Lucy Granville suffers the multiple indignities of the New Deal scheme for the long-term unemployed.
Illustrations by Chris Watson

The morning was spent attending the Discovery Program. I hadn't realised this was what it was known as. I thought it was simply the New Deal Induction Day. I think if I had known about the name it would have put me off going even more than the 9am start. Whatever anyone says about lazy people choosing an easy option by being on the dole, there is only one remotely good thing about life on the social, and that's a lie in.

My Reed employment advisor, Mohamed, (laid on by the New Deal in addition to my half price travel on the tube, London buses and national trains, in kind recognition of my six hard months on the dole) had told me all the New Deal "members" would receive a free breakfast. We had a good laugh after I asked if he needed to know my special dietary requirements. I found out why when breakfast turned out to be biscuits, tea and coffee.

On arrival at the Hackney New Deal Campus just behind Hackney Downs station, I strolled along the narrow street flanked with cars pumping music and youngsters yelling across the street at each other, hanging out. They seemed very busy and industrious, I felt like I was back at 6th Form College. It was 9am. Inside it really was a like a campus, none that I have been to in real life, but the kind you see on TV. The décor was bright and designed for maximum fun for the eyeballs. There was cool, loud music. The majority of the staff was the same age as the 18-24 year old job seekers, and everybody was chatty, happy, and "doing".

Ade and Trevor, the New Deal educators, were a strange couple. One a smiling, panicking African, the other, a weathered pro whose thing is that he knows the score. He defends the role of Reed employment services in the latest back-to-work scheme. "Look, I know what it's like. Reed are really good, honestly. I mean I've been in this

> ## "I know we all say America's shit, but the Discovery programme is also very successful in Australia, where they're more like us"

business for 14 years… when they say they've changed, they really have, they're not like they used to be… they really care about you."

Thus the concept is awakened in all of those who didn't realise it already, that Reed are a bunch of ruthless capitalist foot soldiers that scoop up the unemployed and force them to take that job as a frozen pizza packer because they've done it before, instead of nurturing them through a computer course so they can be the web-designer they always wanted to be.

Trevor compounds the situation by a bizarre admittance that the Discovery program is very successful in America. "I know we all say America's shit, so I understand if that puts you off, but I can tell you that the Discovery program is also very successful in Australia, where they are more like us." Right.

What type of process was I about to encounter? Was I going to morph into a smiling automaton, vacuous eyes lighting up at the barest whisper of the words "well done Miss Smith, Greggs have requested you attend a job interview…"?

Ade deftly deals with a disgruntled Rasta sitting at the back, who has shouted, "This is rubbish, how long's it gonna last?" by telling him not to be silly, that it's like he's got a meal in front of him and he's saying it doesn't taste nice before he's even tried it. He probably uses this line on his children, and to Ade's credit the Rasta is so totally flummoxed by the nonsense inherent in this remark – if your food was rotten with worm holes all over it, you would pretty much know instinctively not to eat it, right? – he

doesn't grace Ade with a reply, and doesn't speak out for the rest of the session.

So, with much further ado, we get stuck in to further introductory stuff about Discovery. I begin to feel desperately sorry for those in the room who are here for the whole three-week course. I don't have to stay for the whole ten yards because I've decided to go for Reed's "self-employment" option.

We are given a test of our basic faculties, which both Ade and Trevor have obviously had problems implementing in the past. They immediately start bad-mouthing the employment services, on whose behalf the test is being carried out, saying to the extremely passive unemployed collective that if they wanted to start a fight, start it with the employment services. Which, as we all know, is like saying argue with a large brick wall until it falls down on top of you.

The test is confusing and I cannot complete the first two questions, designed to test reading skills. This is partly hilarious, and partly desperate, since in the introduction to the introduction we had to introduce ourselves to the group, and I admitted that my past work experience has been in teaching English language. No wonder I'm unemployable as a teacher! I'm illiterate!

The questions all have a slightly sinister "challenge people's justified conceptions about certain crap jobs" agenda. For example:

Some people think working in a factory is boring. They think you often spend all day doing the same thing. But some factories today do try _____ make the work more interesting by _____ you from job to job.

This one's even harder:

In fast food restaurants _____ take-aways the food is _____ as people order. The _____ uses ready prepared food _____ as frozen pies, samosas and pizzas.

I maintain that the questions themselves show a tenuous grasp on sanity let alone the English language. Woe betide anyone in the group for whom English isn't their first language. The grammar and punctuation sections just could not make sense. One question helpfully informed us that we must identify 20 mistakes, when there were only 18 to be had, and all the sentences were in tenses rarely used in any workplace, let alone by your average English person in their day to day communications. So what chance Johnny foreigner? Sod all, judging by the guesses and suggestions flying round the room, in direct contravention of Ade's request that we don't cheat, otherwise he will make us "stand up against the wall".

No one wanted to know who was to see the test, or what function it would have in our "Back to work" program. I was worried. Could employers request to see the test? Would certain jobs not be offered to us because the tests showed our numeracy or literacy skills were not up to standard? If I was to be judged on that test, I would give up now and move to Ibiza, get a job in a bar, and have myself some fun instead of chasing about after what I "really want to do". I was vaguely reassured – but not very – to be reminded that because of the Data Protection Act, no one would be shown the test without my permission, and that anyway, Ade and Trevor considered the test to be pointless because no one looked at it or used it for anything.

Trevor, who had the look of a man who is rarely looked at and still less often used for anything, was so browbeaten that I satisfied myself by scrawling my opinions in the margins.

After the frustrating implementation of The Test the hapless New Dealers were regaled with further introduction, which informed us that we would be finding and examining our "primary fascinations", which before you get excited are the key to the change that Reed has inflicted upon itself to distinguish between the bad old Reed, and the great new one. Basically it means the job seeker says what

Your time is your own at least, even if it is a miserable pisspoor existence

job they actually want to do, and the job centre (aka "Employment Campus") helps them get nearer that job via training, work experience or simply accessing vacancy information for the job seeker.

In the past the pressure was on to get the unemployed person into any old job, never mind that they are bored and unhappy. Worse, nothing about the job would help them towards what they wanted to do in the future. They could actually have their 42 hours a week back for £10 or £20 pounds less wages a week, so why choose a job you hate over a life signing on? Your time is your own at least, even if it is a miserable piss poor existence. So the idea that the New Deal considers the job seeker's choice of career to be relevant is progress indeed.

Over the next few weeks, the New Deal members will learn to recognise their "field of fear" regarding employment. They will learn a skill that ought definitely to help; how to develop "good answers". Plus, they will build up their qsps – yep, you guessed it; their quantifiable selling points.

Intriguingly, the New Deal team promised us that ours would be a partnership that would take on a form that was irrefutably genuine – for every single effort we made to get a job, the New Deal would make the same effort on our behalf. Shouldn't be too long before we all get jobs, though, because like the adverts in the classroom say, Reed has more positions that the *Kama Sutra*.

Oh, by the way, after the session ended (early – the toilets were broken) it was realised that I had found my way erroneously into the 25 upwards group. I should have been in the 18-24 year olds' group. Mohamed joked that I needn't worry, the only difference between the two groups was that the younger one smelled less bad, and I have to admit that, having just sat through a session, I laughed my head off. ☙

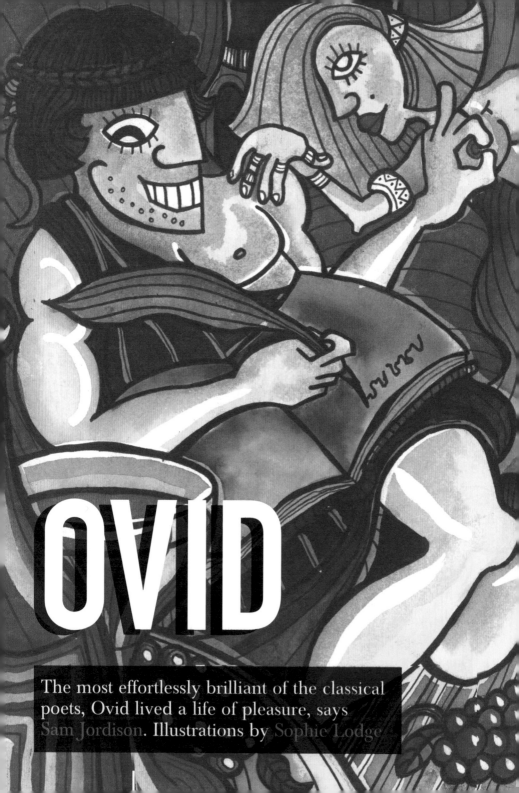

OVID

The most effortlessly brilliant of the classical
poets, Ovid lived a life of pleasure, says
Sam Jordison. Illustrations by Sophie Lodge

Ovid was the consummate ancient idler. He happily turned down an influential, financially rewarding, and unpleasantly strenuous career to dedicate himself to a life of sex and poetry. He wasn't afraid to laugh at the foolish policies and ridiculous arrogance of the most powerful man in his world, and when he was eventually banished, he took the opportunity to invent Crap Towns.

Unfortunately for the lazy Ovid, he lived in a very hectic era. He was born in 43 BC, the year after Julius Caesar's assassination. His boyhood was spent under the shadow of the bloody civil war

He was happy to admit that he "had neither the body, nor the mind" to put up with any kind of work at all

that followed. The three most powerful men on earth, Lepidus, Marc Antony and Octavian battled it out for the control of Rome with a viciousness that has rarely since been equalled. It's hard to say exactly how many people suffered: no one was really counting. However, the decimation of the upper classes in one year, 43 BC, when the three oversaw the execution of 300 Roman Senators and 2,000 *equites* (the two highest strata of society), gives a pretty good impression of what happened to everybody else.

After more than a decade of furious bloodshed, Octavian emerged as the victor. He crushed his enemies with all the shock, awe and overwhelming force the non-nuclear technology of his era allowed. The final act of the war was the battle of Actium in 31 BC when he sank every single ship in the navy of Marc Antony and Cleopatra. He renamed himself Augustus and became the absolute ruler of Rome, with more unrestricted power than any one man had ever had before – or has had since.

Antony and Cleopatra's infamous double suicide was definitely the most sensible response to their unenviable situation after Actium. Only the very bravest – or maddest – crossed Augustus, and nobody got away with it. Not even his own daughter Julia was immune to his wrath, as she discovered when he banished her in 2BC for breaking his stern moral laws on adultery. Equally, only a fool or a hero would turn Augustus down if he offered them a position in his spectacularly powerful inner circle – but that's exactly what Ovid did – before devoting a considerable part of his career to making fun of the image-obsessed dictator.

Ovid, together with his brother, was selected by Augustus because he was looking for someone from their home town, Sulmo (which was about 90 miles from Rome), to help him build up an administration that represented the regions as well as the capital. The young poet managed to skive out of the military service most young men in his position were subjected to (unfortunately, nobody now knows how he managed this) but he didn't avoid being put on the *cursus honorum*, the fast track to political power in Ancient Rome. Augustus made him an *equites* at the tender age of 16 and he was packed off to law school. Ovid went along with this, mainly, he later said, to please his beloved father. And it seems that his traditionalist dad also put considerable financial, as well as emotional pressure on the young poet, ominously warning him that "even Homer died poor."

Luckily Ovid eventually managed to convince the old man that he just wasn't cut out to face what he termed "the burden of power" or any of the "worries of ambition". In fact, he was happy to admit that he "had neither the body, nor the mind" to put up with any kind of work at all. Instead, he loved *otium* (the most evocative Latin term for idleness, our word "negotiation" is its direct opposite). He managed to win the protection and encouragement of the powerful Roman litterateur Messalla, and stepped off Augustus' fast track to dedicate himself to sophisticated city life, getting as much sex as he possibly could and writing fantastic, dazzlingly witty poetry.

Ridiculously, the most common complaint about Ovid's poetry from ancient and modern critics is that he patently didn't suffer for his art. It all came too easily to him. "Whatever I tried to write was poetry," he once complained. He practically thought in verse, the speeches he composed at law school were really all just poems, and as a boy he was even said to have promised that he'd never write another poem to his anxious father – in a perfect elegiac couplet. He enjoyed writing: and jealous puritans have suggested that this devalues his work. However, while it's true that you can never really take him seriously, this doesn't mean his work is without feeling, and it doesn't make his great skill any the less impressive. It's always an easy pleasure to read Ovid, his irrepressible sense of fun bubbling over into everything he wrote. What's more, his poetic gift was rich indeed and his felicity with language unrivalled until Shakespeare. Words were toys to him.

Augustus was accustomed to taking such talents under his "protection" and coercing them to write in praise of his reign. Vergil's patriotic epic *The Aeneid* is the result of this pressure, as are Horace's dreadful military odes (he came up with the "old lie" *dulce et decorum est pro patria mori* to please Augustus). However, not only would Ovid not work to serve the state, he wouldn't even serve the state with his poetry. Instead he dedicated most of his life to singing the praises of the idle life.

Although Ovid found writing poetry so incredibly easy, he didn't actually write that much of it. In fact, until the age of 40, he averaged just 500 lines a year – just under two lines a day, about 10 words. He could happily finish a day's work while dozing in bed before breakfast, and still be confident that he'd done enough to earn himself immortality. He was able to dedicate the rest of his time to research: relaxing in his orchards in the countryside, going to fashionable dinner parties and the chariot races, drinking the finest wines known to humanity, visiting the theatre, staying out until the early morning (when "the cockcrow shatters poor workers' dreams") and arranging dangerous liaisons.

He jokingly called himself the *praeceptor amoris* – best translated as "Dr Love". In *The Amores* he wrote declarations of love and lust for women all over town, celebrating their many trysts and bemoaning the fact that his conquests usually had to go back to their husbands afterwards. *The*

Art Of Love meanwhile is a guide to how best to go about seducing (invariably married) members of the opposite sex.

Ovid gives himself the persona of a brilliant, witty seducer: virile, passionate, tender occasionally sad, but most often amused. And he finds no one funnier or more ridiculous than himself. He may brag about his ability to seduce anyone, and display the "finest cockmanship", and he may boast that he's been able to bring his mistresses to orgasm with a game of footsie, but more often than not we see him completely unable to take his own advice or live up to his self-image. One of his funniest poems is about an attack of impotence that destroyed all his careful arrangements for an adulteress assignation. His would-be-mistress eventually abandoned him in a huff, splashing water on the bed so the maids didn't get the impression that nothing happened. Similarly he undermines his own passionate avowal of fidelity to his most frequent muse, Corinna. She thinks he's been having an affair with her maid, but Ovid fervently declares his innocence asking "What kind of gentleman would fancy making love to a servant?" – especially if he knows how faithful she is, and how likely to give him away. The next poem is addressed to the slave-girl in question, berating her for blowing the gaff and cheekily asking her for more sex

to make up for it.

But Ovid didn't just direct his wit at himself. Augustus was obsessed with promoting old fashioned virtues in his subjects. Ovid delighted in knocking them down. Augustus encouraged *virtutes* – manliness – and the tough military life, Ovid made fun of it in an elaborate metaphor with a salacious punch line: "Every lover acts like a soldier," he claimed. "A commander looks to his troops for gallant conduct, a mistress expects no less, a soldier lays siege to cities, a lover to his girl's doorkeepers… Night attacks are a great thing; catch your opponents sleeping and unarmed… lovers too will take advantage of slumber (her husband's) and thrust home his advantage when the enemy still sleeps." Augustus encouraged his followers to look back on the example of Rome's ancestors for a guide to moral conduct, the *mos maiorum*, exemplified by the early Roman tribe the Sabines whose women faced death rather than betray their husbands. "In the old days things were different," agrees Ovid. "Those Sabine women stuck to one husband apiece. But then," he tells us, "they didn't wash."

In fact, Ovid's whole project was an affront to Augustus' draconian laws against adultery. These laws were more honoured in the breach than the observance – not least by the hypocritical Augustus himself, a well known philanderer who had himself written poems on the subject so disgusting that even the famously dirty Lord Byron claimed they made him feel nauseous. All the same, Ovid's decision to republish his poems on the joys of adultery, the *Amores*, and to issue *The Art Of Love*, his guide to successfully committing adultery in 2BC, the year that Augustus banished his own daughter for her indiscretions – was provocative, to say the least.

Many critics have seen his subsequent work as an attempt to back-pedal and write some more serious poetry in a desperate attempt to make it up to the "injured emperor", as Ovid later termed him. He even states in his introductory lines to *The Metamorphoses* that he's deliberately chosen to write in the epic hexameter, and is going to write on one

"There are no grapes, no fruits. There isn't even any paper. All you can see are naked, empty plains; leafless, treeless"

serious theme for the glory of Rome. The work he actually produced, however, was more like a *Popbitch* of the divine world, a light-hearted account of the misdeeds of the gods, that often had hundreds of themes in the space of as many lines. It's a work of genius, effortlessly intertwining a wealth of mythology and folklore, ingeniously inter-linking the endless variety of stories using the idea of metamorphosis. Characters are turned into birds, fish, insects, plants, flowers, rocks, trees, rivers, fountains, men are turned into women and vica versa, and they all lead seamlessly on from each other. It's our main source for classical mythology and has been plundered for stories for centuries. No lesser writers than Chaucer and Shakespeare make free and easy use of it, and in their famous renditions of the story of Pyramus And Thisbe they both borrow more than a little of Ovid's irreverent tone.

Predictably, this impressive enterprise did not please Augustus at all, not least because Ovid mercilessly ribbed him once again. Ovid's comparisons of the newly deified Augustus to the king of the Roman god's, Jupiter, (who like Augustus holds his councils on a "divine Palatine Hill") should have been warmly received, were it not for the fact that Ovid's Jupiter is a priapic fool, lustily chasing women (and cows) all over heaven and earth, fearfully avoiding his outraged wife Juno, and siring bastard children and man-bull combinations wherever he goes.

Ovid never got to see his masterpiece published in Rome. In AD 8, he was banished. The reason for the exact timing of this has been lost in the mists of time. It may have something to do with the fact that his long-standing friend and protector Messalla died in that year. And perhaps it's just too much of a coincidence that "Dr Love" was banished in the same year that Augustus once again exiled a member of his own family (his granddaughter, also called Julia) for committing adultery.

The outraged emperor chose the most exquisite torture for this dedicated urbane idler. He sent him to a crap town. Ovid was made to go to Tomis, a remote Roman outpost by the Black Sea, where nobody spoke the same language as the talented poet and he was even made to put on a helmet and fight against the barbarians who constantly threatened the borders.

All the same, and despite the two books of poetry he wrote begging to be taken back to Rome Ovid seems to have relaxed into his situation, teaching himself to do a bit of fishing, and even composing in the odd poem in the native Getic. And, although in my vainer moments I like to flatter myself that I came up with the idea for Crap Towns with my fellow Idler Dan Kieran, I'm forced to admit that Ovid, for one, beat me to it by a good 2,000 years.

"I have to live among barbarians," he said, in one of many harrowing descriptions of his new home. "The snow lies continually on the ground, neither sun, nor rain melts it... sometimes it stays for two years. The natives keep out the evils of the cold with skin and pelts, of the whole body, they only dare expose their face... Exposed wine stands upright, retaining the shape of the jar and everyone drinks, not draughts of wine, but fragments! ...I've seen fish fast-bound in the frozen sea...the barbarian enemy... [uses the frozen rivers as an opportunity to attack], and with his far flying arrows, deprives the locality of its populace... Even when there is there is peace, everyone's terrified of another war and nobody bothers to do any ploughing... the soil here is lifeless, abandoned in stark neglect. There are no grapes, no fruits. There isn't even any paper. All you can see are naked, empty plains; leafless, treeless. This is a place – damn it – that no fortunate man should visit."

Tomis, incidentally, is in modern Romania. It's now called Costanza, and by all accounts it's still pretty awful. Although Ovid wasn't best pleased to have been sent to such a miserable place, he must have been secure in the knowledge that, as ever, he was going to have the last laugh. His jokes are still funny after more than 2,000 years. His brilliant poetry has won him immortality while drawing an everlastingly ridiculous portrait of his nemesis Augustus. And, most importantly, he's an example and inspiration to idlers everywhere. ◉

WIT AND WISDOM OF PUBLIUS OVIDIUS NASO

Da requiem; requietus ager bene credita reddit –Take rest; a field that has rested gives a bountiful crop.

Video meliora proboque deteriora sequor – I see the better way and approve it, but I follow the worse way.

In medio tutissimus ibis – Moderation in all things.

Bene qui latuit, bene vixit – One who lives well, lives unnoticed.

Cui peccare licet peccat minus – The person who is allowed to sin, sins less.

Exitus acta probat – The end justifies the means.

Gutta cavat lapidem, non vi sed saepe cadendo – The drop excavates the stone, not with force but by falling often.

Omnia iam fient quae posse negabam – Everything which I used to say could not happen will happen now.

Nil homini certum est – Nothing is certain for man.

Parva leves capiunt animos – Small things please small minds.

Paucite paucarum diffundere crimen in omnes – Do not blame the masses for the crimes of the few.

As est et ab hoste doceri – It's right to learn - even from an enemy.

Saepe creat molles aspera spina rosas – Often the prickly thorn produces tender roses.

Leve fit, quod bene fertur, onus – The burden carried in good spirit is made light.

Rident stolidi verba Latina – Fools laugh at the Latin language.

STORIES

JANET'S TALE

From *Wednesday's Child*, a
forthcoming novel by
Eloise Millar.
Illustration by Edwin Marney

··········

*Janet is eight years old. She lives on the Blackbird Leys
estate on the outskirts of Oxford. Her older brother James
has run away after being beaten by their father, Dick
Roberts.*

On Thursday I stayed at Aunty Net's while Mum
went up the hospital with Nan. I didn't know
why they were going. I just knew that they'd
spent the morning up the doctor's, and that
when they arrived back they told Dick Roberts that
they had to go up to the John Radcliffe, way up in
Headington, and if he looked after the house and
waited for any news, they'd take me over to Net's.

Aunty Net was in the dark, as well.

"Mind your own," Nan had said when she asked
her what was going on. "It would make a bloody
change."

Aunty Net scowled and stood watching them from
behind the net curtains, as they sat at the bus stop
across the road.

"Mind your own," she mimicked irritably,

"Go on, luvvie, I'm half parched, I tell you. I've not had a drop since your brother did a runner"

scrunching up her face. "Mind your own, for a bloody change."

She waited until Nan and Mum had climbed onto the bus and then hurried over to her handbag. She emptied the contents, scattering rusting coins, rumpled tissues, a couple of old screw-top bottle-tops and a DHSS booklet over the floor, until she found what she was after: an old, scuffed leather purse, from which she plucked a battered five pound note.

"There we are," she said, holding it in the air as she smiled at me pleadingly with orange teeth. "Pop up the shops for me would you, ducky?"

I reluctantly took the money and looked down at the queen's face.

"I'm not allowed to go out by myself," I complained, but she brushed my protests aside, pushing me out of the living room and towards the front door.

"Go on, luvvie, I'm half parched, I tell you. I've not had a drop since your brother did a runner."

I knew that wasn't the truth, she smelt a bit funny already. I left the house anyway, wondering as I walked where she had been getting her medicine from without James or I to help her.

When I got back I pushed some clothes, dirty plates and old milk cartons off from the sofa and onto the floor, taking a seat. A trickle of lumpy liquid dribbled out of the carton and onto the carpet, but it didn't really matter. The house was so generally squalid that another mucky puddle wasn't going to hurt. I watched as Manalow, Aunty Net's cat, prowled around the room. He paused briefly at the white trail, sniffing it curiously, before moving on and settling for a piece of old, indistinguishable food on a plate in a corner. He probably ate more than Aunty Net, I thought, although like Aunty Net his eyes oozed and scaled with sticky grunge and his tabby fur—like her hair—was falling out in greasy clumps.

Aunty Net sat in the middle of the living room floor, her own eyes glowing as she unscrewed the bottle. Her legs were tucked beneath her coiled body: she sat, poised like an aged nymph, surrounded by the dirty fibre flowers of the ancient, patterned carpet.

She must have been pretty, once. You could see it shining out from old photos. There was a kind of ravaged beauty about her, even now, at least when she was animated.

"You must miss that little brother of yours, pet," she mumbled, but her thoughts were elsewhere. She scrabbled around until she found an old, cloudy glass, holding it up before her as though it were a diamond-encrusted genie's lamp, filling it right up, up to the very brim with the clear liquid from the bottle.

"Cheers," she giggled, holding the glass high in the air and downing the contents in one go.

She belched, and wiped the spit from her mouth with the back of her hand.

"Mind your own," she repeated sadly, and let out a loud sigh.

Then she filled up the bottle cap with the liquid, and knelt down with her elbows on the ground, holding it out to the cat.

"Manny? Meow? Come and have a drink with your mummy!" she coo-ed.

Manalow carried on eating from the plate, ignoring her.

She turned and held the cap towards me.

"Want it?" she asked. When I quickly shook my head she shrugged, and swallowed the measure herself.

"I don't know," she grumbled. "Bloody swotty kids. I was smoking when I was eight."

She sat silently after that, her eyes swerved purposelessly around the living room until they came to rest on me again. I squirmed uncomfortably, and tried to avoid the intensity of her gaze, focusing on the television, where *Why Don't You* was on.

"I'll tell you something, though," Aunty Net said. "If anyone knows where your brother is, it's you. Isn't that right, little miss?"

I didn't know how to react and sat, trying to wipe the surprise off my face as I mutely shook my head. It was just like her, to come out with something like that.

"Look at you, sitting there as if butter wouldn't melt in your mouth."

She let out a sharp cackle and, reaching out over the floor, patted my head.

"Don't you worry, my little darling," she said. "As long as you're sure he's all right, your secret's safe with me."

Aunty Net got livelier and livelier. She alternated between lying on the floor and performing a strange whirling dance around the living room. The now empty bottle was her partner, she held it tightly to her chest as though it were a fragile and precious child. Eventually she collapsed back onto the carpet, her ragged skirt splayed around her, and began, hiccupingly, to tell me of the Roman soldier a friend of a friend had seen, walking through the park the other day.

"And it occurred to me, didn't it? Didn't it?" she shouted excitedly, wagging her fist in the air. "I tell you, it suddenly hit me that there used to be an old Roman Road around here, and that was why she could only see half his body, because that old road is buried under our one. It's lower down, eh?"

I nodded.

"You see?" she shouted.

She tried to get to her feet but failed, falling back onto the ground.

"I'll get you a cup of tea, Aunty Net." She lifted her face from the carpet and pouted at me.

"It will make you feel better," I hazarded.

Her features continued to darken.

"Listen to yourself. Tea? 'Cup of tea, Aunty Net?' Chip off the old block, you. Bloody Bainbridge through and through."

"It might make you feel better …"

"Oh, listen to it," she spat at an invisible audience. "'It might make you feel better. Cup of tea, Aunty Net? One single cup of tea and you'll never need your medicine again.'"

She picked up a rusting knitting needle that lay by her side and threw it limply across the room at me.

"Just like your mother," she snapped, "but all the tea in China's not changed her rotten luck."

Her body swayed, and then lurched sideways. She toppled down onto the ground and her head landed with a painful thud on the carpet. It didn't seem to bother her though. She didn't move again, and after a few silent minutes she began to snore snoftly.

"Aunty Net?"

I whispered softly in her ear and tugged half-heartedly at her naked, carpet-creased arm. It thumped flaccidly to the ground again as soon as I let go. Her breaths were long and heavy.

"Aunty Net!"

There was no use. A green string of saliva hung from her mouth, trickling down and soaking into the threadbare carpet. Her eyes rolled half open, half closed.

My tummy rumbled.

"Aunty Net?" I said, trying one last time

and placing a tentative hand on her shoulder.

At last she stirred, but it was only to bat me away.

"Leave me be," she managed to groan, before she fell back into sleep.

Despondent, I gave up and wondered into the kitchen, skidding over some oil on the lino as I walked through the door.

It seemed impossible that Aunty Net's kitchen – her whole house, in fact – and ours had an identical layout. They managed to look so different. She had the same kitchen units as us, the ones that had come with the house, but whereas Mum bleached and sprayed and scrubbed ours all day long, Aunty Net just left hers to nature. The surfaces were cracked and peeling, tiles hung off from the ceiling and the floor stuck to your socks. Half eaten food lay everywhere – on the floor, on the tables – rotting like a pitiable homage to Mrs Havisham's wedding feast.

She really didn't care, Aunty Net, but there was a gentleness in the neglect. She didn't subdue anything, she simply let things grow around her.

I pulled open one of the rickety cupboard doors, and rifled through sticky packages of decaying food in the hope of discovering something I could eat. A Nescafé jar lay on its side, the last few grains of coffee dissolving on the plastic; a Yorkshire pudding mix, gnawed open by mice, spewed flour over a couple of tins of Nisa baked beans. I picked one up, but any hope of cooking it dissolved when I turned and took a look at the cooker. In the end, in amongst the multitude of empty bottles and some plastic packets of powdered mash potato, I found some out-of-date jelly babies.

I popped them into my skirt pocket and walked over to the sink, looking for a cloth to mop up the oil, when Nan let herself in.

"Where's Net?" she asked, standing in the kitchen as she took off her scarf.

She wasn't looking at me and didn't seem to need an answer. Her eyes fluttered briefly over the room, taking in the cobwebs and the grease stains sliding up the walls.

"Christ, look at the state of this place," she said, loudly, wrinkling her nose, "and what's that smell?"

She walked over to the bin, flipped open the lid—muttering something about Mum and the worry as she did—and lurched hurriedly away when she saw what was in it. She sighed, rolling her eyes.

"Just nipping to the loo," she said.

She didn't stop to look in the living room before she disappeared upstairs into the toilet.

I held my breath and listened to her footsteps up the stairs, waiting until I heard the toilet door close before hurrying into Aunty Net. She'd be in trouble if Nan found her asleep on the floor. I'd probably be in trouble too.

"Aunty Net, wake up!" I whispered urgently.

I tapped her shoulder, but she lay silent and prostrate, aside from the strange gurgling sound that bubbled up from her lips.

"Aunty Net! Aunty Net!"

The toilet chain flushed.

The toilet door creaked open.

Panicking, I grabbed her dandruffed curls and wrenched her head up into the air. She jerked, and began to rattle and choke. I could hear Nan's footsteps on the stairs. Oh god, I thought, we're in for it – but then Aunty Net came to with a violent start and shook herself awake. She heaved herself up onto all fours, crouching like a downtrodden, stray dog as she retched

> "Just like your mother," she snapped, "but all the tea in China's not changed her rotten luck"

into the already sodden ground. Her cheeks were sweaty with bile and flecked with tiny grains of dirt. One half of her hair stood up on end.

I stood watching her, unsure of what I should do.

"Nan's here," I whispered, helplessly, grabbing her arm and trying to pull her towards the sofa.

But it was too late. Nan was already at the living room door. She stood, her headscarf in her hand, watching Aunty Net as she writhed pathetically, on all fours, on the floor.

"What the hell is going on here?" she asked quietly, her eyes thin slits, her lips pursed. ◉

Wednesday's Child by Eloise Millar is published in April 2004 by Virago

THE HAMMER

Milton Young is going, going, gone.
By Matthew De Abaitua.
Illustrations by Jeff Harrison

....

"Welcome to *The Hammer*. Sell anything you want live on television. Mary is selling five hundred teddy bears she knitted herself, despite her crippling arthritis.

"Former Generals Dirar, Galal and Adow – veterans of the Eritrean-Ethiopian border conflict – want to come around to your house to play Risk, the world conquest board game.

"Sunshine Stone is selling her Orgone Accumulator, a magical box to increase your sexual energy.

"Anton Superman wants to be your poet laureate. He will follow you and your friends around for a month as he writes a collection of verse commemorating your life.

"Register now to bid on these and other fantastic lots as we all go under... *The Hammer*."

Two hours later, Milton Young herded his gang into the limousine idling outside the studio. Honking and whinnying at one another like geese: Roger and Benny and Mimi and Beng and Milton himself, producer and inventor of *The Hammer*, only just thirty and on his way to his first fortune and his big party. He had to shout their destination twice to make himself understood to the driver.

As soon as the car nosed its way free of the kerb, the gang got their phones out, and set about

"Be a naughty clever boy to catch Mummy's eye. Attention is survival. The ignored are the unfed"

clearing their diaries. The spinning wheel of invitations had finally settled. The evening's other responsibilities – hosts, lovers, relatives – were served excuses. For this party could absolutely not be missed. Only Milton refrained from untying himself from prior commitments. His only responsibility, Sylvia, his fiance, would be waiting for him there, despite his best efforts to put her off coming.

He stared out of the window. A terrible cold concreted over his senses - he could not taste or smell, and even his hearing was dull. He had caught the cold off the child of a friend, who had bullied him into kissing the kid goodnight. His blocked sinuses pressed against the nerves beneath his face, each step felt like it was jarring his teeth from his gums. His tongue was a dirty flapping innersole. Veuve Cliquot was wasted on him, a platter of Loch Fyne scallops in a lime jus might as well have been marshmallows in water. Even Marlboro Lights failed to cut through the numbness. The cold placed him at one remove from himself. His mind, deprived of its sensory contact with the outside world, turned inward for stimulus, like a figurehead detaching itself from the prow of the boat to venture below decks.

All this time his eyes had been fixed forward, he had forgotten about all the cargo stored in the hold. Specifically Sylvia, who was still holding him to that old promise to marry her. In his mind's eye, her face was turned modestly to the ground, half-hidden by a wave of blonde hair. This image conflated with another, the face of St. Catherine of Siena, puppying up to God despite her stigmata and her crown of thorns. Sylvia's suffering was likewise an act of faith: she believed that one day Milton would marry her and make her pregnant, despite all evidence to the contrary.

Sylvia was waiting for him to come around. Unfortunately, Milton knew he was about to take off. *The Hammer* was a sensation on the verge of becoming a phenomenon. *The Hammer* meant fuck-you money. *The Hammer* meant that there would be no wedding, no babies, no settling for second best.

The car skirted Soho and jostled through antic crowds, high pressure trapping layers of heat and stale air on the streets. Milton felt it right here – at the bridge of his nose. He massaged his gridlocked sinuses. There was no way out of this head. The good ship Milton Young was marooned in still, windless waters.

He imagined the quarters of this ship. His old gang – the pre-Hammer squadron of old university and school friends - lolled in the hammocks, yet to wake up to the realisation that they essentially despised one another. Soon he would turn them all out, and start again.

He ran down through the decks, past all the younger selves living there. First there was his breakdown in his mid-twenties, drug-induced of course. A minor flare-up of derangement. His housemates woke up one morning to find that he had cooked every foodstuff in the kitchen into one giant breakfast. Even the kettle was full of flour and eggs and milk. He just wanted to make everyone happy. Sylvia stroked his hair and murmured into his scalp until he calmed down.

The remembering drifted down another deck. Milton outside the university library selling his copies of Socialist Worker and shouting at the Tories, because he decided the Socialists should like him. There was the adolescent Milton throwing another party in his parents' town house, the unpopular kids invited then locked out in the garden. Down again, all the way to the anchor. The first urge. To get attention. Be a naughty clever boy to catch Mummy's eye. Attention is survival. The ignored are the unfed.

He had forgotten the discomfort of remembering. He preferred the mode of the urban amnesiac. One day deleting another. Drifting on the winds and the tides and never looking back.

The party was in a bar called Taxidermy, off the Liverpool Road. Milton left the others to pay the driver, and marched straight up to the side entrance.

"This is a private party," said the bored bald woman holding a clipboard.

"Yes," said Milton. "My private party."

Everybody was already there, and he wanted to say hello to them all. He entered with shocking volume, springing out of his introspection and upon the party, acknowledging two or three acquaintances simultaneously with a nod, a catchphrase, a wave, a knowing point. Beneath this ebullience, a sulk was brewing. An itch to punish Sylvia just for being there, just for constraining him. Noting its approach, he decided it would be best for everyone if he nipped off and had more cocaine before he saw her

In the cubicle, he crouched before the toilet seat and divided the heap of white powder into lines, sorting and allocating his favour: one for Roger, one for Benny, one for Beng, two for Mimi, all of whom were huddled behind and about him, *The Hammer*'s famous five crammed in yet another confined space.

"Chopping out lines is my favourite spectator sport," said Benny, his harlequin shirt, outsize wooden-rimmed glasses and crazy shoes the uniform of a housebroken eccentric. Milton helped himself first, whiffling up the line with an ungainly rattle of mucus. The cocaine further

anaesthetised a head swaddled with cold. He pocketed his fiver, and left the others to finish off. In the mirror, he made a quick check on his look - pricking up the gelled surf of his hairstyle, teasing out a stalagmite here and there, checking the left then the right nostril – and he was out again. The DJ was revisiting Stock, Aitken and Waterman. A few guests were dancing ironically. He was pleased to spot that a few celebrities had put in an appearance. Their presence was noted by the civilians with furtive glances, meer cats peering cheekily over new exciting terrain. He was also pleased that he couldn't see Sylvia anywhere. No doubt she was out back in the garden, guarding the buffet. This gave him the opportunity to dally at the bar, make inroads into the free cocktails and get the latest news from his mentor, Sebastian Blast.

"Here he is," announced Sebastian, stepping forward to part his coterie and receive Milton, his golden child. "My most favourite cunt in the whole world. As fabulously late as ever."

"I am only late because the cocaine was late." Milton paused while the coterie adjusted themselves toward him. "The bike had an accident in Tottenham Court Road and they had to send another."

"Can I just say, we all caught the show." Nods and murmurs of approval from the clique. The woman from the channel took this opportunity to compliment him but, between the music and his cold, he didn't catch the precise wording of her praise. There was no such problem with Sebastian, that loud omnisexual lord of Light Entertainment, patting his gut paternally as if it were a baby in a papousse.

"A work of genius, so utterly embodying the *zeitgeist.* It blasphemed spectacularly, reducing those African

"I am only late because the cocaine is late"

"The enemy of promise: the three-wheeler in the hallway and a people carrier in the drive"

generals to a stoned joke, and that poor woman with her misshapen teddy bears - I hope you are not going to let her give all the money to charity. I yawned when she rabbitted on about that blind baby needing an operation on its detached retina. We feel that altruism compromises the ruthless dynamic of the show: *The Hammer* is an amphitheatre of desperation, contemporary life boiled down to its essentials. A conveyor belt of contestants and their lots. Ordinary men and women reduced to the capitalist binary of buy and sell. The grandees of the Garrick have virtually blackballed me for my involvement with it. I say fuck them. I love you and your young friends. You are the future and they are the past."

A croupier of compliments, Sebastian dealt out praise briskly and professionally to the players about him. But Milton had picked up on the *en passant* mention of the old cultural order. His anger sprang up. If only his vitriol had not been so general and raging he would have risked a tirade there and then. He thought: yes, the grandees refuse to go all the way to give people what they want. Their delusion that culture should be improving holds them back from fully embracing the spirit of the age. *The Hammer* was not exploitative entertainment, it was a celebration of consumerism, the contestants and viewers revelled in the debasement. "Is everyone really nothing more than what they have to sell?" bleated the *Guardian*, misunderstanding the masochism of the seller, the sadism of the buyer. Sex sells, selling is sex. The liberals had agoraphobia – etymologically, a fear of the agora, the market place, which stemmed, not from a moral objection, but from their sexual inhibition, too repressed to get off on the basic human urge to use and be used.

Experience had taught Milton that it was unwise to hold a beer and this opinion at the same time. This anger came from an older, thwarted self. It was unbecoming of the new successful Milton, inventor of *The Hammer*, the man who could throw a party on a Thursday night in a fashionable bar somewhere between Islington and King's Cross for the city's cutting edge people.

Sebastian Blast had taught him this: failure loves to talk whereas success chooses its words carefully. And to some people, it has nothing to say at all.

"It was a good show," he confined himself to this observation, "but it must go further, Sebastian. I want to take *The Hammer* to America."

"Of course you do. And we will, I know it. *The Hammer* cannot fail in a continent of extrovert materialists. The networks are already sniffing around. The lawyers are in the paddock. We will be millionaires before the year is out."

"I want to do it now. We need an event on *The Hammer* that will force their hand. Spark a bidding war. Something outrageous. To take us to the next stage."

Hitching his eyebrows at his protégé's impatience, Sebastian patted the backside of this topic to usher it on its way. "I look forward to discussing this further but for now I think we should all enjoy your party." One of Sebastian's coterie passed Milton a drink. "Didn't I see your lovely lady *fiancé* around here earlier? She was carrying a child. I didn't know you were a breeder, Milton."

"It's not ours," he snapped.

"She looked to me like she was trying the baby on for size," teased Sebastian, tempting the coterie back into the conversation with the promise of needling the golden boy. Sebastian certainly had an eye for a man's weak spot. "The enemy of promise: the three-wheeler in the hallway and a people carrier in the drive."

"I'm not ready to settle down yet," insisted Milton.

"Everyone is aware of that," the coterie chuckled. "Well, not quite everyone."

At the back of the bar, the double doors were thrown open to the summer evening. Milton walked down the steps flanked by flickering lanterns, burning off curls of citronella smoke. The production budget only stretched to Anglo-Vietnamese caterers, their barbecue was set up on one side of the walled garden. Although Mimi had arranged the whole thing, Milton had signed off all her suggestions and so felt a certain pride in surveying his scene: media journalists and commissioning editors and gallery producers and a smattering of *The Hammer*'s most notorious contestants: Anders, who sold a vial of his Aryan sperm, Barbara the embittered divorcee who auctioned all her ex-husband's possessions (the lawyers were still mollifying him), a brace of men's magazine models who flogged a lap dance for a grand and a lot of publicity: all micro-celebrities of his own creation. He went immediately toward the models, who stood apart as bored as catyrids.

"Evening ladies. I hope you are not finding my party too tiresome."

A waitress was briskly over with cocktails. Champagne mixed with an imported spiced vodka liqueur called Gold Vasser. Gold leaf drifted in its viscosity like gilded astronauts. He took a sip, and tasted nothing.

"The original distillers were alchemists, who believed gold had a healing quality," said Milton, trying on a little of Sebastian's learned if unctuous charm. It was wasted on the girls however.

"It's murder on my fillings," said the one on the left.

"Is it really expensive?" asked the one on the right.

"Hello Milton," said the one in the middle. Sylvia ushered between the girls and brushed a kiss against his cheek. Such a mischievous entrance, and she knew it. Her smile bared a wall of teeth, to protect herself. When she stepped back, he was horrified to see that she was holding the toddler, a blonde-haired blue eyed little girl who regarded him, sleepy and content, with her head laid in the lee of his girlfriend's neck. What made the sight even more disturbing to Milton was the resemblance between the toddler and Sylvia: the same golden curls, the same hum of innocence. Sylvia's need to love and the child's need for love fitted snug against one another. Milton searched around for something to spoil the moment, saw the reef of dried mucus around the child's nostrils, and said:

"I hope that isn't infecting all my guests."

"We've been having a lovely evening haven't we, Iona?" Sylvia said, ignoring him. "We've smelt the flowers in the hanging baskets, listened to the birdies sing, tasted some of the food. She's been very good, haven't you? You've eaten coconut rice and a little crispy duck. Iona likes the crispy duck, don't you?"

All evening he had been devising schemes to leave Sylvia, reasons to hate her, concocting vengeance for her various heinous crimes, all of which suddenly felt, in the warmth of her presence, to be mere misdemeanours. Ever since she nursed him through his blue period, he responded to her as an errant son to his mother. Sylvia's sing-song cooing spoke both to Iona and the long-buried boy within him. The mother's burble of gentle interrogatives and praise was an incantation that summoned a lost age. Sylvia's soothing chatter was a lullaby that sounded, to Milton, like a lament. When he was away from Sylvia, he thought of her as the ball-and-chain, the bovine herd clopping in his wake. But it was impossible for him to sustain this sulk when he was with her. This was his weakness, the source of all his love and hate for Sylvia.

Also, he was coming down from his last line and that always made him a bit weepy.

"You look tired." Sylvia touched his cheek. She hitched Iona up for a snuggle. "My poor babies both need to go bo-bose."

"It was a difficult show."

"I know."

"I had so much to clear up afterwards."

"I understand."

"It's this cold. I've lost all feeling."

"I am going to give Iona back to her Mummy and Daddy, and then we'll get you some vitamin C. Kiss-kiss."

Sylvia picked her way back through the crowd. Milton looked sheepishly around himself, and saw the two models sneering contemptuously in his direction.

"Kiss-kiss," said the one on the left, blowing two air kisses.

"Bo-bose," said the one on the right, making a little wave with her hand.

....

"Welcome to *The Hammer.* Sell anything you want live on television. Tonight, VooDoo priests will cast a spell on your enemies. Bid for the psychic chicken to contact your dead relatives. Which pop star is going to rent you their entourage for a week? And has this poor bint really come all

this way just to sell you a second-hand Sunblest loaf? Register now to bid on these and other fantastic lots as we all go under…
The Hammer."

After the show, Milton sat in his office surrounded by flowers. Bouquets of red ones, blue ones, yellow ones and phallic ones. He could name perhaps four of the species. He moved some orchids aside so he could open up his laptop. On the keyboard lay a card from Sebastian. It read:

"Jung wrote that flowers are God's thoughts. I send them to inspire you."

On the reverse of the card, Sebastian had scrawled:

"The perfect lot is a sacrifice."

Milton lowered his nose into the trumpet of an exotic bloom and inhaled. He smelt nothing. His cold had thickened to the point where his head was a wax effigy, a smooth unfeeling likeness of itself. It was past midnight. After the ordeal of the live show, his synapses were charred fuse wire. What sacrifice was Sebastian thinking of? The offering of a goat to appease the gods? A nuclear family selling their Labrador only for the buyer to heave it yowling onto a barbecue? Milton poured himself two fingers of Armagnac and set to work.

Cruelty was the key. If there was one factor that had sped Milton Young up the beanstalk, it was his cruel streak. When he first started work, he had merely a wicked tongue. "Will anyone else without a personality please join the queue behind Susan?" "You are thin, sweet and wearing a cheap black dress – my god, woman, you are an after-eight mint." He had said that to Sylvia, when he was first introducing her to the gang. Sebastian had spotted Milton's camp rehearsed wit and

"You are thin, sweet and wearing a cheap black dress – my god, woman, you are an after-eight mint"

"Is this all society is now? Consumers and workers? Buyers and sellers? What happened to faith, meaning?"

promoted him to booker. "You need bitches to book bitches." When it came to devising the tortures for Celebrity Bootcamp, it was Milton who suggested that one wall of each bedroom was a screen displaying a live feed of all the emails and text messages viewers were sending in. The celebrities lay awake at night, messages from their loved ones interspersed with the vindictive, pornographic spite aroused in the deranged wing of the audience. Lay there scanning thousands of madmen who criticised, fantasised and terrorised them in search of a "goodnight daddy", or an "I love you darling." The rest of the gang – Mimi, Beng, Benny and Roger – came up with end-of-the-pier pranks, such as comparing the cocks of former Eastenders with ex-inhabitants of Coronation Street - "Join us as we play Cast Members!" They deferred to Milton when it came to truly compelling humiliations.

The Hammer was devised one Sunday when he had dragged himself home for his father's birthday. The retired councillor was flicking through the *Telegraph* with disgust. "Is this all society is now? Consumers and workers? Buyers and sellers? Whatever happened to faith, meaning? Whatever happened to real life?" This complaint had been a refrain throughout Milton's upbringing, an incessant whinge about the way the world was turning. Milton lay in his old bedroom and concocted a show that opposed every principle of his father. Sell Anything You Want Live On Television. The name was inspired by a phrase his father used whenever he encountered the latest dumb thing. "It's another hammer blow to civilisation." It was mere serendipity that it also recalled the auctioneer's gavel.

Milton tapped at the keyboard, his

thoughts skipping from one lot to the next. Could they get a man to sell himself one finger at a time on ten consecutive shows? Probably, but who would buy them? It's not enough that the item represents a great personal loss to the contestant, it must also be something that inspires a bidding frenzy. Sebastian was half-right. The perfect lot was a sacrifice, but it must also be a must-have for the bidders. Like bone marrow to a person dying of leukaemia. Could he get asylum seekers to sell their kidneys? The problem with both these items was that they would only inspire bids from a tiny proportion of the audience – the dying ones. He wasn't sure how the pictures would play, either. Too medical. Both items had the stink of death to them, a guaranteed turn off.

All he needed was one item that was so unprecedented that it would spur the sale of *The Hammer* format across the world. The item, whatever it was, must also work in each territory – it wasn't enough to have a spectacular one-off, it must be a regular strand that would play as well in Russia as in America, especially America, always America. Next year, he imagined himself in Hollywood, a hostess at his arm introducing him to representatives of sex and power as the young genius who invented *The Hammer*.

He called Benny into his office.

"Benny, what would you least like to sell?"

Benny shrugged and picked motes from the fur cuffs of his gold shirt.

"Dunno. My girlfriend?"

Benny had a thing for girls who didn't have English as a first language. His latest girlfriend was Indo-Croat. He always had to be different.

"That wouldn't be much of a sacrifice. You could always get another girlfriend."

"I wouldn't like to sell my shirts. Some

of them are very rare."

"There is a reason for that, Benny. They are rare because no other fucker wants them."

Offending Benny was like slapping a loyal hound. His bottom lip protruded, showing Milton his upset.

"You've been in a foul mood ever since the party," said Benny.

"There was a child there." Both men made the sign of the cross. "Sylvia was holding it. I had to tell its parents, 'Could you please keep that thing away from my girlfriend?' I think they were trying to convert her, hoping another couple would join their little breeding club. Sylvia told me I was being rude, but the parents started it. You talk to them and you get 30 per cent of their attention at best. They are always looking past you to see how their darling is getting on. Have these people never heard of babysitters?"

"You wonder why they bother coming out at all."

"You wonder why they have children at all. Why do they want them? Why take all that responsibility and pain on, for nothing! To spend a fortune raising someone who will grow up to hate you."

Benny nodded, idly plucking red petals from the head of a rose. "They say that you have to sacrifice everything for them."

Milton saved his work, and slowly closed his laptop. After slipping into his jacket, he stepped around his desk, gently lifted Benny's out-sized glasses from his face, and planted a long slow kiss on his bemused – but not appalled – employee.

"Thank you Benny," said Milton. "As of this very moment, you are my most favourite cunt in the whole world."

....

"Welcome to *The Hammer.* Sell anything you want live on television. Tonight, this yardie gang wants to sell you their respect. Which Hollywood legend will sell you their tumour? And yes, everything you have heard is true. They said it was wrong, they said it was evil, but we believe it is your chance to give someone a new life. Tonight ladies and gentlemen, in a first for British television, we auction this baby live. Register now to bid on these and other fantastic lots as we all go under… *The Hammer.*"

W ho Would Your Man Leave You For?" This question accused Sylvia from the pages of her magazine. A collection of women gave their answers over the next ten pages. Some speculated that their man would leave them for a woman who was their polar opposite. Others imagined a woman who was a younger version of themselves, not yet wise to the man's repertoire of tricks. These love rivals had bigger tits and neater arses, were more adventurous in bed and less demanding out of it, more intelligent and less career-orientated. A woman who wants children or a woman who doesn't. "His mother," joked one.

"I already know what type of woman men leave me for," said another.

The kittens clawed at her calves. Sylvia went out into the kitchen and spooned more cat food into the bowl, then returned to the lounge and her magazine. Who knew men had so many reasons to hate us?

Sylvia wasn't afraid that Milton would leave her. She was afraid that they would stay this way forever. They were in a rut.

The weeks passed in the social equivalent of the washing-up: Thursday night Milton did *The Hammer*, then Friday night takeaway and TV, Saturday night clubbing with old university friends, then a Sunday lunch-and-lager comedown at a gastro pub.

Monday to Wednesday was his free time. Spent with the gang and god knows who else.

At the party she overheard Sebastian Blast pointing her out to his clique. "That is poor Sylvia." She was holding Iona at the time, the little girl trying out the sibilants of her name. Ssssyl. Ssssyl. Poor Sssssyl.

The clique pitied her because of Milton's infidelities, but that pity could not conceal their contempt for her. She was part of his unflattering past, the woman who had nursed him through his "difficult patch." Those dark five months of bed-bound weeping and mortality terrors. When he emerged from this depression, he asked her to marry him. The opinion was that she had trapped him at his most vulnerable moment.

She had only been trying to help.

"Who would your man leave you for?"

"Someone who doesn't know his weaknesses."

Although this episode of *The Hammer* was being watched by pretty much the entire country, Sylvia realised it was addressed to her. The sale of the Iraqi baby was the message Milton could never bring himself to deliver in person.

I know what you want more than anything in the world. Not only am I refusing to give it to you, I am going to give it away for money.

At the press conference, Milton read out a statement rebutting the outrage surrounding the selling of the baby. Sylvia watched it on the news. She could no longer ignore what Milton had become. He sat there behind the bonsai tree of microphones, each labelled with the logos of the major international broadcasters, CNN, NBC, Canal Plus, Sky, BBC. Sebastian's hand rested on his arm for support.

"The looting of the Iraqi hospitals denied Fadel Hamza's wife the care she needed after the birth of baby Ali. Her death left Fadel alone to support four young children. With his country descending into anarchy, with clean water and food hard to come by, Fadel took the agonising decision that his youngest son would be better off being raised in the West. He approached *The Hammer* after reading about the show on the internet. At first, we were appalled by the idea of selling a baby live on television. It was only after Fadel insisted that – not only would baby Ali have a much better chance of survival with an adoptive Western family, but also that the monies raised in the sale would give him the chance to save the rest of his children - that we realised we must put aside out knee-jerk moral objections and review the case more closely."

Milton paused to wipe his nose. His cold had taken a turn for the worse, the pressure upon the nerves numbed the right side of his face, and the corner of his mouth kept twitching. On television, however, these symptoms only indicated a man in the throes of an agonising moral quandary. His illness was his best defence.

"Children are precious, they are the future, and it is a future under threat in Iraq. This very public method of adoption will not only help Fadel and his family, it puts the plight of his people centre stage at a time when the media are brushing over the consequences of the British and American military action.

"These issues aside, it is the welfare of baby Ali that is foremost in our concern. Today the press have raised the spectre of the baby being purchased by a paedophile ring. We assure both the concerned public and, of course, Fadel himself, that we will rigorously screen the winning bidder before we allow the sale to proceed. All day I and my colleagues have heard the objections of the crowds massing outside the studio. We understand their rage and confusion. Equally, we have listened to the objections of the Minister for Media and the complaints raised in the House Of Commons. It does seem, at first glance, that the sale of a baby live on television is an exploitative outrage. But tonight, we will be saving lives. I urge the British public to see the show in this light, and to participate in the auction firm in the belief that they are building a future not only for little Ali, but also for all the children in Iraq, to whom we owe the most onerous responsibility."

On the TV, the opening credits of *The Hammer* rolled. The camera swooped down to focus on an Iraqi man, dressed in an ill-fitting grey suit. In his arms was swaddled the baby Ali, a mite with a heap of black hair. Sylvia picked up her phone, took out Milton's credit card, and registered to bid. ◉

BIRDS, BOOZE AND BILL ODDIE

Being the second installment of the Chronicles of
Peregrine Beer, drunken ornithologist.
By Jock Scot

P erry boarded the coach, gave the driver a cursory nod and made his way to the back seat. Settling there he donned his spectacles, the better to the view the others as they arrived in ones and twos. A few faces he recognised from previous outings. He was pleased to see the pop singer, Edwyn Collins, a keen and knowledgeable birdman, come aboard, though not so happy when the rotund figure of Bill Oddie chortled his way up the aisle. They had never got on and Perry pointedly ignored his greeting by staring out the window at two rather attractive girls strolling by arm in arm and laughing. To his delight, they too boarded and sat down a couple of seats in front of him. "Promising," he thought. The driver announced they would be

leaving in a few minutes after he had collected the fares. As he did this and approached, Perry strained to eavesdrop as he spoke to the young lasses who had caught his eye. Their accent betrayed them as American and their good humour and polite manner won his approval.

Over the years, Perry had found that a jaunt such as today's could be enlivened no end if a couple of foreign lovelies were part of the group and he made it his business to indulge in some gay badinage with any likely types. In fact, it was the main reason he still went on such expeditions, as he had a remarkably high success rate with the ladies on RSPB field-trips. His affable manner, ready wit and staggering knowledge of Ornithological matters would see him strike up conversation with any loose or unaccompanied gals. By the end of the day, if not before, it would be bodily fluids, rather than phone numbers, that would be exchanged. He'd had many a memorable ride in a hide, *al fresco* leg-over in the bushes or sand dunces of nature reserves the length and breadth of the country.

As the driver hovered, kestrel-like, and Perry fingered his wallet then proffered a tenner, he asked him who the girls were. "They're from Tulsa, USA, over here on a Gap Year tour of Europe. They are both studying environmental science at the University of Texas at Dallas and wanted to see a bit of our countryside. Oddie's got his eye on the blonde one, she's called Helen. I didn't catch her pal's name. Lovely girls, very nice."

"Fuck Oddie! Little twat. Oh driver, could you stop at a shop before we leave town? I need a paper and some cigs." With that, he returned to his seat, started her up and they set off. Perry spread himself out on the back seat, content and optimistic. At Carshalton his reverie was interrupted as Driver's voice came over the intercom. "We'll stop here for five minutes, if you need anything this is your chance." Perry spotted an off licence and ducked in, closely followed by young Edwyn. He pulled six purple tins from the fridge and Edwyn chose Budwar, the world's finest bottled beer. "Good to see you again Ed, it could be an interesting day. There's a couple of American birds on board, I'll offer them a can and give them some of the old flannel. How's the wife and kids?"

"They're fine, although William's at that age where he wants a new pair of trainers every month, it's costing me a fortune." Perry paid for his lagers, got forty Regal King Size and they boarded the coach.

Edwyn joined Perry on the back seat and they got stuck into the carry out as the coach headed through suburbia and into the countryside.

"I saw you on TOTP 2 the other week there, those were the days, eh? Number one in 27 countries [sings] "I Never Met a Girl Like You Before". What a great song, not a patch on the early Postcard stuff though. Any good new ones in the pipeline?"

"I'm working on a new concept album, *Lumps in My Porridge*. All the old stuff is coming out on a CD box-set called *My Kilt's On Fire*, and Channel 5 want me to present a birding programme for them, after the success Bill Oddie's had with his one. Maybe I could row you in there as an advisor."

"Oh yeah, I noticed that bearded little dwarf get on. It shouldn't be difficult to top his pathetic efforts. What have you got in mind?"

"I hear the chough has returned and is nesting again in Cornwall, so I'm gonna cover that for the pilot programme. Fancy a trip down West to see if we can capture him on film? The money's good."

"I might take you up on that, the chough's one of my favourites. Do you recall when I tried to re-introduce them in 1970? I netted three pairs in Morocco and released them near Lands End. But a couple of days later a huge fucking storm blew up and we never saw them again. I've still got some Super-8 footage of that debacle, you could use it as an intro. Plus I'd love to put one over on Oddie, the depressing fucking midget. Where is the little twat?"

"He's down there, talking to the American lassies", said Edwyn.

"Boring them to death more like. I'll wring his fucking neck."

As they worked their way thirstily through the bottles and cans the miles melted away and they were soon in Hampshire. It was turning into a glorious day. The sun rays raked over the fields and a light breeze sent the few clouds scudding across a bright blue sky.

As they arrived at the RSPB reserve, Perry experienced a severe, verging on the violent, mood swing and had to be restrained from brawling with

Oddie by young Edwyn. No mean feat, for Perry had worked himself up into an almost heroic state and he had the strength of a squad of Kilburn navvies when the mood was upon him, and it was upon him now. His foul-mouthed tirade of abuse directed at Oddie had gone too far to be funny anymore, beyond the bounds of gay badinage or boisterous banter. It was by turns mean, personal and intimately rude in the sickest fashion.

With all his strength Edwyn wrestled Perry to the floor and the two US girlies sat on him. It had to be done, Perry was now foaming at the mouth, as if in the grip of a mandrake root-induced hallucinogenic orgasm. The girls' presence astride him was not helping to calm him down. Before his verbals had turned too blue, he had managed to lure the gals away from Oddie and to the back seat of the coach to meet Edwyn, his "pop star" friend. (Despite his world-wide fame, they had never heard of him.) They were all getting along famously when Oddie vexed him by trying to stick his oar back in and join them. Perry flew at him in an incoherent frenzy and Oddie fled back down to the bus, screeching "You go to far! You go too far!" like an affronted and feathered Grande Dame in some crap Barbara Cartland bodice-ripper. Such was the state of play as they pulled up at the car park.

Bill Oddie scarpered for the shore in very short order whilst Perry was restrained. He loved restraint, but, in his cups, he seldom showed it. He was still acting up, as if Patrick Thistle had just won the treble. (He dearly loved Patrick Thistle and sometimes, as a drunken chat-up line, he claimed to be his manager. Lingerie models had been known to swallow it.) However, his enjoyment of the girls using him as a sofa was no longer concealed. He was sporting a huge, virile stalk of an erection and such was its vigour and enormity that the strict confines of his Dryzabone could not contain it, and the reader will recall, he sported only pyjamas beneath. He knew this, but had forgotten. He now felt the sea-breeze whistle round his tackle as he was carried from the coach having promised to behave.

Edwyn and the girls managed to adjust his dress before delivering him to the snug of the Hampshire Ham, a nearby hostelry. Acting as if nothing untoward had occurred, he called for a large whisky. He drained the glass in one gracious swallow and then asked for a local ale. He was off. Unbeknownst to the others, he had been working his way through a handful of little white pills which he'd come across in his pocket, thinking at first they were ibuprofen or similar. He always kept a ready supply on his person for hangovers, or pre-empting them. By the time he realised they were something far stronger, it was too late. Far too late. Then, in a flash of total recall, he remembered one of Irvine Welsh's football hooligan mates had sold him forty quid's worth of the latest designer head-spinner. But, like the ex porn-star that he was, he took it all in his stride. (I should perhaps mention here that when times were tight and Perry was short of readies, he had foolishly consented to partake in the filming of some outré shagging which was later released as "Missionary Impossible". It went on to become a much sought after under-the-counter underground classic. He had been heavily drugged on a cocktail of Ritalin, Ketamine and Viagra by the producer and signed away the rights to his filmic endeavours for fifty quid.) *To be continued.* ☜

THE ANTI SANTA

A former elf tries to take the commerce
out of Christmas. By Scott Bradfield.
Illustrations by Marcus Oakley

....

T he last house on the block
was always the toughest.
"Ho ho ho, Jennifer
Williams of seven-seventy-
five West Palmdale Avenue!
Merry Christmas! Merry
Christmas!"

"Are you Mommy's new
boyfriend?"

"Absolutely not, little girl!
Don't you recognize me and my
solar-powered sleigh in the
driveway there? How many
hints do you need?"

"Santa Claus doesn't wear
Levis and a flannel shirt."

"That's because I'm not your
normal, run-of-the-mill,
commercially-approved Santa.
I'm the anti-Santa, Jennifer. But
that doesn't make me anti-

Christmas, oh no. Not by a long shot."

"And his beard isn't blonde and trimmed like
that, and he doesn't wear cologne. You look more
like that cute mountain man in *Dr Quinn, Medicine
Woman.*"

"Why thanks, I don't actually trim it, but look,
we're both in a hurry. Let's dig into our sack of
wholesome treats and see what we have for
Jennifer Williams this Christmas Eve. Why, it
looks like you've been a very good girl. Anti-Santa
has brought you two presents!"

"Let me see! Let me see!"

"As you can tell, Anti-Santa and his elves don't
actually wrap their gifts up in gaudy, meretricious
paper and bows, since that would only reinforce
the fictive nature of high-consumer corporate
propaganda."

"It's a big jar of pills."

"Not just any pills, Jennifer. What you hold in
your hand is five hundred capsules of 1000
milligram timed-release Ester-C, the Cadillac of

Vitamin supplements. You take one of these suckers every morning with your orange juice and you'll enjoy the new year free from sniffles, flues, and long-term viral immuno-deficiency."

"This present sucks, Anti-Santa."

"I'm sure you don't mean that, Jennifer. Anyway, here's another little goody – a parsley plant to grow on the windowsill. Parsley cleanses the bad carbohydrates from your blood, and if you take good care of it, this gift will take good care of you."

"I wanted a Barbie play-set and a cell-phone."

"No you didn't, Jennifer. Not really. That's what commercial culture told you you wanted. What you really want, what the long-term health and integrity of both your body and mind require –"

"These are the two worst Christmas presents I ever received in my life."

"Now honestly, Jennifer, that isn't very polite."

"You're knocking on my door, Anti-Santa. So you'll take what I give you."

"Well maybe, little Jennifer, but try to remember that I'm only –"

"Please leave, Anti-Santa, before I call the cops. Oh, and another thing."

Anti-Santa paused hopefully on the steps before he slung the huge, bulky bag over his shoulder. It was absurd, he thought, how we always hold out

this vain breathless expectation that a bad moment will get better. Even a moment as irredeemable as this one.

"Don't come back next year, Anti-Santa. Just scratch me and Mommy off your list permanent, okay?"

<I'm sure she didn't mean it, Sir> the glowing red eye on the dashboard solemnly intoned. <You know how children get at this time of year.>

The voice was designed to provide the same soft, seductive reassurance as HAL, in Stanley Kubrick's 2001: A Space Odyssey. But since it communicated directly with the Radar Deployment Off-Base Simulator back in Tampa, everybody referred to it (naturally enough) as Rudolph.

"I guess so, Rudolph," Anti-Santa drawled unconvincedly. "But I can't help feeling, maybe for just a few brief moments every so often, that kids don't really like me. They don't seem excited to see me at all."

<All that sugar and heightened expectation. It's a very powerful drug, Sir. The children aren't always in their right mind. They need someone to bring them back down to earth.>

Anti-Santa gazed out at the sparkling night, and wondered if he was the only person in entire the universe to appreciate what it was all about. Simplicity, vastness, cosmogeny and light. Not a lot of third-world manufactured plastic crap adorned with tinsel and shiny foil.

"She said they were the worst presents she ever received in her life."

<She is only six years old, Sir.>

"She seemed to think I was good looking, anyway."

<That's something to build on.>

"And maybe we could, you know – we'd have to discuss it with the elves – but put a few more actual toys in the gift sack next year."

<Those wooden dradles, hand-carved by the native tribes of the Bolivian rain-forest, seem to be quite a hit with the youngsters>

"Yes, they don't actually throw them in my face

or anything. Not like last year."
<*And the comic books. All children like comic books.*>
"Remind me when we get back to order more copies of *Mandela for Beginners.*"
<*You see, Sir, that's what I admire about you. Even in adversity, you're preparing to take the next step forward. And well, uh-oh.*>
The red light evinced a sudden blink, like a desktop PC trying to catch up with its own streaming data.
<*Course-correction requested, Sir. Perhaps it might be best to adjust our longitudinal axis just a half degree eastward or so before* ->
Anti-Santa felt it rise up from the nub of his colon. It wasn't his soy-burger from supper or even the fruit smoothie. It was something at once more intangible and more distinct.
"It's him, isn't it."
<*I see no reason, Sir, especially when you're just starting to feel* ->
"We won't be changing our course for anybody tonight, Rudolph. Especially not for him."
It was as if speaking his presence made it real, and before Anti-Santa could anchor himself to his ergonomically-designed seat a meteor blaze and sonic clap struck the sky with tangle-horned reindeer and snow-dusted hooves and plump piles of velour-sacked prezzies as fairy dust sprayed across the surface of starlight tinkling with a memory of bells. Anti-Santa always thought that he could live with the reindeer and the prezzies – but the fairy dust, throbbing with false cheer and subliminal advertising. The fairy dust was truly unbearable.
"Ho ho ho! Merry Christmas!" cried the Old Man through his fat plummy face, heated into veiny splotches by several generations of imbibing cheap Tokay. "You pretentious, silly little do-gooder! Merry Christmas! Merry Christmas to all and to all a good niiiii –"
And then he was gone again in the flash of his own anticipation, like light chasing itself into a black hole. The sky resounded ominously.
<*Sorry, Sir. I did try to warn you.*>
Anti-Santa felt the fragile truthfulness of night

"**You pretentious, silly little do-gooder! Merry Christmas! Merry Christmas to all and to all a good niiiii-- "

"I just have these sugar-free candied apples to deliver to the residents of your cosy little gated community"

relapse around him, wavering like a mirage. It felt so thin and impalpable now. It made Anti-Santa want to cry.

Seeing the Old Man again was always hard. But seeing him leave was even harder.

"That's okay, Rudolph. We can take anything he throws at us. Now let's get to work and land this boat. It's time to deliver those Amnesty International lifetime memberships to the kids in St Pete."

By four am, it was nearly impossible for Anti-Santa to maintain his spontaneous good will for humanity. Cynical, enervated and footsore, he began speaking his yuletide greetings woodenly, as if reading them from a three-by-five file card.

"Ho ho ho, everybody. Merry Christmas and so forth."

"Hold it right there, pal. Where you think you're going

with that burlap sack?"

"Oh hi, Eugene, it's me. Anti-Santa. I just have these sugar-free candied apples to deliver to the residents of your cosy little gated community, along with the latest paperback edition of Noam Chomsky's *Deterring Democracy*. Could you please be careful where you point that thing, Eugene? You do realize that America suffers nearly twenty thousand needless gun-related fatalities each year, most of which are the result of accident or misuse."

"How'd you know my name? And where'd you get that weird looking UFO-like dingy?"

"You're Eugene Waterbury of six-oh-seven–"

"Hey, cut that out!"

"Your sons, Tony and Derek, are receiving Ammo Attack from, you know, the Old Man this year. Which is why you'll notice a couple of non-confrontational-type playthings from yours truly under the collapsible tree. One's a little board game I invented called Anti-Risk, which isn't about conquering the world or blowing up cities, thank God. Rather, the object is to negotiate peace settlements with your fellow players until you've achieved a world of total parity and mutual cooperation – "

"I'm calling the cops, Anti-Santa. Even if it is Christmas."

"I guess I should warn you, Eugene. I wouldn't do anything to hurt you, but I possess a green belt in Aikido, and my sleigh is equipped with a protective force-field which will deflect any –"

Bang.

"Shit, Eugene. I think you shot me."

"Damn right, Anti-Santa. Now fly your contraption way the hell off my turf, or so help me. Sure as my name's Eugene Waterbury, you'll be digging a bullet out of both thighs."

Anti-Santa lost consciousness somewhere over the forty-second parallel. "I thought Santa wore a red suit and said things like Ho ho ho."

"Help me get him on the gurney, that's it."

"This guy don't look like Santa to me. He looks more like that guy, that mountain man, right? On *Dr Quinn, Medicine Woman.*"

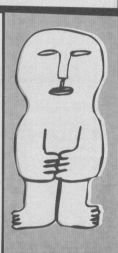

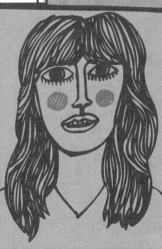

"The Anti-Santa believes in telling it like it is. He hasn't got a publicist, and it's hurt him, media-wise"

"He's not Santa, you idiot. He's the Anti-Santa. I saw a profile of him once on *Sixty Minutes Two*."

"When I was a kid I couldn't wait to visit Santa and his elves when they came through Macy's. Then I got older, right, and I just wanted to see Santa's elves. Hey, he's trying to say something."

"It's the thought that counts. It's the thought that counts. It's the thought that counts."

"Let's get some blood into him and see how he looks in the morning."

"It don't seem right, somehow. Santa Claus sleeping in the hall on a rusty gurney."

"He's not Santa, you idiot. He's –"

"I know, I got you. He's the Anti-Santa, which sounds kind of ominous, don't it? I mean like the anti-Christ, triple sixes and all that. Gregory Peck's wife getting shoved off the roof. I couldn't sleep for weeks after that flick."

"The Anti-Santa believes in telling it like it is. He hasn't got a publicist, and it's hurt him, media-wise."

"Maybe. Or maybe it's those crappy presents he keeps giving."

"Here we go, pal. Maybe this'll help you sleep."

"I mean this one elf, this Chloe, she had legs up to here, and wore this pea-green wraparound slit-skirt. That girl got me through puberty, boy. And Santa – not this guy – but the real Santa I'm talking. He'd pretend he was listening to you tell what you wanted for Christmas? But the whole time he had his big knobby hand on Chloe's ass. I couldn't blame him, neither. That old boy, one look at his ruby-red face and you knew. That was one Santa who knew how to have a good time."

They weren't dreams, exactly; they were more like periodic interventions of the real. Men and women moaning softly; crisp white shoes clacking on waxy linoleum; babies crying; the blossoming scents of disinfectant and blood. He didn't know where he was and he didn't want to be anywhere else. It felt like one of those circular fades in a Looney Tunes cartoon.

"It's the worst time of year to feel unloved or under-appreciated," Anti-Santa whispered softly.

In his medicated fog, he saw his former lover, Chloe, sitting across from him at the sawdust-strewn gingerbread table where they had once worked peacefully together under the beneficent (or so it had seemed) gaze of the Old Man. "You just want to make the world a better place, and pass on some of the wisdom you've gleaned. You see these little kids, these bright little faces, and you want to make that brightness last, see yourself reflected in it somehow, you want to live forever. You don't want to dazzle them with fairy dust. You don't want to watch them grow inflated with consumer dullardry, chewing away obediently at huge genetically-modified steaks on a slab. You want them to grow and learn and maintain their, I don't know. Their natural joy for life, their spontaneous... I guess you'd call it, pleasure. Their ability to be pleased. Their ability to reply to the simple smells and tastes and textures of the world. Eventually, you know it can't last. They'll be reprogrammed by TV and Gameboy and the Home Shopping Network, and they won't take pleasure in anything anymore. They'll stop replying. They'll just start responding. They'll want to possess more plastic doodads than anybody else. They'll want to be better, happier, and wealthier than all their friends at school."

For the first few decades of their personal-slash-business relationship, Chloe had listened to him with obvious concern, her eyes moist, lips slightly parted. But eventually, as further decades passed, her expression grew cold and unresponsive. She began seeing other elves. She stopped returning his calls.

"I guess it might have helped if the Old Man had just, you know, listened to what I was trying to say," Anti-Santa told the last woman who had ever loved him. "If he hadn't just shrugged me off and snarled at all my ideas. And when I decided to start my own operation, he could have been more gracious about it. Maybe wished me luck, or told me to break a leg, I don't know, just something. Instead of calling me Mr Know-it-All, Mr Holier-Than-Thou, after everything he'd done and so forth. And then, I'm sorry, Chloe. I'm sorry to get so emotional. But then never to write or call or ask how I was doing. To just dismiss my whole existence like that, and never. Never try to understand that I was doing my best. That I loved the kids too and I just wanted, maybe once. To make one child happy. One child happy, Chloe. That one child who wanted something most kids never find under their tree on Christmas morning."

In the lull before dawn, a stranger entered the ER and made his way to Anti-Santa's gurney. He was shrouded in fairy dust. The air tinkled synesthetically as he passed.

"Ho ho ho," he whispered. "Merry Christmas." The fairy dust darkled obligingly.

Gunshot victims and overdosed self-abusers and auto accidentees all stopped crying at once. All except for Anti-Santa, who felt wide vertiginous spaces open around him, and the renascence of panic in his addled blood.

It couldn't happen like this. Not after all he had been through.

"Please not the fairy-dust," he moaned dopily. "Anything but that."

"Ho ho ho." The Old Man's words whirled in the stale air like dust. "Merry Christmas, Mr Know-it-All. Merry Christmas, Mr Righteous Do-Gooder. Now let's see who's really been a good boy this year."

Broken hypodermics and twisted condoms lay about the icy, smog-stained sludge like weird leaves

It was just past dawn when Anti-Santa awoke on a broken street in a broken city somewhere in mid-western America. The dashboard lights of his solar-powered sleigh thrummed solidly as they charged. He sat up. He felt his wounded thigh.

It was still bandaged. It still hurt.

"Oh my gosh," Anti-Santa sighed relievedly. "For a moment there I thought. I mean, I must have had the awfullest dream."

<The servo-mechanisms are almost functional again, Sir> Rudolph modulated. *<When you're ready, I can prepare you a mug of soy-enriched egg-nog. And maybe another seaweed-poultice for your leg.>*

It was one of those streets which made even Anti-Santa hesitate. Broken hypodermics and twisted condoms lay about the icy, smog-stained sludge like weird leaves. Houses and telephone poles were scarred with graffiti, gunshot, and police memoranda. And amidst the jumble of all this unwelcome tinny information, it took a while to see anything that was simple, meaningful and discrete.

She was standing directly in front of the sleigh. She was staring directly at him.

"I can't believe you came to see me, Anti-Santa. I can't believe you came to see me on Christmas morning."

She was precisely seven years, three months and twelve days old. Fiona Washington's name had been on all his lists for years now, but this was the first time he had met her face to face.

<Ahem> Rudolph said. And gave Anti-Santa a nudge with the vibratory back-rest.

It took Anti-Santa a second to catch up.

"Ho ho ho," Anti-Santa said distantly. "Merry Christmas. Merry Christmas, Fiona."

"It's so exciting, Anti-Santa. I mean, I've seen you on *Sixty Minutes Two* and I'm like your biggest fan. And here it is, the best part of Christmas already, the brand new morning lying fresh and unruined all around us, before the latest stupid newspaper or driveby shooting has been delivered, and you're here to see me, me, Fiona Washington. I can't tell you how happy it makes me, Anti-Santa. I mean, we've got so much in common it's ridiculous."

Anti-Santa tugged on the lapels of his down parka, feeling naked, off-kilter and abashed. He was secretly ashamed about how much he needed to meet someone exactly like Fiona.

<*Sir, we have a problem.*>

" – I want to go get Mommy but I think she's crashed out on the sofa. Ever since Daddy got arrested she doesn't do anything all day but eat Pringles--"

"What's that, Rudolph?"

<*Well, when you were at the hospital I delivered the last of the presents. I don't think we have anything left except, well, maybe this.*>

Rudolph's mechanical arm extruded itself from the dashboard, bearing the remnants of Anti-Santa's bagged supper. The dolphin-friendly tuna from his long-digested sandwich had stained the brown paper with a macabre silhouette of Mickey Mouse.

It didn't seem possible. But suddenly all the wind went out of Fiona's sails.

"Oh, that's OK, Anti-Santa, that's OK, I guess. I mean, I shouldn't, I didn't expect anything really, I mean. I guess the real present is you came to see me, right? You came to see me, Fiona Washington, and nobody else."

Anti-Santa opened the bag and looked inside. There was only this last little object left in his entire sleigh, the only gift left to give. It wasn't much, but it looked a lot more intact and self-sufficient than Anti-Santa felt right now. He needed to get some sleep. He needed to wake again, like Fiona, to a brand new world.

"It's not much, Fiona," Anti-Santa told her, his voice husky with emotion. "But it's all I've got."

Her bright eyes opened just a fractional bit wider.

"An egg, Anti-Santa? A hard-boiled egg?"

Anti-Santa smiled and shrugged. Sometimes life could be sad and happy at exactly the same time.

"It's like the ultimate container, isn't it, Anti-Santa? I could sit this on my bookshelf for years and it wouldn't rot, or break, or go bad. I mean, I heard these stories about the Chinese and they'd

like save these eggs for hundreds of years before eating them. But I'm never going to eat my hard-boiled egg, Anti-Santa. Because you gave it to me. And every time I look at it, I'm going to remember you, and all the good things you've tried to do for children all over the world."

Anti-Santa was speechless. Then, just before the lapse of words grew too heavy to bear, he found heart enough to use a few old words one more time.

"Ho ho ho," he told her softly. "Merry Christmas."

And rode his sleigh, half asleep and smiling gently, all the way home to Tampa. ☉

THE PRACTICAL
IDLER

THE PRACTICAL IDLER

How to live the idle life? This is the question which has foxed the intrepid indolent for generations. Now we hope to help you with our Practical Idler section, where we have brought together a host of tips for good living at low cost. This section is all about getting your priorities straight. Shop at car boot sales, drink good whisky, find a good barber-shop. If you know of a special place, an outstanding pub, tranquil spot or a delicious cheese, then let us know. Being idle is about quality of life and all knowledge should be shared for the greater good. Just e-mail your tips to: theidlers@idler.co.uk

YOUR GUIDE TO THE EASY LIFE

THE RAMBLER:
THOR'S CAVE

By Albert Fogg

SWEET ALBION

If you drive into the Manifold Valley from the south (in the Peak District, just west of Dovedale) you'll find a small car park and a cycle track along the floor of the millstone grit gorge. High above you, to the south of the valley, is the entrance to Thor's cave, which sits under a jagged sloped hill.

If you walk up the fairly easy path that forks off to the left, you'll eventually come to the cave mouth. Most people clamber in, then walk straight back down again. However, peace, solitude and a warm feeling of superiority can be achieved by going out of the cave via the narrow chink in the dripping rock, on the right hand side. It is wide enough for a person of average width. Hang left up the thickly grassed slope - it's rather steep, but the grass is sturdy enough to cling onto. And when you've climbed up a few metres, settle down in the armchair-like soft grasses and gaze about you.

To the east lie a series of folded Staffordshire hills, green hedgerows marking the field boundaries, and with a church steeple poking out of the middle. Straight ahead is the Manifold valley, topped by stone walls and moorland. If you crane your neck forward, you can look down on the miniscule people below, giving you an unavoidable, but delightful, feeling of godly omnipotence.

The view changes dramatically, according to the seasons, but the best time is high summer, when the gorge is filled with people, but their noise and bluster doesn't reach you, being filtered by the copious foliage below. The grass is also less damp and slippy, reducing the likelihood of accidental death by falling.

Continue upwards, and be rewarded with greater views and a short grassed meadow, soft with clover, buttercups and forget me nots. Walk back towards your car along the stone wall lined pathway, then turn right down the road. ☺

Thor's Cave, Manifold Valley,
Peak District, just west of Dovedale

IDLE PURSUITS:
THE BARBER SHOP

Ivor Smullen celebrates our folk hero, the barber

ZED NELSON

When the late and much revered WC Fields resided in a ramshackle mansion near Hollywood, he stationed, among his furnishings, a resplendent symbol of The Good Life: a barber's chair, complete with towel and aprons. In earlier days he had made the discovery that getting a haircut was one of life's more sybaritic pleasures. Now he was able to ward off insomnia by leaning back in his commandeered chair and dropping off into a welcome doze.

Some years later, a Canadian psychiatrist was to disclose that a safe way to get high on a psychedelic trip was to take a fast spin in a barber's chair.

Both Fields and the psychiatrist were clearly barber-shop connoisseurs, and presumably they also appreciated the stature of the barber in the noble hierarchy of international folk figures.

Unlike wizards, dragon-killers and Elizabeth Taylor, the barber does not seem to be the stuff of which legends are made. The fact is, though, that he hasn't done too badly, and sociologically, he has few peers. A child's first visit to a barbershop is a memory (traumatic or otherwise) he may cosset the rest of his life: at the age of 78 the author Sir Compton Mackenzie wrote that he still treasured the envelope containing the curls he'd snipped off at the age of one. American ad-men once classified barber-shops among such valued publicity media as TV, billboards and the press. In ancient Egypt shaving was virtually a religious rite and barbers ranked almost with priests; at top people's banquets haircuts and shaves were on the house. Free haircuts have also been among the appreciated pay-offs for crooked cops by some discerning New York hotels. Most important of all, the barber-shop has, for hundreds of years, figured, in both life and literature, as a unique haven from nagging women and other assorted burdens: a miniature parliament whose discussions on affairs of state, war, peace and the winner of the next race have become a ritual as formalistic as a Morris dance or a wedding ceremony. One New York barber even went so far as to claim that a barber-shop was a fine place in which to "incubate plots, hatch feuds or plan sudden attacks upon enemies."

Circus clowns used to insist on at least one barber-shop sketch (later taken over by slapstick movie-makers), in which the barber swabbed his victim's chin with a giant brush until both were blinded by great clouds of foam. And there are as many barber-shop legends as there are stories of leprechauns and kidnaps by aliens. Richard Procter, a Victorian barber, wrote in his autobiography: "I remember listening, soon after my initiation, to a tough yarn which was spun... The tale was repeated at short intervals during many years; it has continued to haunt me, like a ghost that would not be laid; and even now the blessed evergreen

THRONES OF FELICITY

salutes my ears, as fresh and virginal as at first. It is an heir-loom of the barber's shop, and I will bequeath it to posterity - if posterity choose to accept the legacy." Posterity did.

The story concerns a traveller returned from foreign parts who observes to the barber that he cannot remember when he last had a perfectly clean shave. He now announces his patience is at an end, lays a revolver on the basin rim, and gives warning that, should the barber be careless enough to draw blood, he will be shot forthwith. When the shave has been smoothly and efficiently completed, the customer, though pleased, expresses surprise at the barber's imperturbability throughout the operation. To which the barber replies that, if anything had gone wrong, he, after all, held the whip – or rather, razor – hand.

Yarns have also been prolific about barbers whose shops were next door to pubs and who could not resist leaving a customer half-lathered, while they disappeared for a noggin. The best variation comes (naturally) from Ireland, where the barber concerned would borrow sixpence (this was a long time ago) from his chairbound victim before slipping out for his Guinness. Cassidy (the name given this *dramatis persona* is altogether more picturesque than his English counterparts. For

instance, he has a cat with whom he communes as if it were human and which has a disconcerting habit of springing on its master's elbow while scraping off a client's sideboard.

The boozing-barber myth, incidentally, is rooted in distressing fact: barbers, as a breed, were once inordinately fond of their tipple. In the early 18th century they had free recourse to the cheap gin they sold on their own premises. A *Sunday Times* writer in 1883 wondered why the law did not insist that every barber, "a tremor of whose hand could mean sudden death", should be teetotal. Six years later a barbers' trade journal admitted that in the 1860s the British barber was generally an unmanageable drunk.

On the brighter side, it should be remembered that barbershops were once entertainment venues. The lute-player of the ancient Roman and pre-Restoration barber-shop was thus transposed into the violinist whose scrapings haunted many a Victorian saloon, and the banjo-twanging shoeshine boys who made the rounds of American barber-shops, many of which were sold sheet music of popular songs. Several barbers were musicians in their own right. In 1908 impresario Oscar Hammerstein (grandfather of the man who wrote *Oklahoma!*) cancelled plans for presenting a Spanish opera on the grounds that the score called for a vast host of guitar players. "I should have been obliged,' he said, "to engage all the barbers of New York." A black Philadelphia barber, Richard Milburn, was famous both for his guitar-strumming and his whistling "bird-calls", usually to his own tune, "Listen To The Mocking-Bird". It is a safe bet that the barber-shop routine of singing originated in a saloon where the barber hummed a melody while his customers (including the man in the chair) provided the bass and counterpoint. The town of Jacksonville, Florida, usually lays claim to the first barbershop quartet, citing four singing black barbers who flourished around the 1880s. The barbershop routine fell into disrepute only during the Roaring Twenties, when everyone was so drunk they sang off-key.

In London one barber collapsed while singing an operatic aria to a customer, and died "from over-exertion", according to a doctor. Five years later, another London barber was reported to have installed a phonograph, the chair "being arranged round the two sides of it, so that the tubes can be placed in the ears of his customers, and they can be shaved to the music of Dan Godfrey's band."

Other barbers were less musically orientated, but, when it came to pulling in the customers, still had an eye for the main chance. Many ensured there was always a draughtsboard on the premises. A Dunoon barber who shrewdly publicised the fact that he has shaved William Marwood, the notorious Victorian hangman, was besieged by scores of prurient clients who declined to depart until the hand that had scraped the chin of an executioner had scraped theirs. A placard stuck on a wall in the centre of Manchester offered a new hat (or its cash equivalent) to anyone who called on a shaving shop run by a "prize hair-cutter from Dublin." Similar tokens of proprietorial gratitude took the form of legs of mutton or small rounds of beef. Some years ago a Scottish barber offered his customers five-guinea season tickets, arguing that in a year they could make large savings; a Redcar barber installed a fruit machine, offering free haircuts for several months as the jackpot prize; and a barber in the City laid on a tape-recorder and telephone in each cubicle so that enchaired stockbrokers could simultaneously dictate to their secretaries. In 1933 a Buckinghamshire barber went to the trouble and expense of providing a special chair for a 24 1/2 stone customer who claimed to be the heaviest man in the country and was clearly worth his weight in publicity hand-outs. Across the Atlantic a Chicago barber's saloon patronised by assorted hoodlums during the Prohibition era of gang warfare had one chair reversed towards the door so the nervous customers could keep a constant look-out for the appearance of rivals with significant bulges in their jacket pockets. This beats home comforts any day. ☺

The Idler staff's favourite traditional barber-shop is Vic Johnson's of Clerkenwell, 6a Laystall Street, London EC1R 4PA. Tel 07977 662972

TEA TIME:
A BRIEF HISTORY OF TEA

In the second of his tea columns, Chris Yates proves that the greatest nations have been tea-drinkers

The first cup moistens my lips and throat,
The second cup breaks my loneliness,
The third cup searches my barren entrails,
The fourth cup raises a slight temperature,
The fifth cup purifies me,
The sixth cup calls me to the realms of the immortals,
The seventh cup – ah, but I can take no more.
　　　　　[Lo Tung, poet of the T'ang Dynasty, 620 – 907 AD]

The reason China became an advanced civilisation so much earlier than the rest of the world was obviously because, in 2737, the Emperor Shen-Nung discovered tea. Apparently the Emperor was very fastidious and always boiled water before drinking it. But one day some leaves from the burning branches round his kettle fell into it, giving the water a unique and refreshing taste. Urgent investigations found that the leaves were from the wild tea shrub and shortly afterwards the Great Wall of China was built to keep the Western barbarians from discovering the First Secret of the Universe. (The Chinese also discovered the second and third Secrets – gunpowder and split bamboo fishing rods).

About 3000 years after Emperor Shen-Nung, the Indian Buddhist saint Dharma set himself the pious but quite idle task of seven years' sleepless contemplation of the Buddhah. After four years, however, he began to feel just a little drowsy (don't forget they had no amphetamines in those days). Absent-mindedly, he picked some leaves from a nearby shrub and began to chew them. The leaves were from the wild tea plant, and the effect was to banish the desire to sleep, leaving the saint entirely refreshed. Shortly afterwards the English firm Brook Bond offered Saint Dharma a large inducement to allow them take cuttings from his "special tree" and then to use his holy visage as a new trademark for their beverage import division. The saint politely declined, leaving Britain to continue wallowing in the Dark Ages.

It was not until the early days of the 17th century that tea first arrived in Britain, though no one is certain how it arrived and who introduced it. Being by nature backward and conservative, it took a few years before our forbears appreciated the full spiritual value of the new herbal drink, but when it was suddenly announced that tea was the new black, the ever mercenary government imposed a heavy tax on it, putting its price beyond all but the wealthiest members of society (£2, 18s, 4d per pound). Thus began a great smuggling trade, with barrels of contraband tea being "run" on to remote West Country beaches, worth as much on the black market as barrels of brandy.

For the first century of British tea drinking it was China, who had evidently begun to feel sorry

CHRIS YATES PREPARES TO ENTER THE REALMS OF THE IMMORTALS

for us, who supplied the leaves. And while China tea still makes a very fine cup, perhaps we owe the quality of most of our present day blends to Major Robert Bruce, who discovered the wild tea plant in Assam in 1833. A year later tea was being cultivated in India, marking the end of China's monopoly of the market.

And so, just a few thousand years after Emperor Shen-Nung, Britain became a civilised country, though it's interesting to note that in many parts of Europe coffee is still the preferred beverage. Germany, of course, lost the Second World War because its armies only drank a kind of ersatz coffee made from acorns while the British army was well supplied with tea. Our victory had nothing whatsoever to do with superior strategies, Spitfires and code-breaking and everything to do with giving our soldiers, sailors and airmen regular intervals of blissful idleness, restoring their spirits with a tin cup of tea.

While in this historical dimension, I must mention the surprising and amazing fact that, since my last missive for the *Idler*, I have made a pot of tea using tea bags – and really enjoyed it! I couldn't admit this to the editorial team who descended on my home yesterday, eager to sample my new mix of Assam and Luaka BOP. But hidden behind the traditional tea caddies was a box of bags. However, these were not just any old bags. Clipper, a Dorset company, produce superb Ceylon, Indian and African blends and their Fairtrade tea bags are almost as good as the real thing. ◉

THE ANGLER:
SOMETHING FISHY

Anglers do not always see eye to eye, says Kevin Parr,
and some are consumed by negative passions

Fisherfolk are a rum breed. One could be forgiven for believing that all piscators live in perfect harmony, and, yet the truth is that anglers as a family are as dysfunctional as the rest of humanity.

Naturally, it is the minority who most ripple the water, and a shared passion is always an instant ice-breaker, but snobbery, both orthodox and inverted, is rife.

The municipal park-pond fisherman may scoff at the archaic attitude of the tweed-clad, ghillie abusing, chalk-stream fly-fisher, whose results would be vastly improved if the tangle of fluff at the end of his line was replaced with a lump of bread. But, that same soul looks upon his own angle as an art. A mastery of deception, with far greater virtue than that hapless fool sitting beside a steaming, stagnant pool, indeed, one who waits for a prize that shall be returned to the water, and not to the oven.

Coarse fisherman, indeed. This conflict of rectitude is prevalent most in the angler's attitude to success, or more importantly those factors that constitute success.

Far too many fishermen get it wrong.

The match angler has an obvious goal: to catch more fish of a greater weight than those around him and therefore win the money and make his journey worthwhile. It is true that for many the fishing match is a social affair. Friendships are freshened, thoughts shared and that human need for competition satisfied, and yet the elements that are required for a successful day are dreadfully superficial. Water, of course, is vital, but a converted swimming pool would do just so long as it contains lots of hungry fish. Trees and other bankside vegetation are obstructive as a rule, as is an uneven bank. Far better is to sit on ready-made platforms so that Nike trainers stay

clean and contact with nature is kept to a minimum. The fish themselves are also something of an irrelevance, in the match angler's eyes a sparkling 15 ounce roach is less beautiful than a slimy 1 lb eel.

Weight counts unequivocally to the specimen angler, too. He, similarly, is consumed with competitiveness, and the location for his efforts towards success is immaterial if the fish are there.

This person knows just one level of ascendancy. He who has caught the biggest fish – for that is the barometer of achievement and with it respect. It is astonishing how many more ten-pound barbel exist, than fish an ounce lighter. That barrier is sometimes more important than honesty. Naturally, it is felt within every fisherman to be aware of the significance of their catch, but for some it is obsession.

Not so for the idling angler.

The very fact that one is sitting beside a vibrant river, and not in a dull, dead office, is joy enough – to catch a fish is merely a sidetrack

Success for him is far less troublesome.

The very fact that one is sitting beside a vibrant river, and not in a dull, dead office, is joy enough – to catch a fish is merely a pleasant sidetrack.

My most successful fishing jaunts have invariably coincided with a distinct lack of fishy action. I do admit that there is occasion when I succumb to greed and follow well trodden paths to seek a monster, but to catch nothing on such occasions is a disappointment. Somehow, a day of unrivalled action is suddenly essential.

Catch nothing, however, after a day spent dozing on the bank-side, with grasshoppers churring and swifts screaming, and only the occasional effort to catch something, is time well spent. For then, the location actually helps to evolve the essence.

I once fished the River Kennet in autumn, somewhere near late September, and I was still waiting to catch my first ever barbel. Martin, my good friend and patient advisor, was yet again navigating my car along a pot-holed track in the hope of fulfilment, and I, despite his reassurance, was doubting his angling acumen.

We parked the car, and instead of heading for the immediate and, for others, productive swims, we took a long stroll down river where the current eased and the flow pulled lazily through a gentle bend before dipping sharply beneath an overhanging willow.

This spot not only looked good, but had the right feel, and not purely in a fishy sense. The tree on the far bank twisted itself away from the river in a defiant pirouette, providing a curious spectacle and, hopefully a root encased sanctuary beneath the water.

I was soon fishing and soon catching bugger-all, but feeling at great ease in my surroundings. Martin and I shared tea and reflections as the afternoon passed gently and without major incident.

Suddenly, the mood intensified.

The sun was rapidly setting and with it the temperature dropped like a stone. A classic autumn mist billowed from nowhere and filtered the pink light of the setting sun into a hazy candy floss veil.

I was transfixed, like a lion in the long grass. Wholly focussed, I could almost sense the fish beneath me.

I could barely breathe, though I was immune to the cold and my eyes were resistant to the darkness.

And then I realised that catching a fish at that moment would actually break the spell. I had almost transcended to some place Aristotle only dreamt of. Well, almost.

Nonetheless, as I packed my rods away and Martin floated up the bank, I knew by his smile that he had felt the same feeling.

Never, had a fruitless fishing trip been so strangely productive. So, learn how to fish, but learn how to fish successfully. ◉

THE BROWSER:
A BOOKSHOP OF NOTE

Sam Jordison visits Michael Moon's antiquarian booksellers

MICHAEL MOON: HAPPILY IMMUNE TO THE TIDYING DISEASE

Few visitors to Cumbria and the Lake District ever make it as far as the isolated west coast town of Whitehaven. But it contains one of the best bookshops in the country, Michael Moon's gloriously eccentric "Literary Emporium".

An ambience of appealing shabbiness, comfortable yet intellectually charged, immediately grabs you on entering. Moon's is a browser's paradise. It's in the air.

All thoughts of quickly finding a specific volume have to be banished because, aside from a few divisions into fiction, biography, history etc, there is no filing system, alphabetical or otherwise. Mr Moon is proud to say that he hasn't fallen victim to "the tidying disease." The only way to approach the healthy chaos in his shop is with an involved, prolonged browse. You'll probably never find the book you originally intended to buy, but you're guaranteed to walk out with at least three more you probably didn't even know existed.

Mr Moon's personality asserts itself in more than just the determined lack of order. The esoteric collection of books clearly follow his interests and areas of expertise and the intriguing labyrinthine building might just as well be an extension of his own cavernous mind. He will charm you with stories of Whitehaven's often hilarious, often tragic swashbuckling industrial history, as well as with his own career in publishing and bookselling, taking as much delight in his failures as his triumphs.

I'd recommend that all *Idler* readers visit Whitehaven one day and spend time Moon's shop. ☜

**Michael Moon's
Antiquarian Booksellers
& Publishers**
19 Lowther Street,
Whitehaven, Cumbria

THE PASSENGER:
VW CAMPER VAN

Be a snail, says Fanny Johnstone. Be free. Get a camper

Me and my friend Liz, her boyfriend Karim, and my ex-boyfriend Sam are in his 1973 Westfalia VW Camper van. It's orange. Sam's had the van ever since his parents gave it to him for his 18th birthday. They'd seen some rock 'n' roll times in it themselves, and wanted him to have some good times too. Sam's folks have since bought themselves a more sedate Autohome for a quieter, more civilised passage through life. But their old VW engine is still growling happily, like a dog pulling on a stick.

We're high up in our seats, lording it over the sunny Cornish roads, with American band Camper Van Beethoven on the stereo shouting out about our "treehouse condominium". We're loaded up with surf boards on the roof, booze in the cooler, fags on the dashboard, lunch in a hamper, and wet suits and towels draped here and there. The engine's puttering along, gurgling cheerfully as Sam

changes down to approach the dangerous bend where Liz nearly broke her back when Karim crashed into it one night. After the operation she spent the whole of last summer in a corset-style plaster cast, so that with her cascading black hair, big boobs and long legs, she looked spookily like an immobile Wonder Woman greeting her surfing hero back from the waves.

But today we're safely past that bend, on our way to Kennack Sands for a day's modest surfing. My bare feet are up on the padded dash board, and my denim cut-offs are getting their first outing of the summer so I'm already topping up my tan through the open window. As I pass Sam a cigarette I can see him flickering a sideways glance over my thighs. I flick him a smile back to let him know he's been caught. We both snigger and, because the sun is out, and because it's a holiday weekend, and because we're in the van which

makes teenagers of us all, we start laughing. The van goes over a bump which makes the fading plastic Jesus on the dash-board wave to us. We wave back.

I've got that priceless feeling that you get when you're a kid, of an entire day stretching out before you, full of adventures. Add the sun - hot and persistent through the van's tinted windows - and the whole feeling makes me so excited but languid that I want to stretch. But here in the front there's not much room to stretch out. Instead I sneak a look at Sam and his long, brown legs and see the golden hairs on his tanned arms as he changes gear again. The view is pure sunshine so I'm sun-bathing in it.

We turn left onto the Goonhilly downs, checking out the churning wind farm to our left, and over the hedges down to the wooded valleys of Trelowarren to our right. Everything seems within our grasp outside the van, just as much as it is inside

coarseness of the bumpy beige and brown tartan seats that feels good against the flesh.

I don't surf because I can't balance to save my life, so I don't need to change, but Sam pulls the van door shut to change into his Gul suit. I'm in there with him, drinking my beer. The sun's beating down, flooding across the melamine, glinting on the metal stove, heating up the sandy floor, warming our skin. Everything suddenly seems intertwined and inextricable.

Every movement we make brushes against one of the varied surfaces. So in such an enclosed space, with everything revolving around us, it's inevitable that sooner or later we'll end up brushing against each other. ⊚

the van. I say to the others "Hey! I've just realised. Being in a campervan is like being on the web - you can travel the world but the interface stays the same." And Sam says "Yeah, but I've always thought it's like being drunk. You feel really happy in it, and everything seems crowded in and egocentric because all the stuff you need in the world is revolving around you."

"Well the smell definitely revolves around you," says Liz from the back. She's right, sadly. Yesterday's wet-suits, Sam's sleeping bag stuffed into one of the roof-bunks, and his break-fast baked-bean pan awaiting salvation in the sink are all mulching together into one big pong. But it's a smell that, over

the years, I've trained myself to find endearing.

Ten minutes later we've pulled up on the beach. Liz and Karim have zipped up their wetsuits and are running into the water with their boards. But Sam and I have decided to have a beer and have a fag before heading in. The sun through the tinted windows makes our skin look immaculately airbrushed, and there's something about the vague

VW Camper vans can start at around £1,500. A good website is www.volkswest.co.uk/campersforsale. And for advice on buying a VW try www.marksvw collectibles.co.uk . He gives great tips on what to look out for in both the VW model and the interior. Like knowing what you want before making a decision because campers are designed for different reasons. While some may be suitable for UK week-ending, they might not be appropriate for European holidays. Meanwhile, no, Sam isn't selling his.

THE IDLER FAN CLUB

Stay cool with a Spanish fan, says
Christie Currie

! TEN CUIDADO NOS ESPIAN !
! Watch out ; We´re being spied on !

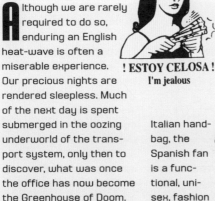

! ME GUSTAS MUCHO !
I like you very much

! ESTOY CELOSA !
I'm jealous

! TE AMO Y SUFRO !
I love you and I suffer

! DESEO HABLARTE !
I'd like to speak to you

Although we are rarely required to do so, enduring an English heat-wave is often a miserable experience. Our precious nights are rendered sleepless. Much of the next day is spent submerged in the oozing underworld of the transport system, only then to discover, what was once the office has now become the Greenhouse of Doom.

Well, swelter no longer, for there is a solution which is both affordable and decidedly kool for kats. Say *Adios* to tube-induced panic attacks, and wave *Ola* to the Spanish fan, welcoming with it a breezy new world of passion and mystique.

Dating back centuries, the fan is not only a traditional costume piece, but a symbol of relaxation and comfort. Lest we forget, the Spaniards are professional Idlers, taking very seriously their daily siestas, and perfecting the art of entirely forgetting the time. Gentlemen don't dismay, for as with the

Italian handbag, the Spanish fan is a functional, unisex, fashion accessory.

A dashing swipe of the fan can be just as commanding as a sweeping cape. Appreciating the fact that sometimes it is simply too hot to talk, the Spanish fan is designed to incorporate its very own language, so you really can flirt and be cool at the same time. Historically, the presence of fans in church was indicative of clandestine flirting amongst the town's adulterers. So next time you're at the Hoxton discothèque keep close eyes on your lover, for their seemingly casual wrist action may be sending saucy signals to the

Señor across the way...

Spanish fans are widely available in numerous styles, and at varying prices. A trip to Barcelona could find you a hand crafted, desirable specimen for anything up to £80. Of course, with our summer lasting ,on average, only a fortnight, you may wish to purchase a modestly priced model at £3.50 from Garcia & Son's off the Portobello road. If you are too hot to leave the house, then jump on the internet and order all kinds of fans from www.boutique-flamenco.com. Or why not customize your own? Just get a piece of paper, write a punchy slogan on it, fold it up and hey-presto! Ultimate cool! ◉

IDLE PURSUITS:
HOT AIR BALLOONING

Sam Jordison went with the wind

They've demystified the skies. Flying on an airline is the most boring thing you can do while still being absolutely terrified. Hot air balloons, by contrast, provide a stately, beautiful and eminently enjoyable way of getting from A to Wherever The Wind Takes You. They bring back the wonder of flight. And do it a pace that will delight even the most indolent soul.

There's no real practical reason to climb into a giant whicker basket and leave yourself at the mercy of the breezes, but it's definitely worth it for the experience. After all, our ancestors always wanted to fly, not because it's a good way of hurtling from meeting to meeting, but because it looks ace. The birds they envied were clearly having fun.

I've been ballooning in the Lake District, and for a while I had a job helping to retrieve the balloons after they'd landed (you have to follow them on the ground in a Land Rover, because you can never know where they'll end up). The view of the mountains is exhilarating, and the feeling of being high in the sky, is euphoric.

The balloon ride is always soothing and calm. Balloons are never flown in anything above a light breeze, and because you glide along with whatever wind there is, everything around you feels perfectly still. Rather than buffet against you, the wind just pushes the basket gently on its way. The only disturbances come when the pilot gives the gas a blast, or when a fellow passenger spots something exciting on the ground.

You can never know which field, or indeed valley, you're going to land in, or how long it's going to take to get there. There's nothing to do other than enjoy the view and chat to your companions. And when you land, you get in the Land Rover and you're taken back to exactly where you started. The flight has served no purpose, other than life enriching pleasure. ◉

Flights in the Lake District are arranged by The High Adventure Balloon Company.
http://high-adventure.co.uk/
At £169 per person, they're expensive, but compare well to most airline flights: the
distance travelled is far shorter but the good memories last far longer.

SLOW BOOZE:
ELDERFLOWER CHAMPAGNE

It's free, it's easy. Chris Yates on the first of the summer wine

Unfortunately for true idlers, the most refreshing, most thirst quenching cold drink in the world is not available in the shops. You have to make it yourself! It's true that you can purchase an approximation of this divine liquid in certain specialist outlets, but anything other than the essentially seasonal real thing is hardly worth the name. That name is elderflower champagne.

The summer of '03 will be remembered by even the eldest elder enthusiasts in the country as the vintage summer for blossom. It began in late May, when the weather suddenly changed from cool and showery to warm and benign, and continued all the way from June into July when the elder trees were still laden with large, dense, beautifully fragrant clusters. From about forty heads of blossom I made five gallons of delectable high quality champagne, but even before the summer had ended we had drunk the lot. Especially when the season is hot, this drink is completely addictive, and because its alcohol content is almost nil my four children know I have no reasonable excuse for hiding the bottles in a locked cupboard. I will always regret the day I allowed one of them a little sip of the bottle marked "dangerous home brew", for such was the duration of the resulting "Mmmmm-mmmmmm..." that the other three dropped whatever they were doing and rushed in to demand a share of this obvious delight. They instinctively knew that the label was a lie and within minutes had consumed every last drop. I consoled myself with the realisation that at least they weren't drinking Coke or Pepsi and, furthermore, they much preferred elder to any of my other less sparkling liquids.

It may come as something of a shock for *Idler* readers when I say that this drink is not only delectable it is also undeniably good for you, elder being rich in organic iron and many other beneficial properties. I'm convinced that, were it available throughout the year, it would prove to be the elixir of eternal youth, though even with its short season it can still vastly improve your spiritual well-being, your general health, your sex life, sleeping habits, appetite, speed from a standing start and ability to leap tall buildings in a single bound.

But enough whittling! Here is the simple recipe for a gallon of "champagne":

TRAJAN HAGUE

HOW TO MAKE ELDERFLOWER "CHAMPAGNE":

When the elder is in full creamy flower, but before the tiny florets turn yellow and start to fall, gather eight flower heads, preferably picking them in full sunshine when they are at their most fragrant. Using a fork, work the florets off the stems into a gallon bucket of water. Then add a tablespoon of wine vinegar, a pound of clear honey, two tablespoons of sugar and the juice and rind of a single lemon. Put a dishcloth over the bucket and leave for 24 hours, stirring occasionally. After 24 hours, filter and transfer the festering concoction into bottles using a jug, a sieve, a large tea-pot and a funnel. [I use screw top plastic ex lemonade bottles.] Store them for just two or three days, depending on the temperature – the warmer the weather the sooner the nectar starts to fizz. Then, if they hiss at you when you loosen the tops, put them in the fridge to chill. Finally, after placing a bottle next to your favourite place, switch off TV, mobile phone and radio, slowly pour yourself a glass, raise it gently to your lips and enter a midsummer dream. ☺

SLOW BOOZE:

THE TALISKER WHISKY DISTILLERY

Dan Kieran has a few drams at the Talisker Distillery on the Isle of Skye, and finds out why Robert Louis Stevenson called Talisker "The King o' Drinks"

The Talisker Distillery lies on the bank of Loch Harport in the shadow of the imposing Cullin Mountains. The first thing you notice about the distillery is that it's much smaller than you'd expect. It is basically a warehouse with three huge stills that look like enormous turnips, a couple of outbuildings and an office. Alistair Robertson, the Talisker's Distillery manager for the last four and a half years, offered to explain how they turn water, barley and yeast into a prize winning single malt. It's in the stills that the liquid, that later becomes the whisky, is boiled and cooled. Alistair took the time to explain through the process of distillation but I got hopelessly confused immediately and just nodded and smiled throughout his explanation. I left none the wiser about how they make whisky, but put my confusion down to the fact that I was drinking my second glass as we walked round. I was also surprised at the total lack of people working there. No one seemed to be around apart from Alistair, the lady who runs the visitor centre and a handful of American tourists. I explained how it wasn't what I'd expected, that I'd had visions of old men in cloth caps who'd been there for forty years talking in an unusual dialect and laughing heartily at my strange modern clothes, but there wasn't a soul around. Alistair explained as we headed for the basement where the casks are laid down. "Those days are long gone I'm afraid, but when I first came here four and a half years ago I had to go to one of the last old boy's retirement do's. There was a guy there called Roddy Alec who I'd been warned about. He was one of the old school, and when I saw him I thought there was something wrong with his leg because he had to be carried off the bus into his retirement party, so I said to somebody, 'what's wrong with him?' 'Oh, just drunk.' This was before the party! Carried off the bus, drunk, into his retirement party! There's a picture of him upstairs in the visitors centre working in the warehouse. The interesting thing is he had an identical twin brother. And Roddy took a big drink. And quite often he couldn't make it into work in the morning so he'd send his twin brother along, and even the guys that used to work with Roddy could never tell the difference, even they weren't sure if it was Roddy or not."

As we enter the basement I feel like I've walked into the warehouse at the end of *Raiders of the Lost Ark*. In front of us there is a glass panel and beyond that hundreds and hundreds of black casks, as

OVER THE SEA TO SKYE

far as I can see, all with "Talisker" stencilled in white paint.

Alistair explained further: "After all that activity, of making it, boiling it, cooling it, squashing it, shunting it through pipes, it ends up in this barrel and doesn't move for ten years. We've gone to all the trouble of putting it through the process, being very careful about the selection of all the ingredients that go into it. Now we want to try and preserve this characteristic of Talisker. The best way to do that is to put it into what we call refilled American oak casks. There it lies undisturbed." I tell him it reminds me of the end scene in Raiders of the Lost Ark and he laughs. "you can imagine it encased in rock and somebody breaks in and finds the stuff."

On the wall there is a sign which says,

"The Angels' Share" and I ask him to explain. "As the casks are maturing the oak breathes, so there are evaporative losses. Now for the first couple of years that tends to be two percent, thereafter it tends to slow down. With a whisky that's 20-25 years old there's not going to be an awful lot left by the end, the casks tend to be about half empty. And that's why it's called the Angels' Share."

We venture out into the sunlight and I begin to realise just how strong Talisker is. Alistair offers me a few more drams of whisky in the tasting room before we visit the shop, I hastily accept his invitation. He pours out a couple more glasses, letting me try a couple of limited edition bottlings. They've just introduced, a 25 year old and a double matured Talisker. He tells me over yet another

SLOW BOOZE HAS NEVER BEEN MORE LEISURELY

dram: "The important thing with a Malt Whisky distillery is that we still do not, as a whole industry, understand what affects the final flavour, so we don't change anything. If we do change something we have to monitor it over a long period of time because we have to make sure it has absolutely no impact on the final quality of the flavour characteristics because a Talisker drinker ten years ago expects it to be the same today."

We chat for a while longer and Alistair admits that he spent the first few weeks of his job just staring out the window of his office, the views of the Loch and the Cullin mountains are breathtaking. He confides in me that being the distillery manager at Talisker "beats working for a living". By the end I'm so overcome with his generosity, the amount of whisky I've drunk and the all round general good vibe that I spend £35 on a bottle of the double matured Talisker in the shop on the way out. When I get home I decide to give the whisky my full attention and open it to see if Stevenson was right. He was. It's cracking stuff. 🔊

The Talisker Distillery

Carbost, Isle of Skye, IV47 8SR
01478 614300

CHEESE REVIEW:

GRANDMA SINGLETON'S EXTRA TASTY

Soft, crumbly but
surprisingly strong.
By Sam Jordison

The soft gold colour, and yielding crumbly texture belie the hidden strengths of this singularly assertive cheese. Unless you intend to blight your afternoon with meetings, this pungent date-killer is strongly recommended as a fortifying lunch time snack.

Nose:

The cheese gives off the kind of honk that the cartoonists from the Beano indicate with wavy green lines, fainting dentists and grinning kids with pegs on their noses. However, in the same way that a damp Labrador's head or your oldest trainers are strangely pleasurable to sniff, so the ripe blasts from a slab of Grandma Singleton's quickly become delightful, evoking feelings of warmth, comfort and potent vitality.

Taste:

Initially delicate and mellow, like a good farmhouse cheddar, becoming increasingly fruity and intense. Just when you're beginning to feel that the cheese has bitten you rather than the other way around, a warm whisky-like glow spreads round your gullet, and life seems suddenly kinder.

Eating and drink:

Strong brown tea, red wine. Best eaten with Thick brown bread, tomatoes. ☻

Grandma Singleton's Extra Tasty
....

Best tried in Lancashire or South Cumbria. Available from Lancaster market and Booth's supermarkets.

IDLE SHOPPING:
CAR BOOT SALES

Daniel Pemberton gets cheap kicks

For me one of the greatest pleasures on a sunny Sunday morning is doing a car boot sale. Time slips by in a most pleasurable manner as your peruse stall after stall of stuff your life is much better off without. Even so it can also be a great place to get a bargain, and if you're too lazy for the whole E-bay shenanigans, a good way to make some cash selling off your junk. The only drawback is they always start at such uncivilised hours.

CAR BOOT SALE I-SPY

One of the joys of a boot sale is you never know what you're going to find. However you can entertain yourself by trying to find the following – they're always there somewhere.

- [ ] a vinyl copy of James Last Hammond A-Go-Go 3
- [ ] Bloke selling a load of batteries that look like Duracells but aren't
- [ ] Golf clubs
- [ ] Something related to Who Wants To Be A Millionaire
- [ ] VHS copy of Gremlins
- [ ] a broken down computer from the late 80's
- [ ] an old typewriter
- [ ] super 8 equipment
- [ ] a shifty looking bloke with a huge box of old "well used" porno mags
- [ ] broken and battered Thundercats toys

TOP TIPS

BUYING

✌ Haggle. If you are not going to haggle you might as well wear a big t-shirt that says "I've absolutely no idea about car boot sales whatsoever" and walk around with a flashing light on your head and a boombox loudly playing the music from TV series *Van Der Walk*. Even if you don't want to haggle,

haggle. It's fun. It's the unwritten law of the car boot.

✌ Make an offer. Similar to haggling but this is best achieved when you are making multiple purchases of something. Eg: "I'll buy these two Chic albums, that bowtie and this broken calculator - for two quid!" "All right". Saving to me : £1.50! Good to throw in a random object that you wouldn't have bought to see if you can get it for free.

✌ Stop to think before you buy something - do you really need it? Do you really need a collection of 1984 Haynes car maintenance manuals even if they are just £2 the lot? No. Think. You wouldn't believe the pointless crap I have bought. One week I bought this totally knackered homemade Turkish guitar that you couldn't even play for

£30. £30! What was I thinking? The next week my mate picks up a fantastic acoustic guitar which he plays every day for the same price while all I can do is make atonal "boingy" noises on one of the few strings that work. Bastard.

✌ Is it going to work? The best approach to the age old is it going to work question is to assume that the price you are going to pay is for the thrill of buying the object rather than the object itself and that way no one gets upset.

✌ If you really really want something buy it straight away but otherwise it's worth "cooling off" before you rush into any purchases. Try to familiarise yourself with the general level of pricing across the sale.

SELLING

✌ Displaying your goods. I am shit at this. For some reason I can never find any trestle tables and the like and usually have to do things out of boxes and laying it on the floor. This is not good. People want to be able to see what's on offer. Most are strangely frightened of actually approaching a stall and prefer instead to stare at it from a distance before they actually move in. I would recommend a couple of trestle tables for general stuff, clothes rails for clothes and boxes for random objects.

✌ You really can sell any kind of shit. You wouldn't believe some of the things people will buy.

✌ Don't arrive too late - arrive too late and you'll get a bad spot and also have hundreds of people poking about while you unpack. I normally insist on

EXPERIMENTAL SELLING TECHNIQUE PROJECT

I decided that I was going to revolutionise the world of car boot selling by starting the first stall to run advertisements over its, erm, PA system (car stereo to be precise). As my own voiceover skills are somewhat lacking I spent the previous evening recording a load of slogans using the computer voice on my Apple Mac. Most of these seem to revolve around either a personal recommendation from Professor Stephen Hawking about the quality and great value of the goods I was offering or phrases to whip people into a spending frenzy (BUY! BUY! BUY!). I also had one that said "spend your money here" that went in a loop for about 20 minutes. The idea was that when sales were slacking I would pump up the stereo, blast this out and everyone would rush to my stall amazed by not only my endorsement from a world famous scientist but also my high tech approach to salesmanship. In practice however I got told off by a moody couple opposite me within about 15 minutes who quickly took offence to computerised slogans such as "everything everyone else is selling is rubbish". If anyone wants to buy the CD with these all on, and I can still find it, it's yours for a fiver.

not selling anything until I'm unpacked otherwise you can't keep track of what's going on.

⚘ Dealing with people who are trying to haggle a stupid price. My technique (which I can proudly boast to have invented) is to simply raise the price of the object in question every time they try to make an offer until they finally agree on my original price. They quickly get the message. For example: "Ere mate how much is that jacket?" "Five quid" "I'll give you two quid for it." "Six quid." "What? Erm, all right, three quid." "Seven quid" "Look here's a fiver OK?".

⚘ If you can get a chance check out some of the prices of similar goods on other stalls. But remember if you end up being too expensive you're not going to sell much.

DAVID GIBSON

THE BARGAIN STORE IS OPEN, COME INSIDE!

⚘ Direct salesmanship. For me this is most of the fun I have when selling. No one seems to do it at car boot sales. Assume you are some kind of wide boy cockney trader, spot someone walking along and just start shouting rubbish at them. "Would you like Oscar winning Hollywood actor Tom Hanks in your living room sir? Well for just £4 that dream can come true when you buy my fantastic DVD copy of *You've Got Mail*. Barry Norman said it's the kind of movie to take a box of tissues to. I watched it and didn't think it was that kind of movie at all but it's still a Hollywooooood classic. And yours for only four pounds sir. Four pounds. Four pooounnndss." Admittedly this actually seems to scare a large number of people off but it did directly help me sell a Phil Collins hat for 50p once. Plus it keeps me amused.

⚘ Good tunes. Always worth getting some good laid back tunes to play on the stereo. And some seats to chill out on. ☻

BOOKS:
TONY'S TEN

Tony White picks his highlights of the last ten years

Shit! It doesn't seem like ten years, but to celebrate we've asked some of the writers who've made an impact during this time to nominate the books which have stood out, for them.

The literary scene of ten years ago seems a moribund place. One or two writers were doing interesting stuff but it wasn't that easy to find in your local bookshop. The science fiction section of the bookshop was a safe bet, but that was still recovering from the cyberpunk scene of the mid-eighties, though by this time it had mutated into San Fransisco hippies doing desperately shite photo-shoots with bits of circuit board on their faces for *Mondo 2000* magazine.

Meanwhile back in the UK, Victor Headley's *Yardie*, and the novels of Stewart Home and Michael Bracewell were about it, weren't they? I'm reading this as I write it, and thinking, no, it can't be right, but I just can't think of anyone else that was worth going down to the bookshop for. Everyone was still reading Martin Amis novels. Which is fine, but... However this is perhaps not as bad as it sounds, because both Bracewell's and Home's novels are incredibly good – and hugely rewarding reads – which is where the similarity ends. Stewart Home had already been in print for a couple of years with *Defiant Pose* and *Pure Mania* (both now out of print), and in 1993 published his short story collection, *No Pity*, swiftly followed in 1994 by his ruthless piss-take of East End regeneration, *Red London*. But these were faint lights in a wilderness. Better, at the time, to go to the late, lamented Compendium Books (run by the late and very lamented Mike Hart; staffed occasionally by the also late and also lamented Liz Young, when she wasn't writing some of the best criticism around – see Serpent's Tail's collection of her journalism, *Pandora's Handbag*) and catch up on whatever they managed to stock in there. I was working for the Post Office at the time, and when I wasn't dodging IRA bombs in Camden High Street (well, one, which went off in a litter bin), I'd spend Saturday lunch times in Compendium and bit-by-bit noticed that things were starting to change. In amongst the crap there were more and more good books and new writers starting to emerge – though this is not to say that there were not, and are not, still, shit-loads of unambitious and boring-as-hell shelf-fillers getting published every year by an industry for whom often the main criteria for going ahead with new books or authors is that they're similar to something else that was once successful. What was interesting in about '93/94 though is that most of the good stuff was coming out of cottage industry micro-publishers, small presses – from Rebel Ink, AK, and Clocktower Press in Scotland, to London's X-Press and Pulp Faction (later to become Pulp Books and now www.pulp.net if you fancy looking them up). There was Creation and the short-lived Attack Books (whose output, including Mark Manning, Steven Wells, Stewart Home, Tommy Udo is finally in a remainder shop near you

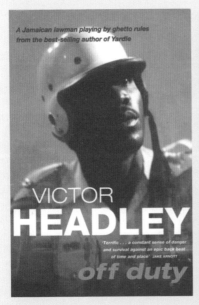

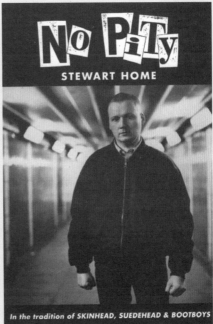

HEADLEY AND HOME: UK STAND-OUTS IN 1993

which means, as Michael Moorcock once said, that finally people can afford to buy them). Also Brighton's excellent Codex, whose list maps the experimental from Kathy Acker to Jeff Noon, from Alan Moore to Steve Aylett. These small publishers were, and in most cases are still, brilliant specifically because they've got nothing to lose: no margins for serious money making, or for the profits that come with economies of scale and the manipulation of print costs and discounts. They were able to publish who they wanted, simply because they thought the work was important and that there was a readership. It's still practically impossible for small publishers to get their stuff in to the bookshops and the debt they're owed for underwriting the risks that larger publishers are or were too scared to take at the time goes largely unacknowledged; un-noticed, even.

What else? Billy Childish and Iain Sinclair have become, in their own ways, kind of national treasures. Michael Moorcock (already one) produced the long-awaited sequel (of sorts) to *Mother London* in *King of the City*. China Mieville and Phillip Pullman each wrote some of the best fantasy fiction to come out of these shores since Christ knows when, all the while completely confounding genre expectations. Victor Headley produced his best novel yet with *Off Duty* (Sceptre 2001), and Michael Bracewell (with *Perfect Tense*, Cape, 2001) produced another "sort-of" sequel to his earlier novel *The Conclave*, which, though ostensibly a novel about the eighties, actually came true – and became a work of prophecy about the "Because you're worth it" nineties.

It's hard to believe that Nicholas Blincoe's debut, *Acid Casuals*, only came out in 1995. He seems to have been around for ever, even before he co-edited *All Hail the New Puritans* with Matt Thorne, which at least got people talking about the short story, despite what Niall Griffiths said to me in Bristol last week. Niall Griffiths! There's another one – and *Stump* (Cape, 2003) is one fuck-off novel – the best pastoral writing since John Cowper Powys's trembling depictions of a near-sentient west country, as seen in (now) desperately unfashionable, but nonetheless astonishing novels like *A Glastonbury Romance*, and *Wolf Solent*. I can almost guarantee you'll find a copy of one of these in your local Oxfam.

Running out of space: Jeff Noon, Steve Beard, (now both collaborating on an on-line remixology fiction project at www.mappalujo.com). John Williams, Toby Litt, Steve Aylett. Stella Duffy's crime novels. John King's stupendous *Human Punk*, even as its idealism disintegrates into smug and self-justificatory rightwing geezer culture, and David Peace's fantastic and terrifying *1980*.

Not forgetting the big ones either – as the politics of necessity which had spawned the experiments in voice of

Linton Kwesi Johnson in the seventies and James Kelman in the eighties gave birth to one big bawling baby in the shape of Irvine Welsh's *Trainspotting* – which became "book-as-brand" once the film publicists got a hold of it; while Alex Garland's brilliant *The Beach* (and even better *The Tesseract* - which disproved the "duff second album" rule that's increasingly applied to novelists these days) did the same; and from somewhere between Oxbridge and Harlesden, came Zadie Smith's big, small novel *White Teeth*, which teetered on the edge of its own modesty for about a nano-second before becoming the must-buy item of whatever year it was now, with a sales curve that mirrored consumer take-up of mobile phones, and thereby created, with Welsh and Garland, a new kind of literary superstar. All of whom are now in some kind of self-imposed exile.

Matthew Collings was right – "Blimey!"

Farther afield, Douglas Coupland's work reached a kind of apotheosis with the beautiful and brilliant indictment of designer-slackerdom which was *Girlfriend in a Coma*, as Scarlett Thomas (herself pretty damn good: her last novel, *Going Out*, contained the best dialogue I've read in a British novel in years) explains below. Out of space (and out of breath), and I've barely scratched the surface, but now I'll hand over to a few other writers who have picked out their favourite books of the past ten years, while I sit back and look forward to the next decade... ☉

Tony White's novel Foxy-T *is published by Faber*

STUPENDOUS, FANTASTIC, TERRIFYING: KING AND PEACE

THE BEST

To celebrate the *Idler*'s anniversary, we've asked a few writers to nominate their favourite reads of the past ten years

SCARLETT THOMAS:

Girlfriend in a Coma
by Douglas Coupland
Flamingo, £6.99

The most intimate, thoughtful book of Douglas Coupland's career so far. Too crazy for some this novel takes a group of suburban Canadian teenagers in 1979 and then throws them like a broken boomerang into the future, via someone else's coma, only to pull them back at (literally) the last minute to ask them what they learnt from the experience. Is this one of the most uplifting books of the last ten years or one of the most depressing? Is this a suicide note or a thank you letter or something in between? Who knows.

TOBY LITT:

The Western Canon: The Books and School of the Ages
by Harold Bloom
Papermac, £12.00

Although not a particularly "Idler" choice, Bloom's monumental work is important for being an unfashionable reminder that literature didn't begin with Modernism. Anyone writing has to take account of the real classics, or suffer from being obviously in ignorance.

NICHOLAS BLINCOE:

Trainspotting
by Irvine Welsh
Minerva £6.99

Trainspotting is driven by one of the most underrated of dramatic forms: the comic monologue. And reading *Trainspotting*, it was a genuine shock to find a novelist from the British Isles who set out with the belief that the contemporary reader - the author's own peers - could be treated with respect.

CHINA MiEVILLE:

The Course of the Heart
by M.John Harrison
(out of print)

Technically this book came out in 1992, but I'm hoping I can nominate it because I read the Flamingo edition printed in 1993. It's the usual Harrisonian concerns – alienation and the bad numinous – expressed with a restraint and an austerity that is humbling. One of the very great books of the nineties.

MCINTOSH AND DUFFY GO FOR JOYCE AND MOSLEY

MATTHEW McINTOSH:

Ulysses
by James Joyce
*Penguin Modern
Classics, £8.99*

Not long ago, I finally read this book called Ulysses by a writer named James Joyce, a book that seems to have something in common with the big Explosion they say brought about the Birth of this Universe. Joyce (re)created the boundries within which the next generations of writers could explore. Some try, but no one yet has reached past *Ulysses*. Most don't come within light years. (Note: If this was supposed to be about favourite books PUBLISHED in the last ten years, simply replace *Ulysses* with *White-Hot Passion on the Slave Galleon* and "James Joyce" with "Vicki Stevens Longfellow".)

MATT THORNE:

The Royal Family
by William T. Vollmann
Penguin (USA only) $17.00

Nothing to do with Charles & Co, it is instead an exhaustive novel about prostitution and one man's search for the Queen of the Whores. A combination of detective novel, love story and sex book, it is the most thrilling read I've ever had.

STELLA DUFFY:

**What Next :
A Memoir Toward World Peace**
by Walter Mosley
Serpent's Tail 5.99

This is far and away the best book I've read in ages. Brief, cogent and compelling, Mosley argues for a better world - and, unlike most of the other authors examining the sorry state of our world, he even suggests a few concrete steps toward making it so.

STEWART HOME:

A259 Multiplex Bomb "Outrage"
by Simon Strong
Codex £5.95

The irrational, all-pervading violence of the modern world is the subject of Simon Strong's hauntingly powerful novel. Through the alchemy of the verbal incantation, Strong transcends today's sexual turmoil and outlines a bizarre new phenomenology of fucking. After I did the five knuckle shuffle with this one handed read, my love life was transformed! ◉

REVIEWS

The Art of the Siesta
Thierry Paquot
Marion Boyars, £8.95

I LOVE these French philosophers. So abstract, playful and confusing. Thierry Paquot is an academic who has produced a terrific defence of the nap as a pleasurable, useful and revolutionary act, and it's all written like this:

> Such an existence inscribes itself through a dialectics of tension and relaxation, of alternation between periods of busyness and calm, motion and rest . According to Bachelard, rest can be "busy" and activity "passive", but each "instance" is unique and its repetition illusory since, by necessity, it must mark the conclusion of something.

Now, I could ponder pleasurably over the meaning of that passage for hours. In fact, I might read it after lunch as I lie down on my day bed for a nap. My siestas begin at two, generally, though in the past they would have been taken at midday, or the "sixth" hour, the original meaning of siesta. Ah, to drift away with Pacquot's dense phrasing whirling in my mind. I could dream about having a nap!

The book, which has a modest title, turns into a damning attack on the whole post-Industrial work-culture, on time as mere duration and the homogenisation of life, and it is an argument for freedom and lolling:

> The word "liberty" has no real meaning without each person having control over their own time. The free use of time is the guarantee of autonomy... availability, awareness and attentiveness are not spontaneous or regular attitudes; they gain greater substance by alternating with pauses, halts and silences. Just as sleep goes through several phases, so too are our activities cyclic... Brothers and sisters! Seize the siesta!

Yes, a great and important work. ☻

Tom Hodgkinson

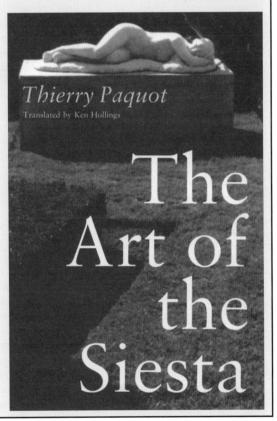

Thierry Paquot
Translated by Ken Hollings

The Art of the Siesta

With the Flow,
and **M Bougran's Retirement**
by Joris-Karl Huysmans,
translated by Andrew Brown
Hesperus, £6.99

At some point in the nineteenth century writers began to notice that large numbers of literate people had somehow been turned into peons. This was not how it was meant to be. Reading and writing had always amounted to a passport to an élite. And the industrial revolution was a kind of promise to liberate people from heavy manual drudgery. Now, somehow, the two were being combined.

There were people it was interesting or instructive to write about, and there were people of no account. But the modern nightmare began to be observed in the middle of the nineteenth century, when the evidence that the souls were being sucked from the populace on a truly industrial scale became too pervasive to ignore. For a start, writers, trapped in such jobs, were suffering from it.

In this country, true machine bureaucracy never truly terrorized much. For one thing, the British civil service had a sense of mission. And it is very possible that the British didn't find this work as utterly soul-detroying as the French. Corruption was not as much of a given; the work either not so mindless, dispiriting and degrading, or the British mind more attuned to the comic aspect of the job. When clerks appear on the English literary scene, they are being gently mocked in *The Diary of a Nobody*.

Things really were worse elsewhere. In France? Ghastly. In Russia it was truly terrible, and the genius of her greatest writer, Gogol, only flowered when he cast his mind back to his two years of experience in the Russian civil service, which operated on a rigidly hierarchical system with ranks equivalent to those in the military. "The Diary of a Madman" is, I think, his first civil service story (it may even be the first civil service story; note, by the way, how the banal form of the diary is appropriated by these two very different writers, as if in tacit acknowledgment that the only people interested in describing such lives would be the people who were forced to endure them), narrated by a man who at forty-two has only achieved the rank of titular counsellor, equivalent to a staff captain in the army, but whose job mainly consists of sharpening pens and being humiliated by his superiors. It is surely the first story in the world which contains the line, an entry in a diary: "Furious with the section chief."

The story could be said to be the last word on the subject, just as it was the first; but the subject is irresistible, a sore patch on the modern achievement that needs constant dressing. An even better story of Gogol's, "The Overcoat", ends, or almost ends, with the death of his put-upon nobody: "And Petersburg was left without Akaky Akievich, as if he had never been there... protected by no one, dear to no one, interesting to no one, who had not even attracted the attention of a naturalist – who does not fail to stick a pin through a common fly and examine it under a microscope ..." The rebuke is to other writers, too – but even Gogol admits to, or rather feigns, the degree to which Akievich exists at the extreme periphery of his interest. (The fate of his possessions after death, "did not even interest the narrator of this story.")

Huysmans, too, addressed the problem, and although he did it some thirty years after Gogol he did so as well as anyone, even Gogol. You may find this surprising if all you know of him is *A Rebours*, the pioneering work of decadence which prefigured and inspired Wilde. But before that Huysmans had worked, meticulously, in the French civil service; and it must have been hell.

> In office life... they went out of their way to take simple things to bits and pieces; they took some legal administrative text whose meaning was clear and precise, and immediately, with the help of turbid and circular arguments, unprecedented precedents, and jurisprudential quibbles going back to the Messidors and Ventôses of Revolutionary times, they turned this text into a hopeless muddle, a contorted piece of literature grinning like an ape, which produced decisions that were the complete opposite of the ones that could have been anticipated.

JORIS-KARL HUYSMANS

With the Flow

Foreword by Simon Callow

Such was the daily professional life that Huysmans lived, keeping both his literary talents and friends hidden from his co-workers; one can only marvel at the discipline and self-control this must have involved. It was Flaubert who had said that in order to be truly radical, one must ape the manners of the bourgeoisie, and while this is indisputably correct, one wonders if he had such lengths as Huysmans went to in mind. But the extraordinary dream, which finds its apotheosis in Kafka, is memorably depicted in the person of Bougran, who, finding himself retired by the department to make way, he plausibly assumes, for a younger relative of someone important, salvages his existence by recreating his workplace at home and performing there exactly the same duties as he used to perform in the office.

With the Flow (*A Vau-L'Eau* in French) is, if anything, more remarkable. Here neither insanity nor death can save the humble Jean Folantin, who begins his story being served a piece of shit cheese (among other things, the story is a hymn of hate to indifferent Parisian cookery), and who ends it in a kind of numb acceptance of his misery. In this he is nobler than the Des Esseintes of *A Rebours*, whom Huysmans contrived to make rich in order to stave off his boredom; it should be stressed, too, that *With the Flow* is funny. Hardly anything happens but the pages grip with the tenacity of a thriller. You are watching a man gazing unblinkingly into the abyss. "To think all this is just a joke, a complete waste of time," sighs Folantin. This is unbeatable. You must read it, now. ☺

Nicholas Lezard

EASY SOUNDS:

FREE TEDDY PAIGE!

Teddy Paige is a lost rock'n'roll legend. Now he's serving
a life sentence for attacking a man with his sword.
Will Hodgkinson reports

In 1999, a huge bearded man wearing a green felt hat, a cape, pointed shoes that curled up at the toes and green tights walked into Sounds That Swing, a rockabilly record shop in Camden that is the first port of call for London's greaser community. Sounds That Swing is a cramped box of a shop, and with most of its limited space taken up by racks of country, rock'n'roll, rockabilly and R&B records there is only room for two or three customers at a time. So a bearded giant dressed as a medieval troubadour didn't take long to come to the attention of Brian Neville, the rockabilly enthusiast behind the counter at the time. After absently thumbing through a few records, this Robin Hood gone to seed asked Neville, in a deep, breathy tone, if he had a copy of a Sun Studios 45 with the catalogue number Sun 400.

It isn't often that people request a record by its catalogue reference. But Neville is a Sun records collector, and he recognised the number as belonging to "Cadillac Man", a 1966 release by Teddy Paige And The Jesters. It was the only record made by the band, which featured Jim Dickinson, later to become a famous producer, on vocals; Sun Studios owner Sam Phillips' son Jerry on bass, and Teddy Paige, who wrote Cadillac Man and its flipside "My Babe", on guitar. It's a much sought-after oddity; a slice of tradtional rock'n'roll made at a time when the style had been eclipsed by the psychedelic innovations of The Byrds and The

Beatles. "I've got a copy myself, but we don't have it in stock," said Neville. "It's very rare. Why do you want it?"

"Well you see," said the man, "I'm Teddy Paige."

Teddy Paige's musical story begins in sixties Memphis. Born Edward McDonald in Newcastle in 1943, Paige fell in love with rock'n'roll as a teenager, and his tastes never developed too far beyond it. By the he moved to Memphis in 1964, Paige was an avid collector of R&B, country and rock'n'roll 45s, and he had no interest in the emerging music of the sixties. This made Memphis a perfect new home: the town held onto its status as the birthplace of fifties rock'n'roll, with Elvis Presley, Carl Perkins and Jerry Lee Lewis coming out of its own Sun Studios, and it wasn't about to let changing times erase its significance. Paige found work in Sun Studios as a session guitarist, working regularly with the bands that recorded there. Typically the backing track would be recorded in one session and the vocals in another, so Paige did not get to meet many of the famous names whose records he played on. But he has vague memories of all the big Sun names: Elvis Presley, Carl Perkins, Jerry Lee Lewis.

Paige's guitar skills saw him rise to being one of Sun's top session men. He also produced a handful of the soul singers who recorded there, and went on the road with Charlie Rich, the rockabilly singer and songwriter who gave Jerry Lee Lewis many of his biggest hits. Paige's chief rival and best friend was the session guitarist Travis Wammack, who matched Paige in virtuosity and the intensity of his musicianship. Paige was there when The James Brown Band, who had just had an argument with their leader and walked out on him, came to Memphis in 1970 to

record "Maceo And All The King's Men", which has since become a soul classic. "Oh man, those guys could play," remembered Paige shortly before ending up in jail. He clearly had no idea that anyone had heard of them; to him they were just fellow backing musicians he did a session with. "I met Bo Diddley too, and I learnt a lot from the way he would tune his guitar." Paige also played a concert with ? And The Mysterians, the teenage Latinos who had a hit with 1966 with the garage classic "96 Tears". "Yeah, they were pretty wild. But I didn't like psychedelic music," said Paige, sticking his fingers in ears.

By the turn of the decade Paige was producing blues records for Sun and later working in A&R for its new boss, the country music-loving Shelby Singleton. He worked closely with Leland Rogers, brother of Kenny Rogers, who signed the Texan psychedelic pioneers The 13th Floor Elevators to his Houston label International Artists. Life was good until one day in 1972. Nobody is

quite sure what happened, least of all Paige himself, but the gist of it is that he and Sam Phillips had an argument and Paige stormed out, never to return. His only subsequent comment on the subject was: "There's a lot of strange folks in Memphis." When box sets of classic Sun recordings were released in the mid-80s, the liner notes for the 60s box stated that Paige had been one of the 911 victims of the mass suicide undertaken by The People's Temple under the leadership of Jim Jones in Jonestown, Guyana in 1978. It was only when Sam Phillips came to London in 1999 that he discovered Paige to be alive, well, and dressed like a medieval troubadour.

From the day he left Memphis in 1972 to the months leading up to his trial in 2003, Teddy Paige actually emulated the life of a medieval troubadour. He developed a belief that his true calling lay in following the ways of the itinerant musicians who performed across Europe at the time of the Renaissance, and he gave up being a session musician to take up a gypsy meander throughout the continent, living with no fixed address and scraping enough money for food and shelter through busking. He made his green jester's outfits himself, and in keeping with his status as a hearty man in tune with the spirit of times long-past, tried to stick to a steak-only diet. "I've been feeling real good since I cut out fruit, vegetables, and all those other bad things that sap your energy," he said in 2000. "Breakfast, lunch and dinner, it's only steaks for me from now on."

Paige performed in castles in Spain and slept under the stars in Italy and France. He never married or had children and remained uncontactable, preferring to arrive in new places and see where his luck took him. His tastes were always steeped in American popular music of the fifties, but he also developed an interest in medieval chamber music. In the mid-nineties he settled in Nottingham and bought a four-track home-recording system, on which he laid down some medieval lute tunes augmented by rockabilly-style echo effects. At the end of the nineties he came down to London, staying in hostels in the West End, busking, and making the occasional semi-professional performance.

At some point on his travels he acquired a three-foot sword, a necessary attention to period detail that was inevitably lost on the authorities: life on the road can be dangerous, and a medieval troubadour does at times have a need to defend himself from churls, varlets and buggery knaves who might rob him of his lute and gold pieces. In 1993 Paige was arrested after he hit a man on the head with a sword, and in 1998, having recently arrived in London, he was walking down Denmark Street when two policemen stopped him for brandishing a dangerous weapon. Feeling the need to defend his property, he didn't hand over the sword without a fight, and ended up spending that night in a police cell, swordless.

"I've been feeling real good since I cut out fruit, vegetables, and all those other bad things that sap your energy," he said in 2000

"He had even gone over to the pub across the road, which is on an estate and is really rough, and done a few songs in there. They all loved it."

In 2000, Sounds That Swing's Brian Neville told Liam Watson, the producer, engineer and co-founder of Toe-Rag studios in Hackney, East London, about his encounter with Paige. Toe-Rag is an eight-track studio made up of vintage equipment from the fifties and sixties; The White Stripes famously recorded their number one album Elephant there in 2002. Watson first met Paige at Come Down And Meet The Folks, a regular Sunday afternoon country, rockabilly and soul session held in a pub in Camden. Paige had already performed there under the name Edward The Troubadour. "I met this guy, who was huge, and in full Robin Hood gear," remembers Watson. "He talked about what he had done in Memphis, and what he was doing now, and he was a very nice man. Eccentric, but relaxed and not at all violent."

Watson invited Paige to have a jam at the studio one evening, with Neville on drums and a friend on bass to flesh out the sound. "I told everyone to come at six. When I arrived at five to set up, Teddy Paige was already there, wearing his curling shoes, cape and little felt hat. Next door to the studio is a bookbinders', and they told me that he had been there since ten in the morning, entertaining everyone with his songs and stories. He had even gone over to the pub across the road, which is on an estate and is really rough, and done a few songs in there. They all loved it."

It occurred to Watson that this returning, long-lost legend was in need of a record contract, especially as the songs that Paige presented at Toe-Rag were pretty good. There was "London Cherry", a polite but swinging rockabilly ode to a peach of a girl from the capital; "Moon Over Mankora", a haunting ballad that Paige sings in the style of a nightclub crooner; an unnamed R&B instrumental and a new version of Paige's classic Sun Studios release "Cadillac Man". Watson got Paige back in the studio to record the tracks under the name Teddy Paige And His New Jesters. "London Cherry" and "Moon Over Mankora" were put out on The Sympathetic Sounds Of Toe-Rag, a compilation of recent Toe-Rag recordings released in 2002 on the Detroit label Sympathy For The Record Industry. Watson played the songs to the London duo The Kills and they loved them. They talked about Teddy Paige to Laurence Bell, the owner of Domino Records, and Bell was keen to meet the troubadour with a view to giving the songs a proper release. The New York-based rock'n'roll label Norton also wanted to bring the portly jester's music to a new generation.

Soon after the recording session, however, Paige disappeared. Contact with him had so far been made through his mobile phone; now its callers received a recorded message of traffic noises. Alan Tyler, who co-runs Come Down And Meet The Folks, had made friends with Paige and had seen him a few months previously, when he had just been thrown out of his hostel. He had since moved to Hastings, and there were vague reports of the residents of Paige's extremely rough estate not being open-minded enough to accept his need to don medieval outfits and brandish a three-foot sword, or to heed his demands to be addressed as Count McDonald.

A clearer picture of what had been going on down there emerged earlier this year. After months of trying to make contact with Paige, we discovered that he had

been arrested. His neighbour, Thomas Blackman, had persistently ignored requests from Paige to turn down his music, and Paige said at his trial that listening to it through his walls "felt like a Chinese water torture". Eventually it proved too much to bear. Paige is reputed to have attacked Blackman with his sword, cutting his flesh to the bone, although he denies the charge. He has variously said that he was asleep at the time of the attack, and that he was in a coma-like stupor due to the medication he had been taking.

On June 25, 2003 at Lewes County Court in Sussex, Edward McDonald was found guilty of wounding with intent. He was sentenced to life imprisonment. Judge Richard Hayward called him "a serious danger to the public". But this eccentric, talented man, who has such a deep understanding of music and its importance as a balm for the soul, is an artist and should be treated accordingly, rather than left in a jail at the mercy of hardened

criminals and prison wardens not always known for their sympathy towards the psychologically unwell. While accepting that Paige may well be too zealous a spirit to co-exist peacefully within polite society, we at the *Idler* feel that the blunt treatment meted out to him is unfair, and indicative of the lack of understanding British law accords to the mentally ill. We demand therefore that Teddy Paige is released from Lewes Jail, and that Cliff Richard is put in his place. ☻

STOP PRESS:
Teddy Paige has been moved to Ashen Hill, a maximum-security mental institution in West Sussex. The Idler is planning to put on a "Free Teddy Paige" benefit gig. If anyone is interested in helping us, please get in touch at theidlers@idler.co.uk. We're also planning Free Teddy Paige t-shirts, with profits going to the campaign.

EASY SOUNDS:

CHAS N DAVE

Mathew Clayton takes a trip down memory lane with
veteran rocker Chas Hodges

He has been sampled by Emimen, been on tour with Beatles, and played with Jerry Lee Lewis and Gene Vincent. But today, forty years into a career as a professional musician, Chas Hodges is best known as one half of Cockney boogie-woogie merchants Chas n Dave. During the eighties they had a string of hit with songs like "Gertcha", "Margate" and "Ain't No Pleasing You". In 2000 they stood in the London Mayor election, their manifesto promises included tax exemptions for bearded men, lager to be made illegal and more types of bitter to be available on tap. They spend the majority of their time on the road, last year notching up over 150 gigs.

MATHEW CLAYTON How did you first get involved in music?

CHAS HODGES My first professional engagement was with Billy Grey and the Stormers in 1960 at a Butlins Holiday Camp. Soon after that we changed our name to the Outlaws. Mike Berry had done a recording session with Joe Meek. Joe loved his voice but wasn't keen on the band. Mike knew us so he got us along with him instead. We went up there and Joe Meek loved the Outlaws and so we started recording with him. I was playing the electric bass then.

CLAYTON: Was that up in his studio in Holloway?

HODGES:: Yes. It was the first and second floor flat on the high road. He hadn't really converted it at all. He blocked off the windows and put a few little bits of soundproofing up. You just sat wherever there was space and recorded. I enjoyed it but Joe Meek was difficult. He could be really nice one minute and then fly off the handle the next. You never knew where you were with him. He was certainly a man of extremes. But we were really impressed with his recording, he knew how to get a good sound.

CLAYTON: And were you playing live also?

HODGES: Yes, we did play live. It was a bit sugary in the charts in the early sixties with lots of ballads going round which I wasn't mad on. But there were a lot of bands like us who still went around playing rock and roll because it was great to perform on stage. We toured everywhere. It was a good live period with people like Screaming Lord Sutch and Johnny Kidd and the Pirates. You took a minimum amount of gear, everyone crammed into the van, and away you went. And hopefully the van wouldn't break down before you got to the gig. The vans never had heaters and in the middle of winter there used to be ice on the inside of the windows. It was good fun but is was harder than touring today.

CLAYTON: Who did you rate live at that time?

HODGES: Well the

NOTHING LIKE A SING SONG ROUND THE OLD JOANNA

American rock and rollers were my heroes. I had seen Jerry Lee Lewis in 1958 and I was still mad on him and I was lucky enough to work with him a little bit later on.

CLAYTON: How did that come about?

HODGES: We heard he was coming over on tour, a double bill with Gene Vincent. There was an ad in one of the music papers.

One of the boys spotted it and we rang up. Don Arden (legendary promoter and father of Sharon Osbourne) was promoting it. And he came down to see us. We had applied for the job backing Gene Vincent. Don liked us and said in fact we had a choice of backing either Gene Vincent or Jerry Lee Lewis. There was no question at the time, me

being a Jerry Lee man. And that was what got me playing the piano as I was watching him for like a month or something. He was quite sensible in those days; he didn't hit the bottle like he did in his later years. And he used to show me a few things.

CLAYTON: Gene Vincent liked to hit the bottle also?

HODGES: When that tour finished we went back out

"Paul McCartney came into our dressing room and said he had a song that would suit us. And that was 'Got To Get You Into My Life'"

on the road with Gene for about six months. And that was a laugh, but poor Gene was a proper alcoholic. I had never experienced it in anyone before. Gene was one of those morose types, he would sit in his room all day with a bottle of whisky. I couldn't understand it. I remember saying to him, "Gene, you haven't been out of your room for two days. Why don't you come out and have something too eat?" But he would just stay there. It was sad.

CLAYTON: So how old were you then, in 1963?

HODGES: I was nineteen.

CLAYTON: What did you do after the Outlaws?

HODGES: In the mid-sixties I joined Cliff Bennett and the Rebel Rousers. We went on tour with the Beatles on their very last European tour. That was when Paul McCartney came into our dressing room and said he had a song that would suit us. And that was "Got To Get You Into My Life". We recorded that and it got to Number 5 or 6 in the charts.

CLAYTON: Where did you tour in Europe with them?

HODGES: In Germany.

CLAYTON: Did you play at the Star Club?

HODGES: Not that time but I had played there earlier with Jerry Lee. The Star Club had a great atmosphere. It was a converted cinema, with the seats took out. A perfect venue for a gig. In Hamburg they were more into the music that I

CHAS AND DAVE WEIRD FACTS

Emimem's hit "My Name Is" includes a sample from a Labi Siffre track "I Got The" featuring Chas and Dave on piano and bass.

In 1996 Tori Amos released two singles that featured Chas and Dave songs on the b-sides. On *Talula*, she covered "London Girls" and on *Caught A Lite Sneeze* she covered "That's What I Like

Mick (The Sandwich Song)".

The Outlaws were Joe Meek's house band. Chas played on hits like John Leyton's "Johnny Remember Me" and Heinz's "Just Like Eddie".

There is a Chas and Dave tribute band called Daz n Chave.

liked – Little Richard, Fats Domino and Ray Charles. I went over there just after the Beatles had left.

CLAYTON: So what was the Beatles tour like? Were they at the height of their fame?

HODGES: It was great but every time they went on stage it was just continual screaming from the girls from start to finish. Which sounds nice but it ain't if you are playing music. It was just like switching on a scream machine. They could have been playing anything.

CLAYTON: And rock and roll music is what you have always been into?

HODGES: Yeah, that is my roots. If you take away the lyrics, Chas n Dave's music is rock and roll. When me and Dave got together that was we wanted to do. Keep the rock and roll but write about the things we knew about and sing in our own accents.

CLAYTON: When did you realise Chas n Dave were going to be a success, was it when "Gertcha" took off or before that?

HODGES: We felt it would work anyway, and that it was just a matter of time for people to hear it. We played here, there, and everywhere to earn enough to pay the rent. And we would sing one or

two of our numbers in between rock'n'roll covers. But then people would come up and ask us about the songs we had written.

CLAYTON: And then "Gertcha" was used in a Courage ad?

HODGES: That gave us a lift. Someone came to see us in a big pub in the East End, the Oxford Arms, where we had gathered a following. They said, "we are thinking about using 'Gertcha' in an ad. Would you mind?" And we said, "No – go ahead". But you know how these things are, people come up all the time and offer you millions of pounds and you go all right. And you never see them again. But this one came through.

CLAYTON: Did you start your own record label as well?

HODGES: EMI had made us an offer but then we got a letter saying they had changed their policy and the terms they were now offering were far worse. So we turned it down. Our manager Bob England said, "I have got some money because I have been getting some big hits with Darts. What if we started our own record company?" So that's what we did, Rockney Records. And all out hits were on that which was great.

CLAYTON: That is brilliant to have done it all yourself?

HODGES: Yes, and because of that we have retained the copyright in all our stuff right to this day. At the time we was thinking, blimey, we have been turned down by all these people but it turned out to be a blessing in disguise.

CLAYTON: And what was the story behind my personal favorite "Ain't No Pleasing You"?

HODGES: We have always believed in the old fashioned way of finding whether a song is going to be successful - by playing to people. You get record companies sitting round desks discussing this and that. The best to find out is to just go out and play it. Our record plugger heard it just after we recorded it and he said, "it's a lovely song, boys, but it ain't a hit'" and we said, "look we have been playing round the halls and people have been coming up and saying, 'what was that song you did, 'Oh Darlin'", and where can we get it?" In the end we did it on a TV show and they got so many phone calls that our manager said we got to put it out. It went straight up the charts to number 2. It was our biggest hit. ◑

EASY SOUNDS:
IN GOD WE TRUST

Sarah Janes meets a pair of rather unusual Christian
rockers from Brighton

I am standing in the lobby of the YMCA on North Road, Brighton, waiting to meet Ashley Fortnam, one half of Christian "rock" outfit, In God We Trust. The receptionist buzzes up to his room and says, "Ashley, are you there?" She adopts that patronising tone reserved for children, old folk and morons. Tumble-driers hum in the laundry room, a top-heavy man with thick NHS glasses, too frequently blinking eyes and a fixed grin, rattles an ice-cube tray full of medication as he shuffles past me.

Ashley finally answers his intercom and I am ushered into the lift and directed to the third floor where I am greeted by the man himself. He's a great ginger Hell's Angel, a hairy hulk of a man, tattooed from knuckle to kneecap. He shifts his weight nervously from one foot to the other. The numerous button badges on his denim jacket twinkle in the anaesthetic light. I shake his hand and follow him into his room.

Gary Jennings, the other half of In God We Trust, is sitting on Ashley's single bed. He is similarly huge and kind of edgy, but looks a little less rock and roll in a zip-up fleece and jeans. Gary does most of the talking and breathes very heavily and sighs a lot.

Ashley and Gary have a history of serious drug abuse and have both been homeless at one time or another. However, after finding, or as they put it, "being found" by Christ, they both landed themselves jobs in a factory and six months later formed the band after discussing their mutual faith over the production line. They've now just finished recording their second album at a Brighton studio.

In God We Trust have an unusual sound, rather dark and tragic. Their lyrics are mainly pulled from the Bible, but much also comes from their own experience. Ashley sings and plays the bass. He delivers the vocals in a melancholy, droney style. Gary accompanies on the keyboard and seems to

There are posters of Motorhead's Lemmy, the Red Hot Chili Peppers, pictures of friends and family, hardcore porn... hang on a minute!

be restricted to two mewing notes, though you wouldn't guess that from the look of intense concentration on his face. Ashley's brother Craig helped out with guitar and drums on the album, but when it's just the two of them they play to a funny little drum machine which keeps a sweetly pitiful rhythm.

"...your pain is over brother, your suffering is over, your hell madness is over..."

I asked them how they thought their involvement in the drug culture influenced their faith. Gary says there's no denying that the addictive personality has a lot to do with it. In 2000 he found himself in a Calvinist church in Manchester and there he had a life-altering religious experience that forced him to turn his back on the drug scene forever. Ashley began attending Bible study classes in Brighton at about the same time.

The support they received from their respective groups enabled them to set about directing their lives in a more constructive way, but there's no doubt about the extent to which their old drug habits have impacted them. I wonder how consciously they entered into Christianity. They spout Bible class phrases with real conviction but there is still something empty about it.

I look around Ashley's room. There are posters of Motorhead's Lemmy, The Red Hot Chilli Peppers, In God We Trust lyrics, pictures of friends and family, drawings, a cardboard skeleton, hardcore porn, hang on a minute... is that hardcore Christian porn, Ashley? "Hmm, I don't know why I put them up there," says Ashley. "Hmm, it's a difficult one," says Gary. "It's very hard for a man to live without a woman. I'll probably take them down sometime,"

GARY AND ASHLEY: GOD GAVE ROCK'N'ROLL TO THEM

says Ashley. "I mean, I'm celibate, so... hmm." Gary interjects: "yeah, I used to have a lot of stuff like that, but I've been a Christian for some years now and it's gradually coming out of my life. I can see why Ashley does it but I don't think it's a good idea... really." Gary sighs loudly. Ashley looks thoughtful. "I mean, I suppose when you're married, sex must be really good. But sex without love is rubbish isn't it?" He looks at Gary, Gary nods, they both look a bit sad. Gary sighs again. We talk for a while longer but nothing after that tells me half as much about them.

"...never mind The Joy of Sex, Jesus Christ is by far the best..."

I bid them farewell. We shake hands again. Before I'm out of the room they both turn to each other and say, "she was really nice."

A while later Ashley leaves nine messages on my answerphone. He asks me if I would like to go out for a drink. I say I don't think it would really be a good idea, but I would like to be their manager.

Their first gig takes place in a small venue in Hove, supporting well-respected Brighton band, The Love Gods. They're second on the bill and get an excellent response. We sell 15 copies of the album and receive numerous t-shirt orders. Several people have phoned me up since to tell me that the album is the same song repeated twelve times but there are subtle differences, I assure you. ◉

In God We Trust will be gigging regularly in Brighton. If you would like more information about them, CDs or t-shirts you can email ingodwetrust@jesusanswers.com.

COLIN BLUNSTONE

Andrew Copeman **meets the** former Zombie

We needn't mention the standout British Beat Groups of the Sixties; there are re-mastered box-sets, weighty historic tomes and reunion tours too numerous to mention. Instead, let us turn our attention to a group of refined, studious chaps who created, quite simply, the greatest pop music of the era.

The Zombies were a complete anomaly, five school boys from St. Albans who looked like a bunch of librarians. Beneath the innocuous façade however, lurked a sophistication that took in Modern Jazz, screaming R&B, Imagist poetry and created a sound that was sinister and quintessentially (Southern) English. If Samuel Beckett wrote a sit-com it would be *Steptoe and Son*, if Harold Pinter formed a band it would be The Zombies. Classics like, "She's Not There", the Zombs' only bona fide UK hit and the three million selling, "Time of the Season" (a US #1) have a fragility and menace unheard of in British pop music before or since. Although completely different in sound and set-up, only Birmingham's, Broadcast come close to tapping the other-worldly noise that the Zombies so successfully channelled.

If The Zombies were just another obscure little sixties beat combo, better than most, they'd just deserve cult status; the fact that they contained two musical geniuses means they demand reverence.

Rod Argent on keyboards, composer of, "She's Not There", "Time of the Season" and with Blunstone, "God Gave Rock'n'Roll To You" (the original!) set the template for viciously intelligent and funky key-work. A fan of Bach, Bartok and Miles Davis, his brooding and groovy runs and solos influenced every sixties American garage-band with a Vox Continental or Farfisa organ. Listen to, "Just out of Reach" and then anything by LA's The Seeds and you'll hear Argent. Plus, there's more than a touch in Ray Manzarek's playing. Most of *The Doors* sounds like Zombies outtakes.

But then there's the singer.

Colin Blunstone, the most distinctive voice in British pop. Breathy, unnerving, soulful, ecstatic and desolate, Blunstone can sound like a demonic choirboy or an abandoned lover, usually in the space of a few bars. He (still!) possesses an R&B scream which tops Steve Marriot

and an emotional range that makes Scott Walker sound like a student busker outside Covent Garden tube. Ask J. Mascis, Beachwood Sparks, Tom Petty and Badly Drawn Boy about the best voice in the business and Colin's will be at the top of the list. His ethereal, English Gothic Romantic influence is all over everything Nick Drake recorded and Julian Cope owes more than a slight debt to the great man. Blunstone's solo albums like, *One Year* and *Ennismore*, still piss all over most contemporary English pop from a K2 height. So, it was with some trepidation that I called a living legend a few days before his June 7th 2003 gig at the Bloomsbury Theatre.

ANDREW COPEMAN: How did The Zombies get together?
COLIN BLUNSTONE: Well, basically The Zombies were a school band, although we did go to two different schools in St. Albans in Hertfordshire. Rod Argent was at St. Albans school with Paul

Atkinson and he had the idea of putting a band together. I went to St. Albans Grammar school and Paul Arnold sat next to me. Hugh Grundy, our drummer, was playing side drum in the school Cadet Corps, that's how he got the gig.

COPEMAN: What sort of age were you? Fourteen, fifteen, sixteen?

BLUNSTONE: Fifteen. Our first rehearsal was put together by Rod Argent's cousin, Jim Rodford, who's now playing in our band (Blunstone&Argent) when we go out and tour. He's the bass player. He's played for about eighteen years with The Kinks and many other big name bands

COPEMAN: Why The Zombies? it's a very clever name. It sounds almost like an American garage-band, with the Horror B-Movie allusions. More important though, are the contradictions that the name throws up; the somnambulant undead and a bunch of nice middle class boys from St. Albans.

BLUNSTONE: Well, to be absolutely honest, we were desperate for a name that no one else had. Our first name was The Mustangs but after a week we realised there were many bands called that.

COPEMAN: This ties in with a question about other bands at the time. The Beatles, certainly in their early days, were marketed as cheeky northern lads, The Troggs and The Animals were marketed as dangerous louts. The Zombies were very different, weren't they?

BLUNSTONE: When The Zombies went for their first meeting at Decca Records and we were introduced to the press department, I can't remember the details of it all, but somehow they picked up this angle that we'd got quite a lot of O-Levels...

COPEMAN: (Laughs)

BLUNSTONE: And, you know, looking back on it, it's a strange thing to say about a band. There were many other bands that had better qualifications than us and I think it did us more harm than good in the long-run. It was just an act of desperation on the record company's part.

COPEMAN: There's a great photograph of, I think it's Rod Argent and Hugh Grundy, at a chess board. So, you see what I mean? The idea of being sold as clean-cut, "nice", southern suburban, faintly bourgeois boys.

BLUNSTONE: Well, we were southern. I'll give you that. (Laughs). I'm not sure about the rest! (Laughs). I mean, I never saw anyone playing chess, except in that photograph.

COPEMAN: There is a classic, southern English feel to The Zombies, though. I pick up on a real sinister aspect too. "She's Not There" is terribly uneasy, there's something which isn't quite right but the listener can't locate what. It's got that killer bass-line, which is very doomy and your vocals which are quite spectral in places. There's a really edgy feeling.

BLUNSTONE: I think it's a wonderful song, a timeless song. That record has got a great atmosphere. It's always easy, looking back, but with the benefit of hindsight I wished we'd have tried to capture a bit

"When we play a US town all the young bands will be in the first few rows because they've been influenced by the Zombies"

of that atmosphere in our immediate follow-up records.

COPEMAN: It stood out at the time (1964) because there was a keyboard solo instead of a guitar solo.

BLUNSTONE: Absolutely. Of course, it was written by Rod (Argent). Then and pretty much now, when he writes a song, a lot of the arrangement is also his. Originally, Rod wanted the solo to be twice as long. The producer, Ken Jones, insisted that the solo be halved.

COPEMAN: The album: *Odessey* (sic) *And Oracle* was The Zombie's masterpiece. Rod Argent's playing and your vocals are incredible.

BLUNSTONE: It's funny, I think in some ways we were lucky enough to anticipate a musical movement, if you like. That album was recorded a year or so before it became really successful, so we were just a bit ahead of the game. This was the first, and of course last, album that The Zombies produced themselves.

COPEMAN: Were you aware that the band was influencing other groups?

BLUNSTONE: No. I don't think we were at the time but we are now, especially when we (Blunstone&Argent) go to America. Firstly, people tell us that we influenced them and secondly, when we go to a town all the young bands will be in the first few rows watching very closely what we do because they've been influenced by The Zombies. I'm sure there were many bands who were influenced by Rod. You can love us or hate us but I think we were unique.

COPEMAN: We've mentioned the record label's attitude to you. At the time of recording, *Odessey and Oracle* what

was the relationship like?

BLUNSTONE: We'd changed labels. We managed to get a one album deal with CBS. I don't think they were terribly committed to the project. They gave us, even in those days, a very small budget; £1,000, to record an album. We were lucky enough to get into Abbey Road and I think we were the first non-EMI act to record there. We worked with two producers who'd come straight from working on *Sergeant Pepper*, so we were very fortunate. We had to record very, very quickly and so there's certainly a spontaneous feel to *Odessey and Oracle* and some of that's due to the

"There's certainly a spontaneous feel to *Odessey and Oracle* and some of that's due to the fact that we didn't have any budget to record"

fact that we didn't have any budget to record.

COPEMAN: Why do you think The Zombies are still so powerful? Why do you think that sound still exerts an influence?

BLUNSTONE: It's always very difficult to judge your own work but one of the things I think that interests young bands is that we had two very good, prolific writers in the band who wrote lots of very good songs. That certainly interests people. We were also part of the "British Invasion", which was a very important time for American music because I don't think it'd ever happened before that another country had dominated their charts. I think there's a lot of interest in all the bands that were part of that... let me ask you a question...

COPEMAN: Yes?

BLUNSTONE: If The Zombies ever got back together again, do you think it would spoil how people perceive the band now? Would it de-mystify the myth? (Chuckles).

COPEMAN: Of course it would. It would de-mystify the myth but then if it meant there'd be forty-five minutes to an hour of genius music being created on stage by geezers pushing their middle ages, I'm all for it. I say; bring on the Vox Continental! I'd be straight down the front!

BLUNSTONE: (Laughs). I was just curious...Yeah... (Laughs).

COPEMAN: I'd be screaming up at the stage; "Sticks and Stones!"

BLUNSTONE: (Laughs) Actually, maybe we should re-examine the early songs. The song you just mentioned, "Sticks and Stones"... there's some good old songs on *Begin Here...*, the first album, and I've sometimes wondered whether we [Blunstone&Argent] shouldn't play some of them.

COPEMAN: Too right. "Kind of Girl"...

BLUNSTONE: Oh yes...

COPEMAN: Fantastic (laughs)

BLUNSTONE: (laughs)

COPEMAN: So, I know you're working on a solo album at the moment with Rod Argent. What are the other members of the band doing? Do you keep in touch?

BLUNSTONE: Absolutely, yeah. Paul Atkinson's (guitar) in California and he's been working for record companies out there for twenty years. He's signed a lot of big acts in his time. He managed to sign ABBA for CBS UK. Hugh Grundy still plays drums and until recently had a pub up in the Midlands. Chris White, our bass player, still writes and produces and is very active in the music business. So, everyone's still playing basically.

COPEMAN: When's your new solo album out?

BLUNSTONE: The one that I'm recording with Rod, I think will be released in the first week of September. No title as yet.

COPEMAN: What label's it on?

BLUNSTONE: It's on, Red House, our own label. We're not signed to a record company; we go straight through a distributor.

COPEMAN: You're also doing a gig at the Bloomsbury Theatre.

BLUNSTONE: Really looking forward to that. We're working a bit more through June, July's off and then we're going to America in August to try and create a bit of interest.

COPEMAN: Colin, it's been a veritable honour for me to speak to The Zombies' mouthpiece.

BLUNSTONE: Thank you.

A BRIEF BLUNSTONE DISCOGRAPHY:

1.) SHE'S NOT THERE: A stone cold classic. Approximately three minutes of brooding, jazzy menace. Chris White's bass-line is beamed direct from *The Twilight Zone*, Colin Blunstone sings like a fallen angel and Rod Argent sets the standard that all other pop/rock keyboardists must match. Never has an electric piano sounded so threatening.

2.) BEECHWOOD PARK: Acid-tinged lament. Blunstone nails the pain and loss with, arguably, one of the best vocal performances of his career: "And we would count the evening stars/As the day grew dark in Beechwood Park."

3.) I DON'T BELIEVE IN MIRACLES: Stand out cut from Blunstone's second solo album, *Ennismore* (1972). Plangent and soulful but too erudite and emotionally raw to be laid back maaan. Beautiful, uneasy listening.

4.) STICKS AND STONES: This proves that The Zombies could stomp effortlessly on any garage-punk R&B band of

the mid-sixties. If this tune had been cut by a bunch of Texas gonzoids, it'd be on every *Nuggets* and, *Pebbles* comp. A real screamer: check Blunstone's wail before Argent gets all smashed/blocked on his Vox Continental organ. Outta sight.

5.) TIME OF THE SEASON: "She's Not There"'s dark psych twin. Chris White's bass is telegraphed from The Outer Limits, Hugh Grundy's drums rasp and snap, there are hand claps with reverb, clipped "Ah's" and Rod Argent's Hammond fairly reeks of sulphur. Only Colin Blunstone could sing so sweetly whilst investing lines like: "It's the time of the season/When love runs high", with the irony and malevolence they deserve. "What's your name? Who's your daddy?/Is he rich like me?" Knocks "Riders On the Storm" into a cocked hat.

Pleased to meet you. ☻

FILM:

O LUCKY MAN!

Lindsay Anderson's savage fable was released thirty years ago. They don't make films like that now and they didn't make films like that, then, says Paul Hamilton

When is a smile a genuine reflection of how one feels? That salesman on your doorstep – why is he smiling? That crap joke somebody's just blown off at you – why are you smiling? Smiles are masks. Smiles spell trouble. "Smile while your heart is aching", instructs the Charlie Chaplin song "Smile". *Smile* is the name of the doomed Beach Boys album that broke Brian Wilson physically and mentally.

Smiles bookend 1973's *O Lucky Man!*, the central segment of a triptych of films by director Lindsay Anderson, writer David Sherwin and actor Malcolm McDowell, the other pieces being *If....* in 1968 and *Britannia Hospital* (1982). The Anderson /Sherwin/McDowell trilogy is a caustic satire on British society, where its prejudices, value systems and moralities are held to the light and squeezed till the underlying venom bursts out. They venture beyond the acceptable

borders of film naturalism and plunge deep into the realm of super-realism, not by depicting real things but, rather, things as they really are.

Britain is symbolised in *If...* and *Britannia Hospital* as, respectively, a public school and a hospital under siege, but *O Lucky Man!* takes the triptych's protagonist, the McDowell character Mick Travis, out of the institutions and on the road into the world of work.

O Lucky Man! begins with Mick Travis, a trainee at the Imperial Coffee manufacturing plant, being handed the job as salesman for the North-West of England. He is given the mission purely on the basis of his beaming smile ("That is a completely sincere smile"). He drives to Yorkshire and meets an enigmatic old man who gives him a gold suit and advises him, "Try not to die like a dog". Driving to Northumberland, he gets lost and is arrested by soldiers who

suspect him of spying on their weapons base. He escapes his torturers and finds the Miller Research Clinic where he is offered £100 to volunteer for "medical research". Discovering a patient who has had his head grafted on to a large pig, Travis makes a break for it and cadges a lift to London in a van carrying Alan Price, his band, and poor little rich girl Patricia Burgess, by whom Travis is besotted. Learning that her father, Sir James, is a multimillionaire, Travis contrives to make his acquaintance. Sir James hires Travis as his personal assistant. Travis escorts him to a meeting with Dr Munda, President of the African state of Zingara, where a deal is made to export napalm. Travis makes the necessary arrangements but is arrested for attempting to export bullion (he's been framed by Sir James) and sent to gaol for five years. Rehabilitated – he's spent

SMILE FOR THE CAMERA, MALCOLM

his time reading philosophy – Travis goes to London's East End where his pocket is promptly picked and he fails to dissuade a working-class housewife from killing herself. Penniless yet with his prison-born sense of altruism he assists a social worker doling out soup and bread to a gang of meths-drinking tramps. They take offence at his charity and attack him. Homeless, beaten and hungry, Travis wanders the London streets. In Leicester Square, a desultory sandwich man ("WANT TO BE A STAR?") wearing Mick's old gold suit gives Travis a leaflet:

"Try your luck". Travis arrives at the audition hall full of hopeful wannabes, is picked out by the film director (Lindsay Anderson) who tells him to, firstly, hold a pile of books and then to pose with a Bren gun, (a reference to the film poster for *If...*) He then asks Travis to smile. He can't; he can no longer perform the action that set him on this journey. The director asks again and again. Each time Travis refuses, until the director whacks him soundly across the head with his film script. Dazed, Travis stares into the camera and his mouth slowly makes a smile...

This précis of the plot fails to do the film's ambition and scope justice since it neglects to mention it's three hours long (but it's so jammed with incident time is forgotten), it utilises various film-making styles, it's a quasi-musical, a meditation on free will... What is apparent from the plot summary is the template employed for *O Lucky Man!*'s epic, poetic development is Voltaire's *Candide* and its seven steps to enlightenment. It is no coincidence that Travis is asked to smile by Lindsay Anderson six times before being bashed on the bonce. This scene

Travis is left empty by all the food, drink and sex

has been misinterpreted as pure megalomania on Anderson's part, instilling obedience in an actor by violent means like Barbara Woodhouse whipping dogs to submission. Critic Stanley Kauffman claimed, "It was the single most sickening, self-indulgent, ego-drooling moment I've seen on film". However, the scene is redolent of Zen Buddhist Tieh Shan's story of attempting to reach the state of *wu*, the Chinese for satori. Failing to attain *wu*, he grabbed the arm of his master, Meng Shan, and pleaded, "Tell me, tell me! What do I lack?" The master slapped Tieh Shan's face three times and said, "Oh, Tieh Shan, it has taken you several years to get here." Tieh Shan arrives at a state of enlightenment at that moment.

Anderson, in his preface to the published script, wrote, "Of course, people must make their their own judgements... and their own interpretations. Personally I can only say that [Travis] seems to me to arrive, after his journeying through a world of illusion, at some kind of acceptance of reality. But acceptance is not conformism."

Unlike most film sequels, one need not have seen *If...* to appreciate, comprehend and enjoy *O Lucky Man!* There are radical differences in Travis' character. He was left at the climax of the first instalment atop a college building machine-gunning away at teachers, soldiers, pupils and their parents in full-on bug-eyed smash-the-system fervour. Logically, he would be behind bars for mass murder, or running a British wing of the Baader Meinhoff Gang, yet five years on and he is the eager-to-please, forelock-tugging, optimistic new recruit at a coffee factory. What wrought this volte-face? What snuffed his revolutionary fire? Travis' teenage attitude was defined by his plaintive, exasperated sigh as the first schoolbell rings in the new term: "When do we live? That's what I want to know." *O Lucky Man!* finds Travis reformed/re-formed as the antithesis of his adolescent self, just like Shakespeare's Prince Hal at his coronation ("Presume not that I am the thing I was. For God doth know and the world shall perceive that I have turned away my former self..."). The adult Travis is a bit of a shit, which displaces our pre-programmed sympathies; for the archetypal screen hero is invariably the renegade, the outsider who refuses to toe the line. Travis lacks heroic qualities. He is a shameless mercenary, presaging the yuppie of the eighties and the geezer of the noughties, and we want him to get his comeuppance. Despite that, we care for him, partly because we recognise in his struggle through life something of our own (he's the aspect of ourselves we won't readily accept or admit to), but principally through Malcolm McDowell's spellbindingly brilliant performance.

Other than sly allusions ("Was your headmaster correct to expel you from school?") there is no explicit comment on how the Travis of *If...* transformed into the Travis of *O Lucky Man!*. Sherwin, Anderson and McDowell leave it to the viewer to join up the dots and fill in the blanks, and that is good. How fascinating would Francis Bacon's triptych "Three Figures At The Base Of A Crucifixion" be if each panel's inherent mystery were explained away?

O Lucky Man! exposes the inhumanity of capitalism. Coffee is the metaphor for capitalist expansionism and colonisation of the Third World. Food and drink provide sexual, political and philosophical connotations throughout Travis' travels. Mick and his trainer at the coffee plant, Gloria Rowe, have a coffee-tasting session ("Mm. Sturdy. Plebeian.

Plenty of body. A vigorous Robusta?") where she dribbles her drink into his mouth like a bird feeding its young. The Imperial Coffee chairman presents Travis with an apple for his journey. He is bribed with booze and is forewarned of a randy hotel proprietess' "treacle tart". Mick, at the point of collapse, is prevented from making a grab at a church's harvest festival display by the vicar's wife ("That's God's food!") who then breastfeeds him. At a private club two white women and a black man engage in a sex act called Chocolate Sandwich. Unforgettably, the term used for the napalm required to massacre Zingaran insurrectionists is Honey.

Travis is left empty by all the drink, food and sex. Like a good Western consumer, his gluttony only fuels his appetites for more of everything. His avarice has made him deaf and blind to human suffering. Drinking champagne with Travis on a London rooftop overlooking the "glass palaces" of multinational

businesses, Patricia describes the cut-throat machinations of her tycoon father: "For every five million pounds he invests, he makes fifty million pounds profit. In Bolivia he drove half a million peasants off their land. They starved to death."

Travis sips some champagne and can only gasp in rapture, "Fifty million pounds profit!"

Sir James Burgess is chillingly played by Ralph Richardson and the model for this ruthless character was the then chairman of EMI, Sir Joseph Lockwood. McDowell and Sherwin met him in 1971 for an explanation of the mysteries of big business. Sherwin in his turbulent, compulsive autobiography *Going Mad In Hollywood* recounts The Great Man's philosophies:

"If you've had failure you'll go on being a failure. If you've had success, you'll go on having success. Unless you go gaga. First thing a successful man in business has got to do is

It feels like a net curtain has been miraculously lifted from your eyes

get rid of non-essentials. Never make wrong decisions. Good health. Sleep well. You should like to make money but not to spend it, unless it's going to make more money. No round-the-world trips with the wife. It's not a question of morals – not morals – it's waste. Once you allow waste it goes right down the company. You end up ruined, be you the United States or a fish and chip shop at the Battersea funfair."

Ralph Richardson was renowned for being absolutely bats. Terry Gilliam contracted him to play God in *Time Bandits*, and had "several meetings at his house where we'd go through every line [...] and he'd say, with absolute assurance, 'God wouldn't say that.'" Richardson in *O Lucky Man!* meets his

match in the oddball stakes with the blinkered boneheaded philosophy of Sir Joseph Lockwood.

Richardson makes an earlier appearance as another tempter, Monty the mysterious tailor, who presents Travis with a gold suit. Is he Lucifer, tempting mortals from a goodly path with material goods? Anderson and Sherwin's decision to use actors in multiple roles lend an air of Brechtian theatricality and surrealism – is this all but a dream of Travis'? – to the film. *O Lucky Man!*'s artifice is heightened by the casting of many well-known faces from TV: Captain Mainwaring, Alf Garnett's missus, Reggie Perrin's brother-in-law Jimmy, Terry Collier, Compo and so on. *O Lucky Man!*'s special genius is in the development of casting familiar faces as outright clichéd characters – its landscape runs rife with corrupt politician, sadistic policemen, mad scientists, braying housewives – and exaggerating them to such an extreme that they appear unfamiliar, fresh, akin to the sensation

experienced on acid where it feels like a net curtain that until then was permanently before your eyes has miraculously lifted. What Anderson and Sherwin have achieved is the elimination of the anaesthetic of sentimentality, exposing our world in all its absurdity.

Arthur Lowe played the African dictator Dr Munda in blackface, alongside actual black actors, but he didn't resort to crass "How-de-do-dere-mon" racial stereotyping. He played it absolutely straight and, because one instantly recognises Lowe through the make-up, the point is established that Munda, though black on the outside, is as white as Sir James Burgess on the inside.

Of course, if *O Lucky Man!* spent its entire 177 minutes ranting about the iniquities of the class system and the abuse of privilege, it would have a narrow appeal, stuck on the shelf with nine-hour Russian films of the Thirties extolling the virtues of one-legged tractor drivers, and brought out and dusted down for a preaching-to-the-converted showing at a *Marxism Today* conference. Will Self defined Bad Satire as "bigotry, as it comforts one group by excluding the other", and Anderson incurred the ire of the Left with his portraits of the working class in the final reels of *O Lucky Man!*

Socialism as a mass popular ideal had been worn threadbare by the betrayal and abandonment of it by Harold Wilson's Labour governments of 1964 to 1970, and Edward Heath's Tory government couldn't control the escalating state of crisis. Revolutionary socialists put their store into the romantic hope of the working class stirring itself into taking control of the means of production. Anderson's depiction of the lowest rungs of the class ladder held no such aspirations. (Anderson was misanthropic: when McDowell asked him what he wanted as an epitaph on his gravestone, Anderson replied, "surrounded by fucking idiots"). Provocatively, he

shows them as mean, petty-minded, slothful and greedy as those occupying the top rungs. Instead of Marxist firebrands in London's East End, Travis meets only stupid, suspicious, politically docile factory fodder. (The only person with a spark of ingenuity is the cutpurse who picks Travis' pocket at a religious meeting.) Like Sir James Burgess and his ilk, money is the number one obsession: Mrs Richards, a drudge, recounts her miserable weekly shopping list to Travis before killing herself as if she was dictating her suicide note. Art and high culture have no place in this world. His quoting Shakespeare and Robert Browning from his poetry anthology fail to dissuade her determination to self-murder. Travis as a last resort even quotes the corny greetings card platitude "Every cloud has a silver lining". Also not listening to Travis is the gang of down-and-outs. They ignore his calls for amity and unity ("Not charity. Not pity. But dignity. Respect! We must love one another. Love!")

and kick the crap out of him. Prior to this incident, Travis walks past a corrugated iron fence painted with the legend "REVOLUTION IS THE OPIUM OF THE INTELLECTUALS". The writing is on the wall.

Thirty years down the line from *O Lucky Man!*'s release, and who can now be counted as lucky? Richard Branson? (Why is he smiling all the time?) That tramp, prostrate outside Pret A Manger in Oxford Street, singing "Fly Me To The Moon" and the theme from *The Great Escape* down a plastic traffic cone – is he lucky? Have we emerged from three hard decades any the better?

If you've found the truth in this world you are a lucky man. Preachers, poets and scholars don't know it, and temples, statues and steeples won't show it. Takers, fakers and talkers won't tell you, and teachers and preachers will just buy and sell you. When no one can tempt you with heaven or hell you'll be a lucky man. And then you can afford to smile. 🍷

FILM:
KEN COLLEY

Jon Fortgang salutes the great bit part actor

The name may be unfamiliar but chances are you've seen Ken Colley's face - gaunt, haunted, witness to terrible things – in more movies than you realise. You may even have heard him speak. As Admiral Piett in *The Return of the Jedi* he has almost three whole lines.

An English actor born in 1937, since the mid sixties Colley has racked up dozens of little roles in dozens of extraordinary films. There's *Performance* (he's the guy who puts James Fox's gangster onto Jagger's shag-palace). There's his portrayal of Christ in *Monty Python's Life of Brian*, there's Slade in *Flame*, most of Ken Russell's seventies stuff, two *Star Wars* sequels and most recently a part in *Brassed Off*.

Clearly a quality actor (hear how he delivers the line, "He'll be here if he's to be found at all", three minutes and fifty-eight seconds into *The Music Lovers*) it's the consistent smallness of Colley's parts that's impressive, and the

SMALL IS BEAUTIFUL: KEN COLLEY IS KING OF THE LITTLE ROLE

fact that pretty much everything he's done has been interesting and unusual.

The only time he's been granted more than two or three straight minutes of screen time was his starring role (we use this term loosely) in an odd little film called *Return To Waterloo*, written and directed by The Kinks' Ray Davies in 1985. A faintly fantastical musical odyssey in which Colley plays a sinister suburban commuter, his looming forehead and dead-fish gaze lend the film a

genuinely chilling air. On the basis of that performance alone he ought to have cornered the market for creepy middle-Englanders of uncertain moral standing. But he didn't.

Whether by accident, design or just because he doesn't like learning lines, Colley never gets much to say. Size however isn't everything and, like The Force, his presence is always strangely compelling. Man of few words, no web-sites and a great many hard-to-find gems, Ken Colley we salute you. ๏

BUMPER BONANZA BACK ISSUE BAZAAR!

1: August '93
SOLD OUT
Dr Johnson
Terence McKenna

2: Nov~Dec '93
SOLD OUT
Homer Simpson
Will Self

3: Jan~Feb '94
£5.00
Bertrand Russell
Charles Handy

4: April~May '94
SOLD OUT
Kurt Cobain
Matt Black

5: July~Aug '94
SOLD OUT
Douglas Coupland
Jerome K Jerome

6: Sept~Oct '94
SOLD OUT
Easy Listening
Richard Linklater

7: Dec~Jan '95
SOLD OUT
Sleep
Gilbert Shelton

8: Feb~Mar '95
SOLD OUT
Jeffrey Bernard
Robert Newman

9: May~June '95
SOLD OUT
Suzanne Moore
Positive Drinking

10: July~Aug '95
SOLD OUT
Damien Hirst
Will Self

11: Sept~Oct '95
£4.00
Keith Allen
Dole Life

12: Nov~Dec '95
£4.00
Bruce Robinson
All Night Garages

To order your back issues:
Go to www.idler.co.uk, or call 020 7691 0320 with your
credit card, or make a cheque out to "The Idler" and
send it to: The Idler, Studio 20, 24-28A Hatton Wall,
London EC1N 8JH. You must include P&P cost as follows:
P&P: Issues 1-24: 50p per issue. Issues 25-31: £2 per
issue. T-shirts/pants: £1 per item. For European
Community, add 50%. For Rest of World, add 100%

13: Jan~Feb '96
SOLD OUT
Stan Lee
Life As A Kid

14: Mar~Apr '96
£4.00
Bruce Reynolds
Will Self

15: May~Jun '96
SOLD OUT
Hashish Killers
Alex Chilton

16: Aug~Sept '96
SOLD OUT
John Michel
World Poker

17: Nov~Dec '96
SOLD OUT
John Cooper Clarke
Cary Grant

18: Spring '97
SOLD OUT
Thomas Pynchon
Ivan Illich

19: Summer '97
£4.00
Psychogeography
Henry Miller

20: Winter '97
£5.00
Howard Marks
Kenny Kramer

21: Feb~March '98
£5.00
The Gambler
Bez

22: April~May '98
SOLD OUT
Alan Moore
Alex James

23: June~July '98
SOLD OUT
Summer Special
Tim Roth

24: Aug~Sep '98
SOLD OUT
Krazy Golf
David Soul

MAN'S RUIN 25: Winter 1999

£15

The first book-format Idler, featuring Louis Theroux's Sick Notes, Will Self, Howard Marks, Adam and Joe and Ken Kesey

PARADISE 26: Summer 2000

£5

Jonathan Coe meets David Nobbs, Nicholas Blincoe on Sherlock Holmes, Tiki Special, Iain Sinclair on the London Eye

THE FOOL 27: Winter 2000

£5

Village Idiots, World Of Pain, Arthur Smith's diary, The Big Quit, James Jarvis's World of Pain, John Lloyd

RETREAT 28: Summer 2001

£10

Louis Theroux meets Bill Oddie, Jonathan Ross meets Alan Moore, Alex James meets Patrick Moore, plus Andrew Loog Oldham

HELL 29: Winter 2001

£10

Crass founder Penny Rimbaud, Crap Jobs Special, Boredom Section, New fiction from Niall Griffiths, Mark Manning, Billy Childish

LOVE 30: Summer 2002

£10

Louis Theroux meets Colin Wilson, Johnny Ball on Descartes, Crap Towns, Devon Retreat, Chris Yates interview, Marchesa Casati

Issue 31:
REVOLUTION
Winter 2002
£10
Dave Stewart, Black Panthers, Saint Monday, Allotments, Riots, Introducing the Practical Idler section

THE VIEW FROM THE SOFA

Bed is a place in the mind, says the lounging, longing Greg Rowland

CHRIS WATSON

HERE WE are again, ten years on from my first column in these pages, and once again I am perturbed by a not very mysterious illness. Today I endure a bout of tummy ache, induced by an over-zealous consumption of pizza. Indeed, last night's pizza appears to be reconstituting its original shape inside my stomach, pushing a disc of 15 inches outwards in a diameter of pure jalapeno-inspired agony.

I have therefore taken to my bed, increasingly mirroring the lethargic winsomeness of some pre-Rapaelite lady of lounging and longing. This is not the first time I have done this. On one celebrated occasion while on tour with my band in Ireland, I forsook the guilty post-imperialist pleasures of "the craic" for a 48-hour bed-life, supplemented only by IRA pot, TV, comics and sweet and sour chicken. The hotel had fortunately supplied four drawers on either side of my bed, which made a highly convenient repository for Chinese take-aways portions in varying degrees of ruin. On my departure the chambermaid's Celtic oaths were of an intensity unheard since Wolfe Tone dropped his favourite stone-clad Shelagh Na Gig on his right foot.

Meanwhile, after a bad experience with Dr Jorst's Sleeping Pills (exclusively available at Zurich Airport on the utterance of the magic phrase "Bitte shoen, haben sie das shlaff-tableten?") I was dragged along the shiny happy floor of Dublin Airport by my sleeves. I was conceptually in bed, however much the situation might have led an observer to think otherwise.

And here, my friends, is the thought for today: bed is where you make it.

Never let the absence of a real bed deny you the pleasures of cosying up.

It's now 48 hours since I began this column, having taken sick leave from it. The exact nature of my malady is now apparent. I am constipated. My loving wife is a paragon of sympathy as ever — combining Victorian notions of the "deserving ill" and a deep pleasure in the metaphorical appropriateness of my situation. I feel like I am a character based on a one-note metaphor, in some early draft of a Martin Amis novel. I am the man who is full of shit.

Those of you who have stayed with us for these long ten years will find this of little surprise or indeed interest. So I take to my bed, secure in the knowledge that metaphor and brute physicality have been united in my person. And so, good night. ☺